MULTILEVEL ACTIVITY & ACHIEVEMENT TEST BOOK

with CD-ROM

SIDE by SIDE Plus

BOOK 4

Life Skills, Standards, & Test Prep

Steven J. Molinsky • Bill Bliss

Contributing Authors

Elizabeth Handley
Sarah Lynn

PEARSON
Longman

D0925335

Correlation and Placement Key

Side by Side Plus correlates with the following standards-based curriculum levels and assessment system score ranges:

	Side by Side Plus 1	Side by Side Plus 2	Side by Side Plus 3	Side by Side Plus 4
NRS (National Reporting System) Educational Functioning Level	Low Beginning	High Beginning	Low Intermediate	High Intermediate
CASAS (Comprehensive Adult Student Assessment System) Reading/Listening	181–190	191–200	201–210	211–220
CASAS Writing	136–145	146–200	201–225	226–242
BEST Plus (Basic English Skills Test)	401–417	418–438	439–472	473–506
BEST Oral Interview	16–28	29–41	42–50	51–57
BEST Literacy	21–52	53–63	64–67	68–75
TABE CLASE-E Total Reading & Writing	395–441	442–482	483–514	515–549
TABE CLASE-E Total Listening & Speaking	408–449	450–485	486–525	526–558

For correlations to other major curriculum frameworks, please visit: www.pearsonlongman.com/sidebysideplus

Side by Side Plus 4 Multilevel Activity & Achievement Test Book

Pearson Education, 10 Bank Street, White Plains, NY 10606

Editorial director: *Pam Fishman*
Vice president, director of design and production: *Rhea Banker*
Director of electronic production: *Aliza Greenblatt*
Director of manufacturing: *Patrice Fraccio*
Senior manufacturing manager: *Edith Pullman*
Director of marketing: *Oliva Fernandez*
Production editor: *Diane Cipollone*
Text design: *Wendy Wolf; TSI Graphics*
Text composition: *TSI Graphics*
Cover design: *Wanda España, Wee Design Group;
   Warren Fischbach; Wendy Wolf*
Illustrations: *Richard E. Hill*

ISBN 978-0-13-234350-3; 0-13-234350-9

Pearson Longman on the Web
Pearsonlongman.com offers online resources
for teachers and students. Access our Companion
Websites, our online catalog, and our local offices
around the world.

Visit us at **pearsonlongman.com**.

Printed in the United States of America
2 3 4 5 6 7 8 9 10 – V011 – 14 13

CONTENTS

To the Teacher

Welcome to the *Side by Side Plus 4 Multilevel Activity & Achievement Test Book!* This volume provides a wealth of reproducible resources for use with the *Side by Side Plus* program: unit achievement tests; assessment tools; worksheets for supplemental practice in life skills and reading; innovative multilevel worksheets providing grammar and vocabulary practice for students at three different ability levels; and activity masters to accompany the activity suggestions contained in the *Side by Side Plus 4* Teacher's Guide.

These materials are also available on the CD-ROM included with the Teacher's Guide. The materials may be reproduced for classroom use only in conjunction with the *Side by Side Plus* instructional program.

TESTING AND ASSESSMENT RESOURCES

UNIT ACHIEVEMENT TESTS assess student progress and prepare students for the types of standardized tests and performance assessments used by many instructional programs. The tests include multiple-choice questions that assess vocabulary, grammar, reading, listening, and life skills; writing assessments that can be evaluated with a standardized scoring rubric and be collected in portfolios of students' work; and speaking performance assessments designed to stimulate face-to-face interactions between students, for evaluation by the teacher using a standardized scoring rubric, or for self-evaluation by students.

Teacher support materials for the Unit Achievement Tests include a listening script, an answer key, and detailed suggestions for developing learners' test-taking strategies to promote success on standardized tests. An answer sheet is also provided to offer students useful and realistic practice "bubbling in" their answers on a separate sheet rather than in a test booklet.

LEARNER ASSESSMENT RECORDS are designed for easy scoring and documentation of student performance on the tests. The forms contain scoring rubrics for all multiple-choice questions, writing assessments, and speaking assessments included on the tests. Each test is scored on a 100-point scale, providing a consistent means to evaluate student achievement of topics, vocabulary, grammar, and listening, speaking, reading, and writing skills. The Learner Assessment Records can serve as documentation of student progress during the course of the instructional program.

A LEARNER PROGRESS CHART enables students to record their test scores and chart their progress. You may want to keep the charts in a folder and have students update them as each test is completed.

WORKSHEETS

The *Side by Side Plus* worksheets are fully coordinated with units in the student book to offer valuable supplemental practice in class or at home.

LIFE SKILLS WORKSHEETS provide realia-based reading and writing activities including personal information forms, checklists, maps, diagrams, transportation schedules, movie listings, product warranties, receipts, safety procedures, apartment ads, utility bills, nutrition labels, medicine labels, safety signs, help wanted ads, a rental agreement, a driver's license application, a bank account application, a household budgeting worksheet, an autobiographical timeline, a consumer complaint form, a medical history form, an accident report form, a job application, a resume, a cover letter, a pay stub, and math practice.

MULTILEVEL GRAMMAR WORKSHEETS contain a variety of word-choice, fill-in, and sentence-completion exercises providing differentiated practice for below-level, at-level, and above-level students on each reproducible page.

MULTILEVEL VOCABULARY WORKSHEETS also offer three levels of differentiated practice through a sequence of word-choice, sentence-completion, and cloze-reading exercises on each page.

GAZETTE WORKSHEETS provide practice with reading comprehension, vocabulary, idioms, and interpretation of charts and graphs, fully coordinated with the magazine-style Gazette sections in the *Side by Side Plus* student book. The bonus Gazette Audio CD that is included with the student book offers entertaining radio program-style recordings of key Gazette features. Students will enjoy listening along as they read the text and do the activities included in the Gazette worksheets. Use these resources to encourage students to extend their language-learning through self-study— building a bridge between the classroom and the home.

ACTIVITY MASTERS

ACTIVITY MASTERS include ready-to-use word cards, graphics, charts, and activity sheets for the multilevel activities and games suggested throughout the *Side by Side Plus 4* Teacher's Guide.

In conclusion, the *Side by Side Plus 4* Multilevel Activity & Achievement Test Book aims to provide you with comprehensive resources for student assessment, multilevel supplemental practice, and dynamic classroom learning through activities and games. We hope that these reproducible materials help you with your lesson-planning and enable you to offer your students an instructional program that is effective . . . responsive to students' differing needs and ability levels . . . and fun!

Steven J. Molinsky
Bill Bliss

A. Choose the correct word. ★

1. If (it will rain   it rains) this weekend, (I'll   I) stay home and study.

2. If (you   you'll) quit your job, (you   you might) regret it.

3. I hope our teacher (won't   doesn't) give us a quiz today.

4. If you (studied   will study) more, (you'll   you'd) get better grades.

5. If Michael (was   were) more graceful, (he'd   he'll) be a better dancer.

6. If I (wouldn't   didn't) have an interview, I (won't   wouldn't) be so dressed up.

7. If I (wasn't   weren't) so tired, (I'd   I'll) be happy to go dancing with you.

B. Choose the correct word and complete the sentences with the correct form of the verb. ★★

| be | do | eat | enjoy | get | go | lose |

1. If (I'll be   I'm) very busy today, _____ lunch in my office.

2. (I   I'll) hope _____ the job I applied for at the bank.

3. If (you'll exercise   you exercised) more, _____ weight more easily.

4. If I (were   was) more careful, _____ a better driver.

5. If I (wouldn't   didn't) like to swim, _____ to the beach every weekend.

6. If my neighbor (wasn't   weren't) so noisy, _____ living in this building.

7. What _____ if you (saw   will see) a bad accident?

C. Complete the sentences any way you wish. ★★★

1. If _____, _____ probably _____.

2. If _____, _____ might _____.

3. I hope _____.

4. I'm not _____. If _____, _____.

5. I'm _____. If _____, _____.

6. What would you do if _____?

Side by Side Plus Book 4
Unit 5 Multilevel Grammar Worksheet

Conditional: Present Real (If ___ Will)
Present Unreal (If ___ Would)
Hope-Clauses

© 2009 Pearson Education, Inc.
Duplication for classroom use is permitted.

5

A. Choose the correct word. ★

1. If I (was   were) you, I (wouldn't   won't) buy that bright blue coat.

2. Do you think the boss (is   would be) upset if (I left   I'm leaving) work early?

3. If (you took   you'll take) that course, (you   you'd) probably (are   be) sorry.

4. To tell the truth, I wish I (work   worked) the day shift.

5. If I (will   could) speak Spanish, (I were   I'd be) able to get a better job.

6. If I (had   didn't have) a meeting, (I'll be able to   I could) have lunch with you.

7. I wish I (wasn't   weren't) "all thumbs." If I (was   were) handy around the house, (I'd be   I'll be) able to repair things by myself.

B. Choose the correct word and complete the sentences with the correct form of the verb. ★★

| drive | get | make | take | teach | visit |

1. I _____ a large dog if I (was   were) you. You might be sorry.

2. If my new laptop (were   will be) lighter, _____ it to work with me.

3. Do you think Dad (would be   is) upset if I _____ his new car?

4. Anthony is a science teacher, but he wishes _____ American history.

5. If I (can   could) knit, _____ sweaters and mittens for my grandson.

6. If our relatives (don't   didn't) live so far away, _____ them more often.

C. Complete the sentences any way you wish. ★★★

1. I _____, if I were you.

2. Do you think my friends would be upset if _____?

3. If you _____, _____ probably _____.

4. I wish _____.

   If _____, _____.

5. I wish _____ (didn't/weren't) _____.

   If _____, _____.

Present Unreal Conditional (continued)
Wish-Clauses

A. Choose the correct word. ★

1. If my alarm clock (rings   had rung), I (would arrive   would have arrived) for work on time this morning.

2. If we (had had   have had) good seats, we (would have   had) enjoyed the play.

3. If I (weren't   hadn't been) tired, I (hadn't   wouldn't have) gone to bed so early.

4. I wish I (had   hadn't) done my work more carefully. If I (had done   have done) that, I (hadn't   wouldn't have) made so many mistakes.

5. I wish I (have   had) a better job. If I (had   will have) a better job, I know I wouldn't (be   have been) so worried about my future.

6. I wish I (prepared   had prepared) for my science test last week. I'm sure that if I (prepared   had prepared), I wouldn't (have gotten   get) a bad grade.

B. Choose the correct word and complete the sentences with the correct form of the verb. ★★

get	go	hand in	have to	taste

1. If I (was   had been) invited, I _____ to the party last night.

2. If my computer (hadn't been   weren't) broken last week, I _____ my paper two days late.

3. If I (had followed   didn't follow) the recipe, my cake _____ so terrible!

4. I wish I (exercise   exercised) more often. If I (exercise   exercised) more often, I _____ go on a diet.

5. I wish I (had had   had) a flu shot last fall. If I (had   had had) a flu shot, I _____ sick so many times during the winter.

C. Complete the sentences any way you wish. ★★★

1. If I had _____, I _____.

2. If I hadn't _____, I _____.

3. I wish I _____. If _____, _____.

4. I wish I had _____. If _____, _____.

Side by Side Plus Book 4
Unit 7 Multilevel Grammar Worksheet

Past Unreal Conditional (If __ Would Have)
Wish-Clauses (continued)

© 2009 Pearson Education, Inc.
Duplication for classroom use is permitted.

7

A. Choose the correct word. ★

1. The plumber called. He said he (can   could) come over tomorrow morning.

2. Aunt Martha called. She said she (would   will) call back later.

3. The landlord called. He said he (is   was) sorry he (forgot   had forgotten) to fix our sink.

4. I didn't know all the chairs and sofas (were   are) on sale this week.

5. My boyfriend asked me (do I want   if I wanted) to get married next year.

6. Amy told me (not to   to not) call her tonight. She said she (has to   had to) study.

7. I didn't know this (was   is) the third time he (had   has) been fired from his job.

B. Complete the sentences with the correct form of the verb. ★★

be	bother	call	get	have	have to	play	want to

1. Our niece called. She said she _____ a big raise last month.

2. I'm very happy. My boss told me I _____ work overtime this weekend.

3. I didn't know our landlord _____ sell the building and move to Hawaii.

4. The job interviewer asked me _____ ever _____ fired.

5. The doctor told me _____ her in the morning if I still _____ a stomachache.

6. My landlord told me _____ my music so loud. He said I _____ all the neighbors.

C. Complete the sentences any way you wish. ★★★

1. _____ called. _____ said _____.

2. You're kidding! I didn't know that _____.

3. _____ asked me why _____.

4. _____ asked me if _____.

5. I'm a little annoyed at _____. _____ told me _____
   _____ said _____.

8

Side by Side Plus Book 4
Unit 8 Multilevel Grammar Worksheet

Reported Speech
Sequence of Tenses

© 2009 Pearson Education, Inc.
Duplication for classroom use is permitted.

A. Complete the sentences. ★

1. I can take pictures here, _____?

2. We haven't seen this movie before, _____?

3. She'll be out of town next week, _____?

4. You remembered to turn off the stove, _____?

5. This building doesn't have an elevator, _____?

6. I'm doing this correctly, _____?

7. You're right. The weather is terrible! It _____ a good day to go sailing, _____!

B. Complete the sentences using the correct form of the verb and the tag question. ★★

arrive	be	break up	going to	look like	want to

1. You still _____ marry me, _____?

2. Our next-door neighbors _____ really _____ move, _____?

3. All the guests _____ already _____, _____?

4. Good morning. We _____ on time for the meeting, _____?

5. You didn't really _____ with your boyfriend last week, _____?

6. You're right! I _____ my mother, _____!

C. Complete the sentences any way you wish. ★★★

1. You _____, _____?

2. We _____, _____?

3. I _____, _____?

4. _____, _____?

5. You're right! _____, _____!

A. Choose the correct word. ★

1. How long (are you   have you been) unemployed?

2. I really don't feel like (taking   to take) a walk today. I (have taken   took) a long walk yesterday.

3. I supposed (you'll   you'd) get tired (to jog   of jogging) in the park if you (jogged   are jogging) in the park all the time.

4. If I (hadn't seen   didn't see) a movie yesterday, (I'll   I'd) see a movie today.

5. If I (hadn't been   weren't) sick, I never (missed   would have missed) the party.

6. If I (weren't   hadn't been) busy, (I'd   I'll) be glad to help you fix your car today.

7. If I (had known   knew) your relatives (were   are) visiting from Seattle, I (wouldn't have called   wouldn't call) you.

B. Complete the sentences using the correct form of the verb. ★★

| be | drive | get | go | have | know | misunderstand | play |

1. I'm sorry to hear about your children. How long _____ the measles?

2. I'm sure you'd get tired of _____ tennis if you _____ tennis all the time.

3. If I _____ shopping yesterday, I'd be happy _____ shopping today.

4. If I _____ sick, _____ happy to help you move today.

5. If I _____ about the parade, I never _____ downtown today.

6. If I _____ the directions, we never _____ lost.

C. Complete the sentences any way you wish. ★★★

1. I don't feel like _____ today. I _____ yesterday.

2. If I _____ yesterday, I'd be happy to _____ today.

3. I'm sure you'd get tired of _____ if _____ all the time.

4. I'm sorry to hear about _____. How long _____?

5. I'm sorry. If I _____, I never _____!

**Review: Verb Tenses,
Conditionals, Gerunds**

Side by Side Plus 4
Multilevel Grammar Worksheets Answer Key

UNIT 1

A.
1. Have you eaten, have
2. haven't seen
3. Has, been, has
4. I've been waiting
5. I had made
6. He had been working
7. has been doing, He's, done, He's, done

B.
1. Have you written, have
2. hasn't gotten
3. has, been leaking
4. has been drawing, He's, drawn
5. We had gone
6. She had been planning

C.
(Answers will vary.)

UNIT 2

A.
1. should have
2. shouldn't have
3. must have
4. might have
5. could have
6. may have

B.
1. should have taken
2. could have been
3. shouldn't have called
4. might have had
5. couldn't have seen
6. must have eaten

C.
(Answers will vary.)

UNIT 3

A.
1. were
2. has been
3. is being
4. was
5. shouldn't be
6. that, been

B.
1. have, been given out
2. is being repaired
3. be used
4. was drawn
5. have, been done, were done
6. was bitten, he's been bitten

C.
(Answers will vary.)

UNIT 4

A.
1. this flight is
2. where they
3. are we going to
4. if parking is allowed
5. if the movie has begun
6. Gary quit
7. if fishing is

B.
1. where the keys are
2. why they moved
3. who the tenth president was
4. what time the train leaves
5. if/whether there's going to be an English quiz tomorrow
6. if/whether anybody here found a black purse

C.
(Answers will vary.)

UNIT 5

A.
1. it rains, I'll
2. you, you might
3. doesn't
4. studied, you'd
5. were, he'd
6. didn't, wouldn't
7. weren't, I'd

B.
1. I'm, I'll eat
2. I, I get
3. you exercised, you'd lose
4. were, I'd be
5. didn't, I wouldn't go
6. weren't, I'd enjoy
7. would you do, saw

C.
(Answers will vary.)

UNIT 6

A.
1. were, wouldn't
2. would be, I left
3. you took, you'd, be
4. worked
5. could, I'd be
6. didn't have, I could
7. weren't, were, I'd be

B.
1. wouldn't get, were
2. were, I'd take
3. would be, drove
4. he taught
5. could, I'd make
6. didn't, we'd visit

C.
(Answers will vary.)

UNIT 7

A.
1. had rung, would have arrived
2. had had, would have
3. hadn't been, wouldn't have
4. had, had done, wouldn't have
5. had, had, be
6. had prepared, had prepared, have gotten

B.
1. had been, would have gone
2. hadn't been, wouldn't have handed in
3. had followed, wouldn't have tasted
4. exercised, exercised, wouldn't have to
5. had had, had had, wouldn't have gotten

C.
(Answers will vary.)

UNIT 8

A.
1. could
2. would
3. was, had forgotten
4. were
5. if I wanted
6. not to, had to
7. was, had

B.
1. had gotten
2. didn't have to
3. wanted to
4. if/whether I had, been
5. to call, had
6. not to play, was bothering

C.
(Answers will vary.)

UNIT 9

A.
1. can't I
2. have we
3. won't she
4. didn't you
5. does it
6. aren't I
7. isn't, is it

B.
1. want to, don't you
2. aren't, going to, are they
3. have, arrived, haven't they
4. are, aren't we
5. break up, did you
6. (do) look like, don't I

C.
(Answers will vary.)

UNIT 10

A.
1. have you been
2. taking, took
3. you'd, of jogging, jogged
4. hadn't seen, I'd
5. hadn't been, would have missed
6. weren't, I'd
7. had known, were, wouldn't have called

B.
1. have they had
2. playing, played
3. hadn't gone, to go
4. weren't, I'd be
5. had known, would have driven
6. hadn't misunderstood, would have gotten

C.
(Answers will vary.)

Student's Name _____

Date _____

A. Choose the correct word. ★

1. If Amy's boyfriend doesn't apologize, she's going to (separate   break up) with him.

2. It must be an important event because everyone is very dressed (up   over).

3. If I hadn't (missed   prevented) class yesterday, I would have gotten the assignment.

4. It's important to learn several emergency (procedures   airways) such as CPR.

5. If a person is (breathing   choking), you should do the Heimlich maneuver.

6. Every home should have a (floor plan   first-aid kit) for medical emergencies.

7. We have a (smoke   fire) detector in our hallway.

8. In case of fire, it's important to have (flammable products   an escape route).

B. Write the correct words to complete the paragraph. ★★

Every household should be prepared for an _____[1], especially a fire.

_____[2] should be installed in hallways. For _____[3]

protection, they should also be installed in bedrooms. Batteries need to be

_____[4] twice a year. _____[5] objects such as curtains and

furniture should be at least three feet away from portable heaters. Every family

should have an _____[6] plan that shows all of the emergency escape

_____[7] to use in case of a fire. Family members should practice the plan

and have an outside _____[8] place.

C. Antonyms are opposites. Look at the words below. Find their antonyms on the pages in parentheses. ★★★

1. tired   (p. 66) _____

2. shy   (p. 73) _____

3. maximum   (p. 78c) _____

4. fail   (p. 14c) _____

5. pay attention (p. 78c) _____

6. outside   (p. 78c) _____

7. discourage   (p. 76) _____

8. advanced   (p. 17) _____

9. go away   (p. 20) _____

10. lend   (p. 46a) _____

17

UNIT 6

Multilevel Vocabulary Worksheet

Student's Name _____

Date _____

A. Choose the correct word. ★

1. Jason is very sorry he (dropped   evicted) out of school last semester.

2. I'm having trouble (concentrating   convincing) on my work.

3. I'd like to (order   open) a savings account at this bank.

4. My husband and I are trying to reduce spending and (cut out   run out of) waste.

5. When Ken opened a new account, the bank (divided   waived) the check fee.

6. I keep important papers in a (safe   certified) deposit box at the bank.

7. I wish I could keep (view   track) of my daily expenses.

8. Whenever you use an ATM, check the (banking   balance) in your account.

B. Write the correct words to complete the paragraph. ★★

Emma is upset with herself. She needs to do something about her _____[1]
situation. Every two weeks she _____[2] her paycheck in the bank and withdraws
some cash from her checking _____[3]. Before the week is over, she often
_____[4] out of cash and has no idea what she spent it on. As a result, she has
decided to make a monthly _____[5]. She's going to list her _____[6]
expenses, such as rent and utilities. Then she'll estimate her spending for groceries, gas, and
other variable expenses. Since she has Internet access, she'll do _____[7]
banking to follow her spending. For daily expenses, she's planning to keep a spending
record to see what purchases she can cut out to save _____[8].

C. Read the following definitions of words in this unit. You can find these words on the pages in parentheses. Write the correct word next to each definition. ★★★

1. _____ areas where people live away from the city center (noun: p. 87)

2. _____ to make someone believe something (verb: p. 90)

3. _____ a plan for how to spend money (noun: p. 94c)

4. _____ without cost, payment, or charge (adjective: p. 94b)

5. _____ to make something become less (verb: p. 94c)

6. _____ a person who likes a sport, a type of music, or a famous person very much (noun: p. 85)

On a separate piece of paper, write a sentence with each of the words above.

A. Choose the correct word. ★

1. My husband and I are very upset. Our mortgage wasn't (convinced   approved).

2. He (scolded   irritated) his sons for riding their bicycles too fast on the sidewalk.

3. I was carefully (shrunk   searched) by the security person at the airport.

4. According to Raymond's doctor, he has a very (rare   swollen) disease.

5. It's important to know more than one emergency (hazard   exit) from a building.

6. Sandra couldn't (set off   swallow), so I thought she was choking.

7. Gasoline is highly (combustible   corrosive). It should be stored outside.

8. Employees must follow safety procedures when using heavy (machinery   guards).

B. Write the correct words to complete the paragraph. ★★

Last month my father was diagnosed with heart _____[1]. We weren't surprised because he seemed tired recently and had been _____[2] weight for many years. According to his doctor, he needs to _____[3] fewer calories each day and avoid foods that are _____[4] in fat, cholesterol, and sodium. This will be difficult for him because he loves french fries, fried chicken, butter, and salt. He needs to read food _____[5] carefully to plan his meals. He also needs to exercise _____[6]. He has started taking a new _____[7] that will lower his blood _____[8]. I'm relieved that he's finally taking care of himself.

C. For each sentence, add a comma if it is needed. ★★★

1. If I had taken the train I wouldn't have been late for work.

2. I wish I knew my neighbors.

3. Do you think your brother would be upset if we borrowed his car?

4. If you exercised every day you would probably lose weight more quickly.

5. I wish I hadn't spent so much money on my new camera.

6. Do you know where I can find a good medical clinic?

7. If you win the competition will you have a big celebration?

8. She wouldn't have been confused if she had read the directions first.

19

Student's Name _____

Date _____

A.   oose the correct word. ★

    an always (convince   depend) on Samantha to arrive promptly.

    What do you (advise   hope) me to do about transferring to another department?

    'm getting a degree in (computer science   correspondence).

    I need to attend two weeks of (duties   training) for my new job.

    Manuel often translates for patients since he's (reassured   bilingual).

. An administrative assistant has many (clerical   certified) duties.

7. I'm looking for a full-time position as a dental (assistant   practice).

8. Are there opportunities for promotion and (abbreviation   advancement) in this company?

B. Write the correct words to complete the paragraph. ★★

I'm starting a job search for a new position. My _____[1] is to find a job as an office manager in a doctor's office. First, I need to _____[2] my resume so that it shows my most recent job. I also need to add that I've received my associate's _____[3] in business administration. Then I need to check the help _____[4] ads in the newspaper and online. In preparation for an _____[5], I need to make a list of my strengths and _____[6]. I know that one strength is my three years of _____[7] as an administrative assistant in a clinic. Another strength is that I am a good _____[8], since I enjoy talking with people and I listen well. On the other hand, I need to improve my writing skills, and I need to be more _____[9] about making my own decisions.

C. Above each underlined word, write *n* (noun), *v* (verb), *a* (adjective), or *p* (preposition). ★★★

1. Abigail felt <u>reassured</u> by her supervisor's good <u>advice</u> <u>about</u> the problem.

2. The <u>training</u> for the new software program is <u>planned</u> <u>for</u> next week.

3. I was <u>annoyed</u> when I <u>saw</u> that my roommate had <u>spilled</u> coffee <u>on</u> our new rug.

4. The father <u>told</u> his son to stop <u>complaining</u> about his homework.

5. The position <u>requires</u> state <u>certification</u> and drug <u>testing</u>.

20

Student's Name _____

Date _____

A. Choose the correct word. ★

1. Lanna and Marco are (engaged   dedicated) and plan to get married next year.
2. The driver thought the speeding ticket was (upset   unfair).
3. Excuse me. Am I (labeling   filing) the cans correctly?
4. Do I need to have the (basic   original) document, or is a copy okay?
5. Many companies offer life (insurance   plans) to their employees.
6. A (free   personal) day may be used to take care of a family member.
7. For questions about benefits, contact the Human (Resources   Research) office.
8. Ramona was promoted due to her hard work and (accusation   dedication).

B. Write the correct words to complete the paragraph. ★★

Peter is faced with a difficult decision. He has two job offers, and he has to

_____[1] which one to accept. He's comparing the benefits offered by each

company. The first company offers basic _____[2] insurance, including

prescription drugs. He would only have one week of paid _____[3] the first year,

but after that he would receive another week. However, unused days cannot be

_____[4] over to the next year. They offer a 401(k) _____[5] and ten

paid days of _____[6] leave a year. The second company offers better benefits

but a lower salary. The additional benefits include five personal _____[7], dental

_____[8], and free gym membership.

C. Many nouns end with the suffix *-ment, -tion,* and *-ship.* Add suffixes to these words and put them in the correct column. ★★★

advance	champion	employ	leader	relation
celebrate	dedicate	examine	manage	retire
certificate	educate	invest	member	scholar

replace**ment**	communica**tion**	friend**ship**

Student's Name _____

Multilevel Vocabulary Worksheet

Date _____

A. Choose the correct word. ★

1. It isn't difficult to (assemble   replace) this bookcase if you follow the instructions.

2. The picnic table was (tipped over   set up) by the heavy wind.

3. His telephone was (deleted   disconnected) because he hadn't paid his bill.

4. You can only vote in an election if you're a (permanent   registered) voter.

5. The jury reached a verdict about the (innocence   legality) or guilt of the person.

6. (Low-income   Domestic) residents can get free legal assistance.

7. Divorce and child custody are issues related to (criminal   family) law.

8. If you're a (taxpayer   resident), you pay the government a percentage of your earnings.

B. Write the correct words to complete the paragraph. ★★

Every person is considered a _____[1] of his or her community. Citizens enjoy many privileges, but they also have duties or _____[2] to their communities. Citizens are also protected by local, state, and federal _____[3] that are written to keep people safe. A special privilege for legal citizens is the _____[4] to vote in elections. A person has to _____[5] to vote by filling out an application. There are many important duties for citizens. For example, citizens must _____[6] the law, pay _____[7], and keep _____[8] about local, state, and national issues.

C. Fill in the chart with the missing words. ★★★

	Verb	Noun	Adjective
1.	replace	replacement	X
2.	evict		X
3.	X		naturalized
4.	adapt	X	
5.	X	nation	
6.	refer		X
7.			registered
8.	recommend		

22

Side by Side Plus 4
Multilevel Vocabulary Worksheets Answer Key

UNIT 1

A.
1. ferry
2. maternity
3. memo
4. participate
5. limit
6. joined
7. absence

B.
1. grade
2. concentrate
3. attention
4. unable
5. learning
6. counselor

C.
1a. value — noun
1b. value — verb
2a. limit — noun
2b. limit — verb
3a. interest — noun
3b. interest — verb
4a. concern — verb
4b. concern — noun

Student Sentences: (Answers will vary.)

UNIT 2

A.
1. Financial
2. stuck
3. registration
4. illegal
5. outreach
6. cause
7. cooperate

B.
1. lights
2. stop
3. pulled
4. officer
5. nervous
6. license
7. registration
8. issued/given
9. violation

C.
1a. frightened — verb
1b. frightened — adjective
2a. surprised — adjective
2b. surprised — verb
3a. experienced — verb
3b. experienced — adjective
4a. stained — verb
4b. stained — adjective

UNIT 3

A.
1. rebuild
2. architect
3. established
4. unemployment
5. attack
6. discrimination
7. required
8. controlled

B.
1. World War II
2. invaded/attacked
3. joined
4. Allied
5. enter
6. bombed
7. won
8. destroyed

C.

1. build	building	X
2. create	creation	X
3. X	democracy	democratic
4. organize	organization	X
5. X	economy	economic
6. attack	attack	X
7. X	color	colorful
8. invent	invention	X

UNIT 4

A.
1. means
2. check with
3. robbed
4. refund
5. membership
6. defective
7. damaged
8. manufacturer

B.
1. consumer/customer
2. defective
3. refund
4. service
5. exchange
6. warranty
7. complaint
8. hotline

C.
1. teacher
2. employer
3. inventor
4. manager
5. manufacturer
6. supervisor
7. driver
8. interviewer
9. governor
10. mediator
11. purchaser
12. instructor

UNIT 5

A.
1. break up
2. up
3. missed
4. procedures
5. choking
6. first-aid kit
7. smoke
8. an escape route

B.
1. emergency
2. Smoke detectors
3. maximum
4. replaced/changed
5. Flammable
6. escape
7. routes
8. meeting

C.
1. energetic
2. outgoing
3. minimum
4. succeed
5. ignore
6. inside
7. encourage
8. beginning
9. come back
10. borrow

UNIT 6

A.
1. dropped
2. concentrating
3. open
4. cut out
5. waived
6. safe
7. track
8. balance

B.
1. financial
2. deposits
3. account
4. runs
5. budget
6. fixed
7. online
8. money

C.
1. suburbs
2. convince
3. budget
4. free
5. reduce
6. fan

Student Sentences: (Answers will vary.)

UNIT 7

A.
1. approved
2. scolded
3. searched
4. rare
5. exit
6. swallow
7. combustible
8. machinery

B.
1. disease
2. gaining
3. consume
4. high
5. labels
6. regularly/more
7. drug/medicine/medication
8. pressure

C.
1. If I had taken the train, I wouldn't have been late for work.
2. (No comma needed)
3. (No comma needed)
4. If you exercised every day, you would probably lose weight more quickly.
5. (No comma needed)
6. (No comma needed)
7. If you win the competition, will you have a big celebration?
8. (No comma needed)

UNIT 8

A.
1. depend
2. advise
3. computer science
4. training
5. bilingual
6. clerical
7. assistant
8. advancement

B.
1. goal
2. update
3. degree
4. wanted
5. interview
6. weaknesses
7. experience/employment
8. communicator
9. confident

C.

1. Abigail felt <u>reassured</u> (a) by her supervisor's good <u>advice</u> (n) <u>about</u> (p) the problem.

2. The <u>training</u> (n) for the new software program is <u>planned</u> (v) <u>for</u> (p) next week.

3. I was <u>annoyed</u> (a) when I <u>saw</u> (v) that my roommate had <u>spilled</u> (v) coffee <u>on</u> (p) our new rug.

4. The father <u>told</u> (v) his son to stop <u>complaining</u> (v) about his homework.

5. The job position <u>requires</u> (v) state <u>certification</u> (n) and drug <u>testing</u> (n).

UNIT 9

A.
1. engaged
2. unfair
3. labeling
4. original
5. insurance
6. personal
7. Resources
8. dedication

B.
1. decide/choose
2. health
3. vacation
4. carried
5. plan
6. sick
7. days
8. insurance

C.

advancement	celebration	championship
employment	certification	leadership
investment	dedication	membership
management	education	relationship
retirement	examination	scholarship

UNIT 10

A.
1. assemble
2. tipped over
3. disconnected
4. registered
5. innocence
6. Low-income
7. family
8. taxpayer

B.
1. citizen
2. responsibilities
3. laws
4. right
5. register
6. obey
7. taxes
8. informed

C.

1. replace	replacement	X
2. evict	eviction	X
3. X	naturalization	naturalized
4. adapt	X	adaptable
5. X	nation	national
6. refer	referral/reference	X
7. register	registration	registered
8. recommend	recommendation	recommended

A. Choose the words that best complete each sentence.

1. The wheel _____ in 3500 B.C.
- A. is invented
- B. invented
- C. was invented
- D. has invented

2. The Taj Mahal _____ in the 17th century.
- A. was built
- B. has built
- C. built
- D. was building

3. All students _____ to take the final exam.
- A. be required
- B. are required
- C. requiring
- D. have required

4. The instructions _____ on the ___ ·d.
- A. were writing
- B. written
- C. wrote
- D. were written

5. The stop sign _____ by a ck last night.
- A. is hit
- B. hit
- C. was hit
- D. was being hit

6. Children _____ t _ e that movie.
- A. should not a'
- B. should not ; wed
- C. should not e allowed
- D. should n e allowed

B. Look at the sentences. Choose the sentence that is rect and complete.

7.
- A. The oil in my car was changing.
- B. The oil in my car be changed.
- C. The oil in my car being changed.
- D. The oil in my car was changed.

8.
- A. He be taken to the hospital.
- B. He took to the hospital.
- C. He was taken to the hospital.
- D. He was took to the hospital.

9.
- A. The new curtains were hung.
- B. The new curtains be hung.
- C. The new curtains been hung.
- D. The new curtains being hung.

10.
- A. The use built in 1953.
- B. The ouse was built in 1953.
- C. T' house has built in 1953.
- D. house being built in 1953.

11.
- A. e been told about the meeting.
- she not be told about the meeting.
- She being told about the meeting.
-). She wasn't told about the meeting.

1 .
- A. The winner be chosen soon.
- B. The winner chose soon.
- C. The winner will be chosen soon.
- D. The winner was chose soon.

A. THE MUSIC OF WISHES AND HOPES

Read the article on text page 79 and answer the questions.

1. Which song was made popular by a singing group?
   A. "If I Were a Rich Man"
   B. "If I Were a Bell"
   C. "If I Had a Hammer"
   D. "If I Could Change the World"

2. _____ of the songs described in the article were first performed in musicals.
   A. Two
   B. Three
   C. Four
   D. None

3. In _____ of the songs, the wish is for money.
   A. one
   B. two
   C. three
   D. four

4. Lee Ann Womack is a _____.
   A. folk singer
   B. rock singer
   C. Broadway singer
   D. country music singer

5. You can infer that a Grammy Award is given for _____.
   A. songs
   B. books
   C. acting
   D. writing a poem

6. In "If I Had a Million Dollars," the word *exotic* means _____.
   A. expensive
   B. beautiful
   C. unusual
   D. very large

7. In all of these songs, the common wish of the singers is to have _____.
   A. love
   B. peace
   C. time
   D. happiness

8. From this article, you can infer that the music of wishes and hopes is _____.
   A. always about relationships
   B. found in many different types of music
   C. the most popular music theme
   D. loved by everyone

B. SONG SEARCH

Look at the Fact File on text page 79 and answer the questions.

1. The word _____ is the most popular of the three words in song titles.
   A. "hope"
   B. "wish"
   C. "if"

2. The word _____ is not in any of the song titles in the article.
   A. "hope"
   B. "wish"
   C. "if"

MAKING WISHES

Read the article on text page 80 and answer the questions.

1. You make a wish if you catch something in _____.
   A. Jamaica
   B. Japan
   C. Korea
   D. Ireland

2. If you hear coins splash into water three times in _____, your wishes will come true.
   A. the United States
   B. Asia
   C. South America
   D. Europe

3. Make a wish when you blow out candles on a cake _____.
   A. in the evening
   B. at midnight
   C. on your birthday
   D. when you look at the moon

4. Coins are used for making wishes in _____ of the traditions described in the article.
   A. two
   B. three
   C. four
   D. five

5. _____ of the traditions described in the article involve looking at the sky.
   A. One
   B. Two
   C. Three
   D. Four

6. People in the United States are likely to make a wish with a wishbone on _____.
   A. Valentine's Day
   B. July 4th
   C. Thanksgiving
   D. New Year's Day

7. "Star light, star bright, first star I see tonight" is a _____.
   A. wish
   B. tradition
   C. custom
   D. poem

8. In the New Year's Eve tradition with grapes, the *chimes* of the clock refer to _____.
   A. the sounds of the clock
   B. the hands of the clock
   C. grapes
   D. midnight

9. If you throw a *pebble* into a well to make a wish, you throw _____.
   A. a leaf
   B. a nut
   C. a small stone
   D. a candle

10. The tradition for making wishes with _____ requires two people.
    A. a wishbone or a coin
    B. a nut or a leaf
    C. candles or grapes
    D. a wishbone or a nut

A. INTERVIEW

Read the interview on text page 81 and answer the questions.

1. The man on the left wouldn't want to quit his job because _____.
   A. he has too much free time
   B. he loves his job
   C. he works very hard
   D. he wouldn't know how to use his time

2. _____ of the people would stop working.
   A. One
   B. Two
   C. Three
   D. Four

3. _____ of the people would help family members.
   A. One
   B. Two
   C. Three
   D. Four

4. _____ of the people would save the money.
   A. One
   B. Two
   C. Three
   D. Four

5. You can infer that *debts* are _____.
   A. money you owe
   B. banks
   C. people
   D. jobs

6. One man would give money to charities. You can infer that _____.
   A. he's retired
   B. he already has a lot of money
   C. he's generous
   D. he works

B. INTERVIEW A CLASSMATE

Interview a classmate. Use the chart below to record your classmate's answers. Then tell the class what you learned.

What would you do if you won a million dollars?	
Would you keep working or going to school? Why or why not?	
Would you give money to people? Who would you give it to?	
Would you give any money to charities? Which ones?	

A. Choose the correct idiom to answer each question.

> You're breaking my heart.
> You light up my life.
> You're a heel!
> You've got me wrapped around your little finger.

1. What would you say to someone who always makes you feel happy?

_____

2. What would you say if a boyfriend or girlfriend hurt your feelings?

_____

3. What would you say to someone you would do anything for?

_____

4. What would you say to a friend who isn't nice to other people?

_____

B. Complete the conversation with the correct idioms.

> weren't a heel
> wrapped around her little finger
> breaking my heart
> lights up my life

1. A. I'm sorry, but our relationship has to end.

   B. Oh, no! You're _____.

   A. Well, I wouldn't have to break up with you if you _____.
   You never return my phone calls.

2. A. Do you enjoy spending time with your two-year-old grandson?

   B. I certainly do! He _____.

3. A. Robert does everything his girlfriend asks him to do.

   B. I know. She has him _____.

C. Answer these questions on a separate piece of paper. Then talk with a classmate about your answers.

1. Who lights up your life? Why?

2. Who has broken your heart? How?

3. Who is a heel? Why?

4. Who do you have wrapped around your little finger? Explain.

A. Choose the words that best complete each sentence.

1. We hope they _____ on time for dinner.
   - A. will
   - B. are
   - C. will be
   - D. be

2. He hopes he _____ a raise.
   - A. is going to get
   - B. will get
   - C. is getting
   - D. gets

3. They hope it _____ tomorrow.
   - A. is raining
   - B. will rain
   - C. doesn't rain
   - D. won't rain

4. She hopes the bus _____ late.
   - A. isn't
   - B. won't be
   - C. is going to be
   - D. will be

5. I hope I _____ for the team.
   - A. will be chosen
   - B. am chosen
   - C. will choose
   - D. am choosing

6. We hope we _____ the train.
   - A. won't miss
   - B. are missing
   - C. don't miss
   - D. aren't going to miss

B. Look at the sentences. Choose the sentence that is correct and complete.

7. A. If I was tired, I wouldn't go with you.
   B. If I weren't tired, I would go with you.
   C. If I weren't tired, I will go with you.
   D. If I wasn't tired, I would go with you.

8. A. If she wasn't busy, she would help us.
   B. If she isn't busy, she would help us.
   C. If she weren't busy, she would help us.
   D. If she was busy, she would help us.

9. A. If he is sick, I would call the doctor.
   B. If he were sick, I will call the doctor.
   C. If he was sick, I would call the doctor.
   D. If he were sick, I would call the doctor.

10. A. If it weren't funny, I wouldn't laugh.
    B. If it weren't funny, I won't laugh.
    C. If it wasn't funny, I wouldn't laugh.
    D. If it wasn't funny, I won't laugh.

11. A. If I was you, I would leave now.
    B. If I was you, I will leave now.
    C. If I were you, I would leave now.
    D. If I will be you, I would leave now.

12. A. She was upset if he is late.
    B. She will be upset if he was late.
    C. She were upset if he would be late.
    D. She would be upset if he were late.

A. POLISH UP YOUR INTERVIEW SKILLS!

Read the article on text page 125 and answer the questions.

1. The most important tip for a successful interview is to _____.
   A. be prepared
   B. brag about yourself
   C. write a thank-you note
   D. fill out an application

2. A good way to find out about a company is to _____.
   A. read job ads
   B. ask the interviewer
   C. look up the address
   D. use the Internet

3. During the interview, you should _____.
   A. tell about your family
   B. answer questions honestly
   C. ask about benefits
   D. ask about vacations

4. In paragraph 2, *dress appropriately* means _____.
   A. stand out from the crowd
   B. wear casual clothes
   C. dress neatly and in nice clothes
   D. dress in comfortable clothes

5. The interviewer will probably NOT ask about your _____.
   A. age
   B. education
   C. strengths
   D. plans for the future

6. You can expect an interviewer to _____.
   A. arrive late
   B. tell you about his or her background
   C. ask about your weaknesses
   D. ask you to come to a follow-up interview

7. *Get along with* in paragraph 3 means _____.
   A. supervise
   B. give instructions to
   C. do the same job as
   D. be friendly with

8. You can infer from the article that an interview _____.
   A. will probably last for an hour
   B. is an important way that companies evaluate job applicants
   C. is easy if you've never had one
   D. isn't challenging for most people

B. HOW PEOPLE FIND JOBS

Look at the Fact File on text page 125 and answer the questions.

1. The second most common way to find a job is to _____.
   A. network
   B. go to an employment agency
   C. read the want ads
   D. write to or call the company yourself

2. More than one-third (1/3) of job applicants find their jobs by _____.
   A. reading the newspaper
   B. contacting an employer directly
   C. communicating with other people
   D. using an employment agency

35

A. WHO GOT THE JOB?

Read the article on text page 126 and answer the questions.

1. When asked about her experience, Sarah Jones _____.
   A. only talked about her education
   B. talked about her family
   C. gave a lot of information
   D. asked about the company

2. Sarah wants to leave her current job because _____.
   A. it isn't challenging enough
   B. it's too challenging
   C. she wants to travel more
   D. she has a lot of weaknesses

3. Sarah thinks she needs to _____ better.
   A. use computer software
   B. ask questions at an interview
   C. write follow-up notes
   D. write business letters

4. Bob wasn't familiar with the company's products because _____.
   A. he didn't need any software
   B. he hadn't prepared for the interview
   C. the interviewer didn't tell him
   D. he didn't have Internet access

5. Sarah made a better impression because _____.
   A. she asked about vacation days
   B. she wanted to work shorter hours
   C. she knew about the company
   D. she hadn't thought about her weaknesses

6. You can infer that Bob's interview _____.
   A. was longer than Sarah's
   B. was cancelled by the interviewer
   C. was successful
   D. was shorter than Sarah's

B. AROUND THE WORLD

Read the article on text page 126 and answer the questions.

1. In the U.S., interviewers do NOT usually ask about _____.
   A. language skills
   B. marital status
   C. educational background
   D. future plans

2. Eye contact is an example of _____.
   A. body language
   B. formality
   C. rudeness
   D. personality

3. A firm handshake is unusual in _____.
   A. Mexico
   B. Germany
   C. France
   D. the U.S.

4. The main idea of the article is that interviews _____ around the world.
   A. are similar
   B. are informal
   C. are formal
   D. are different

A. INTERVIEW

Read the interview on text page 127 and answer the questions.

1. Monica Salinas interviews _____.
   A. about 10 people a week
   B. about 50 people a day
   C. about 50 people a week
   D. about 100 people a year

2. She asks applicants about weekend activities because _____.
   A. she learns about applicants this way
   B. she's interested in hobbies
   C. they need to work weekends
   D. she's a friendly person

3. One applicant ate his sandwich during the interview because _____.
   A. he was nervous
   B. he was confident
   C. he wasn't prepared
   D. he was hungry

4. An employee from Brazil received a bonus check because _____.
   A. she sent money to her family
   B. she was a hard worker
   C. she was promoted
   D. she was given a raise

5. According to Monica Salinas, the best advice for interviews is to _____.
   A. reschedule them
   B. talk only about yourself
   C. be serious and honest
   D. be relaxed and be yourself

6. You can infer that Monica Salinas _____.
   A. works overtime
   B. will be promoted
   C. enjoys her job
   D. works in an international company

B. INTERVIEW A CLASSMATE

Interview a classmate. Use the chart below to record your classmate's answers. Then tell the class what you learned.

Tell me about your background and experience.	
How would a friend describe you? (Suggest at least 4 words that person might use.)	
What do you enjoy doing on the weekend? Do you have any hobbies?	
What would you be able to contribute to a company?	

A. Match the expression with the _opposite_ meaning on the right.

_____ 1. I inflated my resume.

_____ 2. I put my foot in my mouth.

_____ 3. I talked her head off.

_____ 4. I beat around the bush.

a. I gave complete and honest answers.

b. I didn't say very much.

c. I was honest about my experience.

d. I spoke very carefully.

B. Choose the best response.

1. Aunt Dorothy talks my head off.
   A. Did you call her back?
   B. I know. She never says much.
   C. Yes. She's a good speaker.
   D. It's true. She's never quiet.

2. Frank really put his foot in his mouth.
   A. I was surprised it fit.
   B. I think he should apologize.
   C. He was very prepared.
   D. It was a nice thing for him to say.

3. Our boss never beats around the bush.
   A. It's good that she says exactly what she's thinking.
   B. Is she a gardener?
   C. That can be confusing.
   D. Is it difficult to understand her?

4. I think Richard inflated his resume.
   A. That was a good idea.
   B. It's good to have a long resume.
   C. He should have been honest.
   D. I know. It's very short.

C. Write the correct idiom to complete each sentence.

beat around the bush	inflate	talk your head off	put my foot in my mouth

1. It's a big mistake to _____ your experience in a job application. Employers usually find out when someone isn't telling the truth.

2. If you want a day off, just ask your boss directly. Don't _____.

3. I really _____ when I asked my teacher how old she was.

4. If you ask Stan for his opinion about politics, he'll _____.

D. Answer these questions on a separate piece of paper. Then talk with a classmate about your answers.

1. Tell about a time when you put your foot in your mouth.
2. Describe someone you know who talks your head off.
3. Do you sometimes beat around the bush? When do you do that? Why?
4. Why do you think some people inflate their resumes?

A. Choose the words that best complete each sentence.

1. Marcy said she wouldn't be able to come to the party. She said she _____ sorry.
   - A. is being
   - B. had been
   - C. will be
   - D. was

2. We heard from Uncle Carl. He said he _____ visiting us this spring.
   - A. has been
   - B. can be
   - C. wouldn't be
   - D. had been

3. The tenants told the owner of the building they _____ upset with the superintendent.
   - A. been
   - B. were
   - C. will be
   - D. have been being

4. All the students in our class knew that Sacramento _____ the capital of California.
   - A. is
   - B. being
   - C. be
   - D. been

5. They asked me where yesterday's meeting _____ held.
   - A. is
   - B. has been
   - C. had
   - D. had been

6. Our teacher told us that making eye contact _____ considered rude.
   - A. hasn't
   - B. isn't
   - C. being
   - D. hasn't been being

B. Look at the sentences. Choose the sentence that is correct and complete.

7.
   - A. She told me she was surprised.
   - B. She told me she has surprised.
   - C. She told me she had surprised.
   - D. She told me she being surprised.

8.
   - A. He said he hasn't going to be late.
   - B. He said he wasn't going to be late.
   - C. He said he hadn't going to be late.
   - D. He said he not going to be late.

9.
   - A. I knew that the Nile be in Egypt.
   - B. I knew that the Nile being in Egypt.
   - C. I knew that the Nile is in Egypt.
   - D. I knew that the Nile been in Egypt.

10.
   - A. He asked me where the bank be.
   - B. He asked me where the bank was.
   - C. He asked me where the bank being.
   - D. He asked me where the bank been.

11.
   - A. Nobody knew where she is.
   - B. Nobody knew where she be.
   - C. Nobody knew where she been.
   - D. Nobody knew where she had been.

12.
   - A. They said they could help us.
   - B. They said they can help us.
   - C. They said they helping us.
   - D. They said they be helping us.

A. TECHNOLOGY IN OUR LIVES

Read the article on text page 159 and answer the questions.

1. In general, the article states that technology has _____ our lives.
  - A. limited
  - B. improved
  - C. increased
  - D. protected

2. The most changes in technology have come in the past _____.
  - A. year
  - B. 10 years
  - C. 100 years
  - D. 200 years

3. The first telephones didn't have any _____.
  - A. receivers
  - B. operators
  - C. calls
  - D. dials

4. Doctors use _____ to help people in remote areas.
  - A. satellite communication
  - B. scanners
  - C. ATMs
  - D. "smart highways"

5. Nowadays, a cashier can _____ to enter the price of an item.
  - A. pay by credit card
  - B. scan a bar code
  - C. use a cell phone
  - D. take a picture

6. Currently, people are NOT able to _____.
  - A. use a "smart highway"
  - B. send digital photos by e-mail
  - C. do banking online
  - D. use a store scanner without a cashier

7. *Smart homes* in paragraph 3 means homes where computers _____.
  - A. clean rooms
  - B. destroy privacy
  - C. control home appliances
  - D. enter and leave rooms

8. You can infer from the last paragraph that the author of this article believes _____.
  - A. technology is always good
  - B. lonely people like technology
  - C. technology protects personal information
  - D. protecting the privacy of information is important

B. INTERNET USERS

Look at the Fact File on text page 159 and answer the questions.

1. There were approximately _____ Internet users in 1996.
  - A. 50
  - B. 50,000
  - C. 5,000,000
  - D. 50,000,000

2. The number of Internet users increased by about _____ between 1995 and 2000.
  - A. 40 million
  - B. 200 million
  - C. 280 million
  - D. 320 million

TECHNOLOGY IN ACTION

Read the article on text page 160 and answer the questions.

1. Many people use _____ to communicate with family members who live far away.
   A. video conferences
   B. scanners
   C. telemedicine
   D. e-mail

2. _____ are used to provide electricity in Sudan.
   A. Satellite dishes
   B. Solar batteries
   C. Utilities
   D. Scanners

3. In Japan, eye-scanning technology is used to _____ a person's identity.
   A. name
   B. ask about
   C. verify
   D. take a photo of

4. In many _____, scanners are used to screen luggage.
   A. airports
   B. hospitals
   C. homes
   D. stores

5. Telemedicine allows a doctor to _____ a patient.
   A. only talk with
   B. see and talk with
   C. talk with and touch
   D. do a blood test on

6. Many cars have _____ that allow drivers to see a map.
   A. video cameras
   B. keyboards
   C. computers
   D. scanners

7. In some very remote areas, television service is received by a _____.
   A. DVD
   B. satellite dish
   C. cable system
   D. solar battery

8. Businesspeople from different locations can have a meeting using _____.
   A. a video conference
   B. a tape recorder
   C. telemedicine
   D. a meeting room

9. New technology is used _____.
   A. mostly by businesspeople
   B. only by people in remote areas
   C. only for personal enjoyment
   D. by businesses and individuals

10. You can infer that technology makes distances between people seem _____.
    A. more important
    B. shorter
    C. longer
    D. more difficult

A. INTERVIEW

Read the interview on text page 161 and answer the questions.

1. _____ people who were interviewed said they used technology to stay in touch with family or friends.
   A. Two
   B. Three
   C. Four
   D. Five

2. For the boy who was interviewed, technology provides _____.
   A. entertainment
   B. education
   C. cell phone service
   D. exercise

3. One person likes instant messaging more than the phone because it's _____.
   A. easier
   B. faster
   C. more fun
   D. less expensive

4. One woman says people *can always reach me.* This means people can always _____.
   A. touch her
   B. e-mail her
   C. contact her
   D. telecommute

5. A glucometer is used for _____.
   A. telecommuting
   B. medical reasons
   C. instant messaging
   D. global positioning

6. You can infer that a GPS device would also be useful for _____.
   A. a teacher
   B. a doctor
   C. a secretary
   D. a hiker

B. INTERVIEW A CLASSMATE

Interview a classmate. Use the chart below to record your classmate's answers. Then tell the class what you learned.

How much time do you spend on the computer each day?	
Which technology do you use to keep in touch with your friends?	
What is your favorite type of technology? Why?	
How has technology changed your life in the last five years?	

A. Choose the best response.

1. Our computer must be out of memory.
   A. Yes. I forgot it.
   B. Let's turn it off.
   C. Yes. We have too much information on it.
   D. That's okay. We can telecommute.

2. Oh, no! My computer is frozen!
   A. Since nothing is happening, you should restart it.
   B. You can't use it when it's so cold.
   C. That's okay. It will just work slowly.
   D. My software doesn't work either.

3. Do you think my computer has a virus?
   A. Yes. You should call a doctor.
   B. Yes. None of the programs are working correctly.
   C. Yes. You need a new computer.
   D. Yes. It feels very warm.

4. I think this software has a bug.
   A. Look carefully. Can you see it?
   B. That software often has problems.
   C. It must be very old.
   D. That's because it doesn't have enough memory.

B. Complete the paragraph with the correct idioms.

out of memory	have a virus	a bug in the software	froze

Ken had a terrible time with his computer yesterday. First, one of his game programs wasn't working very well. He thought that there could be _____[1]. He decided to install a new game program. But when he tried to install it, his computer displayed the message "_____"[2] because there were too many games and programs on his computer. Ken decided to delete a few of his old games. This would give more space for his new game. While he was deleting a game, his computer suddenly _____[3]. The screen was blank. Now he couldn't do anything at all. He called his friend Kim and explained the problem to her. She said that his computer must _____[4]. That was why nothing was working properly.

C. Answer these questions on a separate piece of paper. Then talk with a classmate about your answers.

1. Do you use a computer? Where?

2. Have you ever had a problem with a computer? Describe the problem. What did you do about it?

A. Choose the words that best complete each sentence.

1. It's a good idea to _____ English after finishing this book.
   A. take a break from studying
   B. keep studying
   C. stop studying
   D. only study

2. Most students _____ grammar.
   A. should stop studying
   B. don't need to learn more
   C. should forget about
   D. should keep studying

3. Watching movies is a good way to _____.
   A. improve your English
   B. enjoy your classes
   C. communicate with people
   D. learn grammar rules

4. Studying in class and using English outside the classroom _____.
   A. have to be done with a teacher
   B. will confuse you
   C. are both important
   D. are very similar

B. Look at the sentences. Choose the sentence that is correct and complete.

5. A. Luisa been studying for three years.
   B. Luisa has been studying for three years.
   C. Luisa is studying for three years.
   D. Luisa has studying for three years.

6. A. At first, she had trouble understanding spoken English.
   B. At first, she has trouble understanding spoken English.
   C. At first, she has had trouble understanding spoken English.
   D. At first, she is having trouble understanding spoken English.

7. A. Now she had been more confident.
   B. Now she was more confident.
   C. Now she is more confident.
   D. Now she has been more confident.

8. A. If she had worked so hard, she wouldn't have learned so much.
   B. If she has worked so hard, she wouldn't have learned so much.
   C. If she hasn't worked so hard, she wouldn't have learned so much.
   D. If she hadn't worked so hard, she wouldn't have learned so much.

9. A. Luisa wishes she has spoken more English with her classmates.
   B. Luisa wishes she had spoken more English with her classmates.
   C. Luisa wishes she had spoke more English with her classmates.
   D. Luisa wishes she had been spoken more English with her classmates.

10. A. Tomorrow she's taking her final test.
    B. Tomorrow she taking her final test.
    C. Tomorrow she's take her final test.
    D. Tomorrow she's taken her final test.

11. A. She didn't feel like studying now.
    B. She not feel like studying now.
    C. She doesn't feel like studying now.
    D. She doesn't feeling like studying now.

12. A. However, if she doesn't study, she will do well.
    B. However, if she doesn't study, she doing well.
    C. However, if she doesn't study, she didn't do well.
    D. However, if she doesn't study, she won't do well.

Side by Side Plus 4
Gazette Worksheets Answer Key

GAZETTE 1
Worksheet 1: Reading/Fact File

A.

1. C	5. B
2. B	6. D
3. D	7. A
4. A	8. C

B.
1. D
2. B

Worksheet 2: Around the World

A.

1. C	6. B
2. D	7. C
3. B	8. A
4. D	9. D
5. C	10. A

Worksheet 3: Interview

A.

1. D	4. D
2. C	5. C
3. B	6. A

B.
(Answers will vary.)

Worksheet 4: Fun with Idioms

A.

1. B	3. C
2. A	4. D

B.
1. held up in traffic
2. in the dark
3. blown away
4. given the ax

C.
(Answers will vary.)

Worksheet 5: We've Got Mail!

A.

1. C	4. D	7. D	10. B
2. A	5. C	8. C	11. D
3. B	6. D	9. A	12. C

GAZETTE 2
Worksheet 1: Reading/Fact File

A.

1. C	5. A
2. A	6. C
3. B	7. D
4. D	8. B

B.
1. C
2. B

Worksheet 2: Around the World

A.

1. B	6. C
2. D	7. D
3. C	8. A
4. B	9. C
5. D	10. D

Worksheet 3: Interview

A.

1. D	4. B
2. A	5. A
3. B	6. C

B.
(Answers will vary.)

Worksheet 4: Fun with Idioms

A.
1. You light up my life.
2. You're breaking my heart.
3. You've got me wrapped around your little finger.
4. You're a heel!

B.
1. breaking my heart; weren't a heel
2. lights up my life
3. wrapped around her little finger

C.
(Answers will vary.)

Worksheet 5: We've Got Mail!

A.

1. B	4. A	7. B	10. A
2. D	5. B	8. C	11. C
3. C	6. C	9. D	12. D

GAZETTE 3

Worksheet 1: Reading/Fact File

A.
1. A
2. D
3. B
4. C
5. A
6. C
7. D
8. B

B.
1. D
2. C

Worksheet 2: Reading/Around the World

A.
1. C
2. A
3. D
4. B
5. C
6. D

B.
1. B
2. A
3. C
4. D

Worksheet 3: Interview

A.
1. C
2. A
3. D
4. B
5. D
6. C

B.
(Answers will vary.)

Worksheet 4: Fun with Idioms

A.
1. C
2. D
3. B
4. A

B.
1. D
2. B
3. A
4. C

C.
1. inflate
2. beat around the bush
3. put my foot in my mouth
4. talk your head off

D.
(Answers will vary.)

Worksheet 5: We've Got Mail!

A.
1. D   4. A   7. A   10. B
2. C   5. D   8. B   11. D
3. B   6. B   9. C   12. A

GAZETTE 4

Worksheet 1: Reading/Fact File

A.
1. B
2. C
3. D
4. A
5. B
6. A
7. C
8. D

B.
1. D
2. C

Worksheet 2: Around the World

A.
1. D
2. B
3. C
4. A
5. B
6. C
7. B
8. A
9. D
10. B

Worksheet 3: Interview

A.
1. B
2. A
3. D
4. C
5. B
6. D

B.
(Answers will vary.)

Worksheet 4: Fun with Idioms

A.
1. C
2. A
3. B
4. B

B.
1. a bug in the software
2. out of memory
3. froze
4. have a virus

C.
(Answers will vary.)

Worksheet 5: We've Got Mail!

1. B   7. C
2. D   8. D
3. A   9. B
4. C   10. A
5. B   11. C
6. A   12. D

Side by Side Plus Book 4
Gazette Worksheets Answer Key (#2 of 2)

46

© 2009 Pearson Education, Inc.
Duplication for classroom use is permitted.

Side by Side Plus 4
Life Skills Worksheets

The *Side by Side Plus 4* Life Skills Worksheets provide realia-based reading and writing activities including personal information forms, checklists, maps, diagrams, transportation schedules, movie listings, product warranties, receipts, safety procedures, apartment ads, utility bills, nutrition labels, medicine labels, safety signs, help wanted ads, a rental agreement, a driver's license application, a bank account application, a household budgeting worksheet, an autobiographical timeline, a consumer complaint form, a medical history form, an accident report form, a job application, a resume, a cover letter, a pay stub, and math practice. The worksheets are fully coordinated with the *Side by Side Plus* units to offer valuable supplemental practice in class or at home for all students or for those students who require additional support or enrichment.

Student's Name _____

Date _____

Giving Directions

Look at the map. ̶omplete the directions with the following words. There is one extra word.

first	left	Maple	second	straight	two
Law̶ ̶	light	right	stop sign	three	

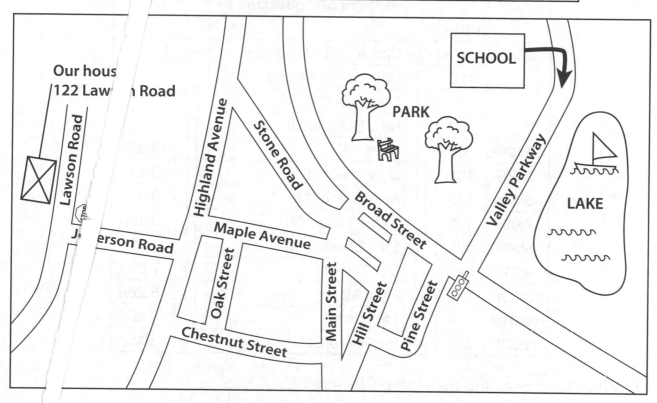

Directions to Our House from School

̶urn right on Valley Parkway. Go _____¹ until the traffic

_____². Turn _____³ on Broad Street. Take the third

_____⁴ onto Main Street. Go _____⁵ blocks. Turn right

̶ ̶ _____⁶ Avenue. Take the _____⁷ left onto Highland

̶venue. Take the _____⁸ right onto Jefferson Road. At the

_____⁹, take a right on _____¹⁰ Road. Our house is on

the left.

Student's Name _____

Date _____

Train Schedule: *Chicago*

Look at the train schedule. Answer the questions.

Chicago • Kalamazoo • Battle Creek • Port Huron

Blue Water 364 Daily	Mile		◄ Train Number ► ◄ Days of Operation ►		Blue Water 365 Daily
3:00P	0	Dp	Chicago, IL Union Station	Ar	11:14A
	16		Hammond-Whiting, IN		
	52		Michigan City, IN		
	62		New Buffalo, MI		
5:38P	89		Niles, MI		10:25A
5:50P	102		Dowagiac, MI		10:10A
6:34P	138		Kalamazoo, MI		9:41A
7:09P	160		Battle Creek, MI		9:12A
8:21P	208		East Lansing, MI		7:43A
9:07P	238		Durand, MI		7:02A
9:32P	256		Flint, MI		6:26A
10:01P	274		Lapeer, MI		6:00A
11:03P	319	Ar	Port Huron, MI	Dp	5:15A

1. What time does the train leave Chicago? _____

2. What time does the train leave Port Huron? _____

3. What time does the train from Port Huron arrive in Kalamazoo? _____

4. What time does the train from Chicago arrive in Kalamazoo? _____

5. What time does the train from Chicago arrive in Port Huron? _____

6. Which states does the Blue Water Train travel through?

   _____ _____ _____

7. How many miles is it from Michigan City, Indiana to Flint, Michigan? _____

8. How long does it take to get from Battle Creek to Chicago? _____

Student's Name _____

Date _____

Train Schedule: *Louisiana–Texas–New Mexico–Arizona*

Look at the train schedule. Answer the questions.

SUNSET LIMITED
NEW ORLEANS • HOUSTON • TUCSON

1			◄ Train Number ►		2
	Mile				
11:55A	0	Dp	New Orleans, LA	Ar	**4:00P**
1:25P	56		Schriever, LA		**1:08P**
2:51P	127		New Iberia, LA		11:46A
3:19P	145		Lafayette, LA		11:20A
4:50P	219		Lake Charles, LA		9:34A
6:43P	281		Beaumont, TX		8:10A
9:13P **9:50P**	363	Ar Dp	Houston, TX	Dp Ar	6:15A 5:45A
3:00A 5:40A	573	Ar Dp	San Antonio, TX	Dp Ar	1:00A **10:25P**
8:35A	742		Del Rio, TX		**6:37P**
11:10A	868		Sanderson, TX		**4:11P**
1:24P	959		Alpine, TX		**2:20P**
5:10P **5:55P**	1178	Ar Dp	El Paso, TX	Dp Ar	9:00A 8:16A
7:26P	1265		Deming, NM		6:15A
8:21P	1325		Lordsburg, NM		5:20A
9:26P	1444		Benson, AZ		2:20A
11:20P	1493	Ar	Tucson, AZ	Dp	1:20A

1. What time does the train leave New Orleans? _____

2. What time does the train leave Tucson? _____

3. What time does the train from New Orleans arrive in Houston? _____

4. What time does the train from Tucson arrive in Houston? _____

5. What time does the train from New Orleans arrive in Tucson? _____

6. How many miles is the trip from San Antonio to Tucson? _____

7. How long does it take to get from El Paso to San Antonio? _____

8. How long does the train from Tucson stay in Houston? _____

Student's Name _____

Date _____

Train Schedule: *Southern California*

Look at the train schedule. Answer the questions.

PACIFIC SURFLINER SOUTHBOUND
Los Angeles • Irvine • Oceanside • San Diego

Train Number ▶			564	566	572	578	582
Days of Operation ▶			Daily	Daily	Daily	Daily	Daily
	Mile		☕	☕	☕	☕	☕
Los Angeles	222	Dp	7:20A	8:30A	11:10A	2:00P	4:10P
Fullerton	248		7:50A	9:00A	11:40A	2:30P	4:40P
Anaheim	253		7:59A	9:09A	11:49A	2:39P	4:49P
Orange	255			9:13A		2:43P	
Santa Ana	258		8:08A	9:20A	11:58A	2:50P	4:58P
Irvine	268		8:22A	9:31A	12:11P	3:01P	5:09P
Laguna Niguel/Mission	277			9:41A		3:11P	
San Juan Capistrano	280		8:40A	9:48A	12:25P	3:18P	5:23P
San Clemente Pier	288			10:00A			
Oceanside	309		9:13A	10:23A	12:59P	3:48P	5:55P
Solana Beach	325		9:29A	10:39A	1:19P	4:08P	6:18P
San Diego (Old Town)	347		9:58A	11:08A			
San Diego (Tijuana)	350	Ar	10:10A	11:20A	1:55P	4:50P	7:00P

1. How many stops does Train 572 make after Los Angeles? _____

2. How long does it take for Train 564 to get from Los Angeles to Irvine? _____

3. How long does it take for Train 566 to get from Los Angeles to Solana Beach?

   _____

4. How many miles is it from Orange to San Diego (Tijuana)? _____

5. If you leave from Anaheim at 9:09 in the morning, what time will you arrive at

   Oceanside? _____

6. If you want to arrive in San Juan Capistrano at around noon, which train should

   you get from Los Angeles? _____

7. If you want to arrive in Laguna Niguel in the morning, which train should you

   get from Fullerton? _____

Train Schedule: *Florida*

Look at the train schedule. Answer the questions.

CROSS FLORIDA SERVICE

- Orlando
- West Palm Beach
- Miami

Silver Meteor 97 Daily	Mile		◄ Train Number ► ◄ Days of Operation ►		Silver Meteor 98 Daily
1:10P	0	Dp	Orlando	Ar	1:43P
1:32P	18		Kissimmee		1:16P
2:24P	56		Winter Haven		12:30P
3:05P	97		Sebring		11:44A
	139		Okeechobee		
4:54P	200		West Palm Beach		10:17A
5:23P	218		Delray Beach		9:52A
5:39P	229		Deerfield Beach		9:38A
6:02P	243		Fort Lauderdale		9:20A
6:18P	250		Hollywood		9:04A
6:55P	254	Ar	Miami	Dp	8:40A

1. What time does the train leave Orlando? _____

2. What time does the train leave Miami? _____

3. What time does the train from Orlando arrive in West Palm Beach? _____

4. What time does the train from Miami arrive in West Palm Beach? _____

5. What time does the train from Orlando arrive in Miami? _____

6. How many miles is the trip from West Palm Beach to Miami? _____

7. How long does it take to get from Fort Lauderdale to Winter Haven?

_____

8. How long does it take to get from Sebring to Hollywood? _____

Student's Name _____

Date _____

Train Schedule: *Northeast*

Look at the train schedule. Answer the questions.

Boston • New Haven • New York • Philadelphia • Washington, DC

		Northeast Regional	Acela Express	Acela Express	Northeast Regional
Train Number ▶		95	2153	2251	99
Days of Operation ▶		Mo–Fr	Mo–Fr	Sa	Sa–Su
BOSTON, MA South Station	Dp	6:05A	6:15A	8:10A	8:40A
PROVIDENCE, RI	⇩	6:55A	6:50A	8:49A	9:20A
NEW HAVEN, CT	Ar	8:42A	8:18A	10:18A	11:08A
	Dp	8:45A			11:11A
NEW YORK, NY	Ar	10:20A	9:45A	11:45A	12:50P
	Dp	10:35A	10:00A	12:00P	1:05P
NEWARK, NJ	⇩	10:52A	10:14A	12:14P	1:22P
PHILADELPHIA, PA		11:57A	11:07A	1:10P	2:29P
WILMINGTON, DE		12:21P	11:26A	1:31P	2:55P
BALTIMORE, MD		1:15P	12:11P	2:15P	3:38P
WASHINGTON, DC	Dp	2:00P	12:47P	2:50P	4:25P

1. What time does Train 2153 leave New Haven? _____

2. What time does Train 2153 arrive in New York? _____

3. How long does Train 99 stay in New York? _____

4. How long does it take to get from Boston to Washington, DC on Train 2251?

_____

5. How long does it take to get from Boston to Washington, DC on Train 95?

_____

6. What days does Train 99 operate? _____

7. What days does Train 2153 operate? _____

8. Which states do the trains travel through?

_____ _____ _____ _____

_____ _____ _____ _____

Student's Name _____
Date _____

Train Schedule: *Sacramento–San Jose*

Look at the train schedule. Answer the questions.

Westbound Weekday

Sacramento • Emeryville • Oakland • San Jose

Train Number ▶			541	543	545	547	549	551	553
On Board Service ▶			☕	☕	☕	☕	☕	☕	☕
	Mile								
Sacramento	35	Dp	2:10P	3:35P	4:40P	5:40P	6:40P	7:40P	9:10P
Davis	49		2:25P	3:50P	4:55P	5:55P	6:55P	7:55P	9:25P
Suisun-Fairfield	75		2:49P	4:14P	5:19P	6:19P	7:19P	8:19P	9:49P
Martinez	93		3:10P	4:35P	5:40P	6:40P	7:40P	8:40P	10:10P
Richmond	112	Ar	3:35P	5:00P	6:05P	7:05P	8:05P	9:05P	10:35P
Berkeley	118	Dp	3:42P	5:07P	6:12P	7:12P	8:12P	9:12P	10:42P
Emeryville	120		3:48P	5:13P	6:18P	7:18P	8:18P	9:18P	10:48P
Oakland	125		4:08P	5:26P	6:38P	7:31P	8:38P	9:38P	11:08P
San Jose	168	Ar		6:45P		8:50P		10:50P	

1. How many stops does Train 549 make after Sacramento? _____

2. How long does it take to get from Davis to Berkeley? _____

3. How long does it take train 543 to get from Martinez to San Jose? _____

4. How many miles is it from Sacramento to San Jose? _____

5. If you leave from Suisun-Fairfield at 2:49 in the afternoon, what time will you arrive at Oakland? _____

6. If you leave from Berkeley at 6:12 in the evening, what time will you arrive at Oakland? _____

7. If you want to arrive in Emeryville at around 7:30 in the evening, which train should you get from Davis? _____

8. If you want to arrive in San Jose at around 11:00 P.M., which train should you get from Berkeley? _____

Student's Name _____

Date _____

Plan a Trip

Look at the map. Complete the directions.

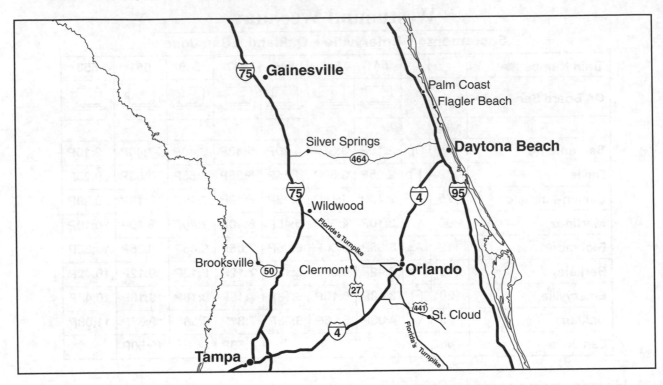

You want to drive from Gainesville to Clermont. What's the best route?

Take Interstate _____¹ south from Gainesville to Wildwood. Take the Florida

Turnpike south. Then take Route _____² south to Clermont.

You want to drive from Orlando to Flagler Beach. What's the best route?

Take Interstate _____³ northeast to Daytona Beach. Take Interstate _____⁴
north to Flagler Beach.

You want to drive from Silver Springs to Brooksville. What's the best route?

Take Route _____⁵ west. Take Interstate _____⁶ south. Then take Route

_____⁷ to Brooksville.

You Decide: You want to drive from Palm Coast to St. Cloud. What's the best
route?

Student's Name _____

Date _____

Movie Listings

Read the movie listings and answer the questions.

CINEMA PLEX 1
West Indies Square, Salem   516-555-1221
Baby Bonzo (G) (11:30, 2:00, 4:30) 7:00
Young Hearts (PG) (10:30, 1:00, 3:35) 6:05, 8:40
Speed Runner (PG-13) (12:50, 3:50) 7:00, 9:00, 11:00
The Listener (R) On 2 screens (12:20, 12:50, 2:50, 3:20)
5:10, 5:40, 7:25, 7:55, 9:50, 10:20

ROYAL Theater &
3209 Weston Way, Salem   516-555-2525
Baby Bonzo (G) (12:30, 3:00) 5:30, 8:00
Young Hearts (PG) (11:45, 2:15) 4:45, 7:15, 9:40
Speed Runner (PG-13) On 2 screens (11:40, 12:10, 2:10,
2:40) 5:30, 6:00, 7:55, 8:25, 10:10, 10:40
The Listener (R) (12:50, 3:50) 6:45, 9:00, 11:10
Traveling Titans (NR) (11:30, 1:45, 4:00) 7:15, 9:50
Metal Man (R) (11:15, 1:55, 4:35) 6:50, 9:35

MOVIE DIRECTORY KEY:
( )   Bargain shows
&   Handicapped access

G
General Audience
All ages admitted.

PG
Parental Guidance Suggested
Some material may not be suitable for children.

PG-13
Parents Strongly Cautioned
Some material may be inappropriate for children
under 13.

R
Restricted
Under 17 requires accompanying parent or
adult guardian.

NR
Not Rated

1. How many times is Cinema Plex 1 showing *The Listener* today? _____

2. How many times is Royal Theater showing *Traveling Titans* today? _____

3. What is the latest possible showtime for *Speed Runner*?

   Showtime: _____ Movie theater: _____

4. You want to see a movie with your 7-year-old child. Which is the most

   appropriate movie to see? _____

5. You want to see *Metal Man* at around 7:00. Which is the best showtime
   and movie theater to go to?

   Showtime: _____ Movie theater: _____

6. What is the latest possible time for a bargain show of *Young Hearts*?

   Showtime: _____ Movie theater: _____

7. You want to see *The Listener* at around 7:00 and you need handicapped
   access. Which is the best showtime and movie theater to go to?

   Showtime: _____ Movie theater: _____

63

Traffic Accident Report Form

Think of an accident. Complete the traffic accident form.

Traffic Accident Report Form		
Date of Accident:		Time:
Location:		
Weather Conditions:		
Road Conditions:		
Driver's Information	**Your Car**	**Other Car**
Name:		
Phone Number:		
Driver's License #:		
License State:		
Vehicle Information	**Your Car**	**Other Car**
License Plate Number:		
Year/Make/Model of Car:		
Vehicle Identification Number (VIN):		
Passenger Name & Number/ Describe Injury, if any:		
Passenger Name & Number/ Describe Injury, if any:		
Describe Damage to Car:		
Insurance Company Information	**Your Car**	**Other Car**
Name of Insured Person:		
Relationship to Driver:		
Insurance Company:		
Policy #:		
Agent/Agency Name:		

Traffic Accident Report Form (continued)

Police Report Information
Responding Department:
Officer's Name & Badge Number:
Police Report Number:
Description of Accident:

Diagram of Accident

DRAW A DIAGRAM IN THE SPACE BELOW

1. Number your vehicle as #1, other vehicle(s) as #2, #3, etc.

2. Show pedestrian by: O

3. Show direction of travel by an arrow. Example: 1→   ←2

4. Show which parts of the cars came together.

5. Give names or numbers of streets or highways.

6. Show traffic signs and signals.

7. Indicate North by arrow in box: ☐

Application for a Driver's License

Complete the form.

APPLICATION FOR DRIVER'S LICENSE OR IDENTIFICATION CARD   Use black ink only.

DRIVER'S LICENSE ☐   IDENTIFICATION CARD ☐

NAME _____   _____   _____
         FIRST   MIDDLE   LAST

ADDRESS _____   APT. #
        NUMBER   STREET

_____
        CITY   STATE   ZIP CODE

HOME PHONE _____   BUSINESS PHONE _____

SSN _____ - ____ - _____   DATE OF BIRTH _____   PLACE OF BIRTH _____

PERSONAL INFORMATION	SEX ☐ M ☐ F	EYE COLOR	HAIR COLOR	RACE	HEIGHT FT. IN.	WEIGHT LBS.

REQUIRED INFORMATION FROM ALL APPLICANTS:

   YES   **NO**

1. ( )   ( ) Have you ever had an identification card from this state?
         Number_____ When?_____

2. ( )   ( ) Have you ever had a license or instruction permit in this state?
         Number_____ When?_____

3. ( )   ( ) Have you ever had a license or instruction permit in any other state? State(s)_____
         Number(s)_____ When?_____

4. ( )   ( ) Are you a citizen of the United States?

5. ( )   ( ) Would you like to complete a voter registration application form today? You must be eligible.

6. ( )   ( ) Do you have a health condition that may impede communication with a police officer?
         If yes, please list:

         _____

REQUIRED INFORMATION FROM DRIVER'S LICENSE APPLICANTS:

   YES   **NO**   **DRIVING HISTORY INFORMATION**

7. ( )   ( ) Are you enrolled in or have you completed a driver education course?

8. ( )   ( ) Is your driver's license currently suspended, revoked, canceled, denied, or disqualified in **ANY** state?
         Where?_____ When?_____ Why?_____

9. ( )   ( ) Has your driver's license or driving privilege ever been suspended, revoked, canceled, denied, or disqualified in **ANY** state?
         Where?_____ When?_____ Why?_____

10. ( )   ( ) Are you currently placed out of service for operating a commercial motor vehicle?
         Why?_____

SIGNATURE OF APPLICANT (APPLICATION NOT COMPLETE WITHOUT SIGNATURE)

I have reviewed the Application Form and swear, under the penalties of perjury, that the information I have provided is true and complete.

Signature: _____   Date: _____

Key Words: *World War I–World War II*

A. Key Words: *Places*

Write the numbers of the places on the map in the correct circles.

1 Austria-Hungary
2 England
3 France
4 Germany
5 Italy
6 Japan
7 Pearl Harbor
8 Russia

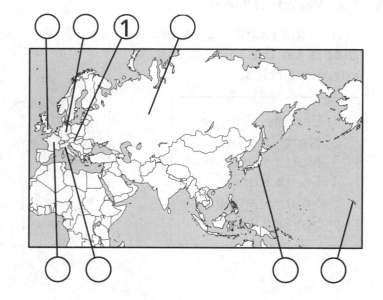

B. Key Words: *People and Events*

Complete the sentences.

Adolf Hitler	Franklin D. Roosevelt	Holocaust	Pearl Harbor	World War II
Allies	Great Depression	New Deal	World War I	

1. _____ started in 1914 and ended in 1917.

2. _____ started in 1939 and ended in 1945.

3. England, Russia, and France were the _____ in World War II.

4. _____ was the leader of Nazi Germany from 1933 to 1945.

5. _____ was the president of the United States from 1933 to 1945.

6. In the _____, hundreds of banks closed and many people in the United States lost most of their money.

7. The _____ is when the Nazis killed over 6 million European Jews.

8. In the 1930s the U.S. government gave unemployed people jobs to build roads, parks, bridges, and buildings in the _____.

9. The U.S. entered World War II when the Japanese bombed _____.

Key Words: *The United Nations–The Civil Rights Movement*

A. Key Words: *Places*

Write the numbers of the places on the map in the correct circles.

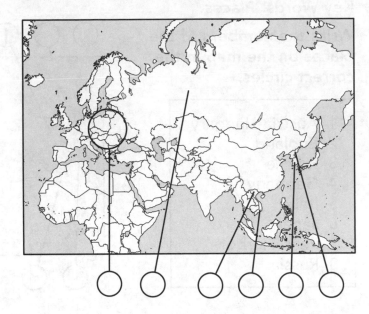

> 1 Eastern Europe
> 2 North Korea
> 3 North Vietnam
> 4 South Korea
> 5 South Vietnam
> 6 Soviet Union

B. Key Words: *People and Events*

Complete the sentences.

Cold War	Martin Luther King, Jr.	United Nations
Korean War	superpowers	Vietnam War

1. The _____ is an international organization established to keep peace among countries around the world.

2. Between 1945 and 1991, the world's two _____ were the Soviet Union and the United States. They had allies and interests around the world.

3. In the _____, the Soviet Union and the United States competed economically and politically.

4. In the _____, the communist North fought against the non-communist South from 1950 to 1953.

5. In the _____, the communist North fought against the non-communist South from 1964 to 1973.

6. _____ was the most famous leader of the civil rights movement in the United States.

Key Words: *September 11, 2001–The War in Iraq*

A. Key Words: *Places*

Write the numbers of the places on the map in the correct circles.

1 Arlington, Virginia
2 Boston
3 New Jersey
4 New York
5 Pennsylvania
6 Washington, D.C.

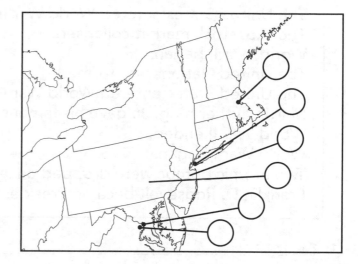

B. Key Words

Complete the sentences.

Afghanistan	Saddam Hussein
George W. Bush	weapon of mass destruction
Pentagon	

1. _____ was the dictator of Iraq from 1979 to 2003.

2. _____ was the president of the United States from January 2001 to January 2009.

3. The United States sent troops to _____ in 2001.

4. The _____ is the headquarters of the U.S. military.

5. The atomic bomb is a _____.

Student's Name _____

Date _____

U.S. History Timeline

Write these events on the correct lines in the timeline below.

> The United States entered World War II.
> The U.S. stock market collapsed.
> World War II began.
> The United Nations was formed.
> The United States entered World War I.
> Martin Luther King, Jr. gave his famous "I Have a Dream" speech.
> World War II ended.
> World War I began.
> Two atomic bombs were dropped on Japan.
> Franklin D. Roosevelt became President of the United States.

1914 _____

1917 _____

1929 _____

1932 _____

1939 _____

1941 _____

1945 _____

1945 _____

1945 _____

1963 _____

Life and Work History Timeline

A. **Brainstorming.** Think about important events in your life such as the following:

> When were you born?
> When did you start school?
> When did you graduate from school?
> When did you take your first English class?
> When did you have your first job?
> When did you get a pay raise or a job promotion?
> When did you move to the United States?
> When did you meet your spouse?

B. **Writing.** Write a timeline of important dates and events in your life.

Month/Year	Event

Explaining Problems with Products

A. Complete the conversation using the words below.

broken	less	receipt	stuck
charge	problem	repair	warranty

A. I bought this notebook computer here, and it's _____[1].

B. What seems to be the _____[2]?

A. Some of the keys get _____[3].

B. I see. Do you have your _____[4]?

A. Yes. Here it is. Will there be a _____[5] for the

_____[6].

B. No. It's still under _____[7] because you bought it

_____[8] than a year ago.

B. Complete the conversation using the words below.

exchange	may	return
matter	refund	work

A. _____[1] I help you?

B. Yes. I'd like to _____[2] this electric toothbrush.

A. What's the _____[3] with it?

B. The switch doesn't _____[4].

A. Would you like to _____[5] it?

B. No, thanks. I'd like a _____[6], please.

A. All right.

Student's Name _____

Date _____

Number Practice: *Estimating Costs*

Read the ad and answer the questions.

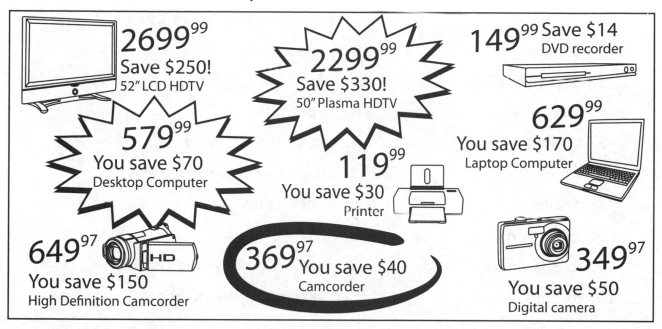

1. The Rodriguez family wants to buy the 50-inch plasma TV and the DVD recorder. How much will their purchases cost?
   a. about $2450   b. about $2550   c. about $2850

2. Steve wants to buy the laptop computer and the printer. How much will his purchases cost?
   a. about $650   b. about $750   c. about $775

3. Linda wants to buy the desktop computer and the printer. How much will her purchases cost?
   a. about $680   b. about $690   c. about $700

4. The Chan family wants to buy the digital camera and the printer. How much will their purchases cost?
   a. about $450   b. about $470   c. about $490

5. The Batiste family wants to buy the 52-inch LCD TV and the high definition camcorder. How much will their purchases cost?
   a. about $2950   b. about $3070   c. about $3350

6. Sue and Bill want to buy the camcorder and the desktop computer. How much will their purchases cost?
   a. about $950   b. about $1150   c. about $1550

Warranty Vocabulary

A. Match the warranty terms with their meanings.

____ **1.** bill of sale

____ **2.** defect

____ **3.** disposable

____ **4.** purchaser

____ **5.** to ship

____ **6.** workmanship

____ **7.** dealer

____ **8.** to exchange

____ **9.** to guarantee

____ **10.** to obtain

a. a problem with the product

b. to get

c. person who sells a certain kind of product

d. to promise

e. can be thrown away

f. to send something in the mail

g. to get a new one

h. quality of work

i. person who buys the product

j. a receipt for the purchase

B. Complete the story with the following words.

bill of sale	defect	shipped
charge	exchange	warranty
dealer	guaranteed	workmanship

Bob bought a new refrigerator from an appliance _____1.

The store _____2 that the refrigerator would have no problems.

Three days after it was _____3 to his house, Bob found that the

_____4 was very bad. The door had a _____5

and he wasn't able to open it. Bob took the _____6 and the

refrigerator tag back to the store. He showed the papers to the salesman and

said, "I want to _____7 the refrigerator for a new one." The

salesman said, "We can't replace your refrigerator, but we'll send a repairperson to

your house to fix the door. There will be no _____8 because you're

still under _____9."

Number Practice: *Interpreting Charts and Prices*

Read the store repair and replacement plans and answer the questions.

Big Buy Small Electronics Replacement Plans	
Purchase Price	1 Year Plan
$0–$49^{99}	$4^{99}
$50^{00}–$99^{99}	$9^{99}
$100^{00}–$149^{99}	$14^{99}
$150^{00}–$199^{99}	$19^{99}
$200^{00}–$249^{99}	$29^{99}
$250^{00}–$299^{99}	$39^{99}

Big Buy Small Electronics Service Plans		
Purchase Price	2 Year Plan	4 Year Plan
$300^{99}–$399^{99}	$49^{99}	$99^{99}
$400^{99}–$499^{99}	$59^{99}	$139^{99}
$500^{99}–$799^{99}	$99^{99}	$169^{99}
$800^{99}–$999^{99}	$149^{99}	$199^{99}
$1,000^{99}–$1,999^{99}	$229^{99}	$299^{99}
$2,000^{99}–$4,999^{99}	$279^{99}	$349^{99}

- The plan begins upon expiration of manufacturer's labor warranty. During the manufacturer's warranty period, any parts or labor are the sole responsibility of the manufacturer.
- Product replacements only for failed products under $300.

The Hanson family bought a $259^{00} DVD player with a 90-day manufacturer's warranty. They also bought a replacement plan.

1. How much did they pay for the replacement plan?
   a. $14^{99} b. $29^{99} c. $39^{99}

2. If their DVD player doesn't work two months later, which warranty will take care of the problem?
   a. The manufacturer's warranty.
   b. The Big Buy Service Plan.
   c. The Big Buy Replacement Plan.

The Yamamoto family bought a $1199^{97} camera with a 1-year manufacturer's warranty. They also bought a 4-year service plan.

3. How much did they pay for the service plan?
   a. $229^{99} b. $299^{99} c. $349^{99}

4. If the camera doesn't work 16 months later, what can they do?
   a. Repair it with the Big Buy Service Plan.
   b. Repair it with the manufacturer's warranty.
   c. Replace it with the Big Buy Service Plan.

Consumer Tip: Read service plans and replacement plans very carefully! They aren't always worth the extra expense. Usually they aren't effective until the manufacturer's warranty expires. The manufacturer's warranty comes free with the product purchase.

Warranty Card

You bought a vacuum cleaner at an electronics store. Here's the receipt. Complete the warranty card.

```
        Welcome to Electronic World
                 Weston, CT
               Keep your receipt.

                              08/05/10

    A850284   Z710XE              $129.99
    Orelco Vacuum Cleaner
```

Orelco Product Warranty Card

1. ☐ Mr.   ☐ Mrs.   ☐ Ms.   ☐ Miss

FIRST NAME   INITIAL   LAST NAME

STREET   APT. NO.

CITY   STATE   ZIP CODE

E-MAIL ADDRESS

2. YOUR DATE OF BIRTH
   ☐☐ / ☐☐ / ☐☐☐☐
   Month   Day   Year

3. PHONE NUMBER
   (☐☐☐) ☐☐☐ ☐☐☐☐

4. DATE OF PURCHASE
   ☐☐ / ☐☐ / ☐☐☐☐
   Month   Day   Year

5. PRICE PAID (EXCLUDING SALES TAX)   ☐ RECEIVED AS A GIFT
   $☐☐☐ . ☐☐

6. MODEL NUMBER
   [A]☐☐☐☐☐

7. SERIAL NUMBER
   [Z]☐☐☐☐☐

8. Where was this model purchased?
   01. ☐ Received as a Gift
   02. ☐ Office Supply Store
   03. ☐ TV/Appliance Store
   04. ☐ Hardware Store
   05. ☐ Electronics Store
   06. ☐ Mail Order
   07. ☐ Other

9. How did you first learn about this product?
   01. ☐ Received as a Gift
   02. ☐ Newspaper Ad
   03. ☐ Magazine Ad
   04. ☐ Television Ad
   05. ☐ Friend or Relative
   06. ☐ Salesperson
   07. ☐ Store Display
   08. ☐ Other

Consumer Complaint Form

Complete the consumer complaint form with your own story of a consumer problem or with information from one of the consumer problems on student text page 64c.

Please use black ink only.

Consumer Complaint Form

Name _____ _____ _____
            FIRST   MIDDLE   LAST

Address _____ _____
              NUMBER   STREET   APT. #

_____ _____ _____ E-mail _____
         CITY   STATE   ZIP CODE

Home Phone _____ Cell Phone _____

1. How did you learn about the company?
   ☐ Someone came to my home.
   ☐ I went to the company's place of business.
   ☐ I received a telephone call from the company.
   ☐ I received information in the mail.
   ☐ I reponded to a radio/television ad.
   ☐ I responded to a print ad.
   ☐ I responded to a website or e-mail ad.

2. Where did the purchase take place?
   ☐ At home
   ☐ At the place of business
   ☐ By mail
   ☐ Over the phone
   ☐ Over the computer
   ☐ Other _____

3. Please describe your complaint in detail (attach extra sheets if necessary).

   _____

   _____

   _____

   _____

4. Have you complained to the company?   No ☐   Yes ☐   If so, when? _____
   What was the company's response?

   _____

   _____

   _____

Signature _____ Date _____

CPR Instructions

1. CALL

- If the person isn't responding to anything, call 911.

2. BLOW

- Tilt the person's head back and listen for breathing.

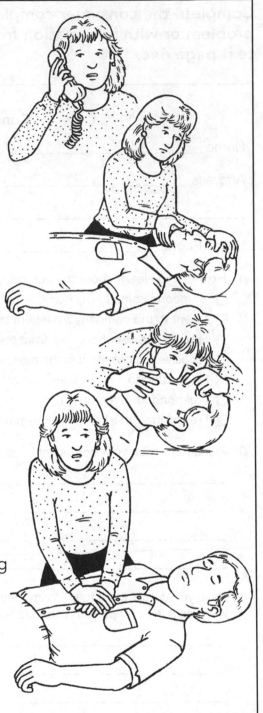

- If the person isn't breathing, press the person's nose closed and cover the mouth with your mouth.

- Blow into the person's mouth until you see the chest rise. Blow two times. Each blow should take 1 second.

3. PUMP

- If the person still isn't breathing normally or isn't coughing or moving, begin pressing the chest.

- Push down on the chest 1½ to 2 inches 30 times. Pump at the rate of 100 times a minute, faster than one pump per second.

Student's Name _____

Date _____

The Heimlich Maneuver

A. Read each statement and circle *True* or *False*.

1. The Heimlich maneuver is for emergency use only.   True   False

2. If a person is coughing, you should perform the   True   False
   Heimlich maneuver.

3. If a person isn't breathing, he or she can't speak or cough.   True   False

4. If a person can't breathe for four seconds, he or she will have   True   False
   brain damage.

5. The Heimlich maneuver pushes food out of a person's stomach.   True   False

6. The Heimlich maneuver can injure a person.   True   False

7. The Heimlich maneuver can save a person's life.   True   False

B. Number the steps of the Heimlich maneuver from 1 to 6.

_____ Grab your fist with your other hand.

_____ Make a fist with one hand.

_____ Press into the person's abdomen with four quick inward and upward thrusts.

_____ Put the thumb side of your fist below the person's rib cage.

_____ Repeat until the object comes out.

___1___ Stand behind the person.

Student's Name _____

Date _____

Your Escape Plan

Draw a floor plan of your home. Show rooms, doors, windows, and stairways. Use the symbols below to show the location of your fire extinguisher, first-aid kit, utility shutoff, smoke detectors, and outside meeting place. Draw an escape plan for your home. Make sure you draw two exits from every room!

KEY

← normal exit route	Ⓢ smoke detector
◄┄┄ emergency exit route	▥▥ stairway
Ⓕ fire extinguisher	Ⓤ utility shutoff
⊞ first-aid kit	═ window
∕ door	✗ meeting place outside

Student's Name _____

Date _____

Home Fire Safety Checklist

Read the checklist. Check (✓) *Yes* or *No* for each question.

	Yes	No
1. Do you have a fire extinguisher in your kitchen?	___	___
2. Do you have smoke detectors in your home?	___	___
3. Do you change the batteries in your smoke detectors every six months?	___	___
4. Do you store flammable products away from heat?	___	___
5. Do you keep space heaters away from flammable materials?	___	___
6. Do you have an escape route plan?	___	___
7. Do you have a meeting place in case of fire?	___	___
8. Do you have a first-aid kit?	___	___
9. Do you practice your escape plan twice a year?	___	___
10. Do you know how to shut off your utilities?	___	___

Reading a Smoke Detector Diagram

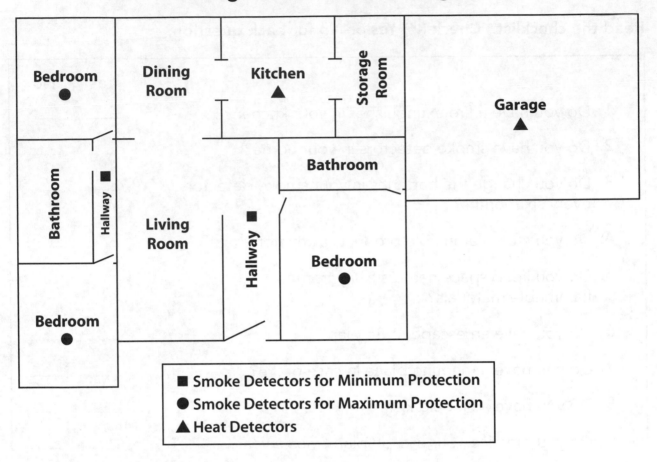

1. Which areas should have smoke detectors for minimum protection?
   a. The bedrooms.   b. The hallways.   c. The kitchen and garage.

2. Which areas should have smoke detectors for maximum protection?
   a. The kitchen and garage.   b. The bathrooms.   c. The bedrooms.

3. Which areas should have heat detectors?
   a. The bedrooms.   b. The kitchen and garage.   c. The hallways.

4. Which areas of the home don't need smoke detector protection?
   a. The dining room and living room.   b. The storage room.   c. a and b.

5. According to the diagram, how many smoke detectors are needed for minimum protection?
   a. One.   b. Two.   c. Three.

82

Reading Apartment Ads

A. Read the abbreviations and write the full words.

air conditioning	bedroom	elevator	included	parking
available	building	heat	large	transportation
basement	dining room	hot water	living room	utilities
bathroom	eat-in kitchen	immediately	near	washer and dryer

1. BR _____bedroom_____
2. W/D _____
3. A/C _____
4. EIK _____
5. DR _____
6. LR _____
7. BA _____
8. elev. _____
9. bldg. _____
10. pkg. _____

11. trans. _____
12. ht. _____
13. incl. _____
14. hw _____
15. immed. _____
16. nr. _____
17. bsmt. _____
18. lg. _____
19. avail. _____
20. util. _____

B. Look at the apartment ads. Read the sentences. Write the letter of the apartment next to each sentence.

A	B	C
CHELSEA Avail. now. Lg. 3 BR apt. 1 BA, LR, EIK, W/D, A/C, $1600 plus util. Pkg. Call Rick 413-555-2948.	SUMMERHILL 1 BR apt. 1.5 BA, elev. in bldg. A/C, W/D in bsmt. $850. Util. incl. Nr. trans. Avail. 6/10. Call 312-555-0295.	WESTVILLE 2 BR, 1 BA apt. Lg. kit. LR, DR, nr. shopping. $1200. Ht. hw. incl. Avail. immed. Call owner 971-555-1352.

_____ 1. It has two bedrooms.
_____ 2. It has an eat-in kitchen.
_____ 3. It's not available now.
_____ 4. It has parking.
_____ 5. Utilities are not included.

_____ 6. It has one and a half bathrooms.
_____ 7. Heat and hot water are included.
_____ 8. It's near public transportation.
_____ 9. There's an elevator in the building.
_____ 10. It doesn't have air conditioning.

83

Reading a Rental Agreement

Read the rental agreement. Circle T for *True* or F for *False*.

Rental Agreement

THIS AGREEMENT IS BETWEEN:

_____Trini Parramon_____ as LANDLORD and _____Lisa Shaw_____ as TENANT.
The LANDLORD leases to the TENANT apartment number: __3B__ at _291 Center Street_ Tampa,
Florida 33651 for the term of _____twelve months_____ beginning _____June 1, 2011_____ and
ending on _____May 31, 2012_____.

TERMS AND CONDITIONS OF THIS AGREEMENT:

1. **RENT:** The total rent for the apartment is __$12,000.00__. The monthly rent is __$1,000.00__
   due on or before the _____first_____ day of each month.

2. **UTILITIES AND SERVICES:** The TENANT will pay the following utility and service charges:
   _____Electricity, Telephone, and Internet_____.
   The LANDLORD will pay the following utility and service charges:
   _____Gas and Water_____

3. **APPLIANCES:** The apartment is rented with the following appliances:
   _____Refrigerator and Dishwasher_____
   The LANDLORD will repair appliances that the LANDLORD owns. The TENANT is responsible for
   repairing any other appliances.

4. **SECURITY DEPOSIT:** The TENANT will deposit with the LANDLORD a security deposit of
   __$2,000.00__. If the apartment is in good condition when the TENANT moves out, and all rent is
   paid, the LANDLORD will return the full amount of the security deposit within 30 days.

5. **ENTRY TO APARTMENT:** The LANDLORD has the right to enter the apartment if the
   LANDLORD gives 24-hour notice.

6. **CONDITION OF APARTMENT:** The TENANT agrees to take good care of the apartment. When
   the agreement ends, the TENANT will return the apartment in good clean condition. The LANDLORD
   agrees to maintain and repair the structural components of the dwelling (roofs, floors, walls) and to
   provide adequate locks and keys, and to maintain electrical, plumbing, heating, and other appliances in
   good working order.

---

1. The apartment has a stove.   T   F

2. The landlord is responsible for the repair of all appliances.   T   F

3. The landlord can come into the apartment with 24-hour notice.   T   F

4. The rent is $12,000 a month.   T   F

5. The tenant is responsible for maintenance of floors and walls.   T   F

6. The landlord must provide the tenant with keys and locks.   T   F

7. When the agreement ends, the landlord must leave the   T   F
   apartment in good condition.

Bank Services

A. Complete the sentences with the correct words.

account	make	sign
certified	order	send
deposit	savings	withdrawal

1. I'd like to _____ a deposit.

2. I'd like to _____ more checks. I'm running out.

3. I'd like to get a _____ check.

4. I'd like to make a _____. I need $100.

5. I'd like to _____ money overseas.

6. I'd like to open a _____ account.

7. Please _____ and date the form at the bottom.

8. How much would you like to _____ to open the account?

9. I'd like to open a checking _____.

B. Put the conversation in the correct order (1–11).

_____ All right. Please read this information carefully. Then sign and date it at the bottom.

_____ And what's your address?

_____ And your zip code?

__1__ How may I help you?

_____ How much would you like to deposit today to open the account?

_____ Okay. What's your name, please?

_____ $100.

_____ 72 Pine Street, Centerville, Texas.

_____ 75833.

_____ I want to open a checking account.

_____ Armando Ortiz.

85

Number Practice: *Money*

Solve the word problems.

Maria is at the bank.

1. She has $1,325 in her savings account. She makes a deposit of $850.00. How much is in her account? _____

2. The next day, Maria makes a withdrawal of $280 from her savings account. Now how much is in her savings account? _____

Ivan is at the bank.

3. He has $1,185 in his checking account. He makes a withdrawal of $540 to send overseas. Now how much is in his account? _____

4. He orders more checks. The bank charges him $5.60 for the checks. They make the withdrawal from his checking account. Now how much money does Ivan have in his account? _____

5. Ivan makes a deposit of $230 in his checking account. Now how much money does he have in his account? _____

Eliza is at the store.

6. She has $80 in her wallet. She wants to buy the following items: a blouse for $24.00, socks for $5.50, a skirt for $29.00, and a pair of pants for $15.00. Does she have enough money to buy all the items? _____

7. There are no taxes on clothes in her state. How much change does Eliza get back? _____

Kenji is at a gift store.

8. Kenji is buying a $15.99 clock. The sales tax is an additional $.96. What is the total cost of the clock? _____

9. Kenji gives the cashier a $50 bill for the clock. What is his change?

_____

Julia is at the supermarket.

10. The total cost of Julia's groceries is $63.54. Julia gives the cashier $70.00. He gives her $7.44 in change. Is that the correct change? _____

11. The cashier notices his mistake. How much does Julia have to return to him?

_____

Bank Account Vocabulary

Match the bank words on the left with their definitions on the right.

____ **1.** daily balance

____ **2.** monthly fee

____ **3.** opening deposit

____ **4.** record keeping

____ **5.** interest

____ **6.** minimum balance

____ **7.** online banking

____ **8.** waive a fee

____ **9.** safe deposit box

____ **10.** passbook

a. bank services a customer can use on the Internet

b. writing down the information about what goes in and out of an account

c. the money a bank customer earns by leaving his or her money in a bank account

d. a small booklet that records all the money coming in and going out of a savings account

e. the amount of money in an account at the end of one day

f. a small storage unit in a bank to keep valuable items such as jewelry or legal documents

g. a required amount of money a customer must keep in a bank account

h. the first amount of money a customer puts in a new account

i. money a customer pays a bank 12 times a year to have an account

j. to allow a customer *not* to pay a bank charge

Bank Account Application

Complete the application for a checking account.

Midtown Bank Account Application

For a Personal Checking Account

What account do you wish to open?
- ☐ Basic Checking   ☐ Regular Checking   ☐ Checking Plus
- ☐ Individual   ☐ Joint

For a Personal Savings Account

What account do you wish to open?
- ☐ Statement Savings   ☐ Passbook Savings   ☐ Money Market Savings
- ☐ Individual   ☐ Joint

PRIMARY APPLICANT

Last Name _____ First Name _____ MI _____

Social Security Number _____ Date of Birth __ __ / __ __ / __ __ __ __

Home Address _____
               STREET   CITY   STATE   ZIP CODE

Home Phone No. _____ Work Phone No. _____

Cell Phone No. _____ E-mail Address _____

How do you prefer us to contact you? ☐ e-mail   ☐ mail   ☐ cell phone   ☐ home phone

JOINT APPLICANT

Last Name _____ First Name _____ MI _____

Social Security Number _____ Date of Birth __ __ / __ __ / __ __ __ __

Home Address _____
               STREET   CITY   STATE   ZIP CODE

Home Phone No. _____ Work Phone No. _____

Cell Phone No. _____ E-mail Address _____

OPENING DEPOSIT

   ☐ check   ☐ cash   ☐ transfer from account #: _____

I certify that the above information is correct and that I have read the account agreement and will follow the account requirements.

Primary Applicant Signature _____ Date _____

Joint Applicant Signature _____ Date _____

Budgeting Worksheet

Complete the budgeting worksheet.

Housing Expenses	**Monthly Payments**	
Rent or Mortgage	$_____	
Utilities	$_____	
Insurance	$_____	
Repairs	$_____	
Taxes	$_____	
= Total		$_____
Car/Travel Expenses		
Loan Payment(s)	$_____	
Gas	$_____	
Insurance	$_____	
Maintenance & Repairs	$_____	
Public Transportation	$_____	
= Total		$_____
Debts		
#1 _____ Balance _____	$_____	
#2 _____ Balance _____	$_____	
= Total		$_____
Miscellaneous Expenses		
Groceries, Lunches, Meals Out	$_____	
Childcare	$_____	
School Fees/Supplies	$_____	
Medical Care	$_____	
Prescription Medicines	$_____	
Entertainment, Cable, DVD Rentals	$_____	
Clothing	$_____	
Gifts	$_____	
(Other): _____	$_____	
(Other): _____	$_____	
= Total		$_____
Monthly Expense Totals		
Housing	$_____	
Car	$_____	
Debts	$_____	
Miscellaneous	$_____	
= Total Expenses		$_____
Total Take-Home Income		
– Total Expenses =		$_____

Student's Name _____

Date _____

Number Practice: *Utility Bills*

Read the utility bills and answer the questions.

Florida Energy
P.O. Box 2145
Miami, FL 33166
Floridaenergy.com

Account Number: 03-112-8846

Martin Morales
15 Bella Vista
Coral Gables, FL 33155

Billing Summary	
Previous Bill	$57.49
Payment – Thank You	– 57.49
Total Cost Electricity	53.71
Amount Due on May 14	**$53.71**

Electricity Used

April 29 2009	Actual Read	29608 kWh	
March 29 2009	Actual Read	29345 kWh	
31 Day Billed Use		263 kWh	

Delivery Charges .0925 x 263 kWh	24.33
Generation Charge .1117 x 263 kWh	29.38
Total Charge for Electricity	**$53.71**

Mobile Talk
P.O. Box 926653
Cincinnati, OH 45724

Statement for: **Cathy Lin**
Account Number: 9925364
Amount Due by 6/27/09   **$86.28**

Phone Accounts	Monthly Charges	Taxes and Surcharges	Total Current Charges
312-555-2435	69.94	4.65	$ 74.59
773-555-7243	9.99	1.70	$ 11.69
Total	**79.93**	**6.35**	**$ 86.28**

Account Service Detail

Monthly Phone Account Charges	**$ 79.93**
Family Plan	49.99
Unlimited Instant Messages	19.95
Added Line	9.99
Taxes Fees and Surcharges	**$ 6.35**
Federal Universal Service Fund	1.00
State Sales tax	3.55
State 911	.60
Regulator Programs Fee	1.20
Total Charges	**$ 86.28**

Number Practice: *Utility Bills* (continued)

Martin Morales's Bill

1. Martin has to pay his bill on or before _____.

2. Last month Martin paid _____ for electricity.

3. This month Martin must pay _____ for electricity.

4. Martin used _____ kWh of electricity in April 2009.

5. $_____ of Martin's electric bill is for Generation Charges.

6. $_____ of Martin's electric bill is for Delivery Charges.

7. Martin pays about $_____ for every kWh of electricity he uses.

Cathy Lin's Bill

8. Cathy Lin has a total cell phone bill of _____.

9. She has to pay her bill on or before _____.

10. She has to pay a total of _____ in Monthly Phone Account Charges.

11. The phone number account of 312-555-2435 has two detail charges. One

    charge is $_____ for the Family Plan and the other charge is

    $_____ for Unlimited Messaging.

12. Cathy thinks there's a mistake on her cell phone bill. She's going to call
    Customer Assistance and ask about two new charges that she hasn't seen
    before—the Federal Universal Service Fund and the Regulator Programs Fee.

    Together these add $_____ to her phone bill.

Student's Name _____

Date _____

Community Health Provider Information Form

Name of Health Provider: _____

Address: _____

Phone Number: _____   Hours of Operation: _____

	Yes	No
Types of Visits		
drop-in		
by appointment		
Population Served		
serves children		
serves adults		
Medical Specialties		
dental care		
physical therapy		
women's health care		
counseling services		
eye care		
other:		
other:		
Language Services *		
interpreters on phone		
interpreters in person		

* Languages _____

_____

Symptoms and Medical Advice

A. Complete the sentences with the following words. There is one extra word.

bump	low-fat	swollen
exercise	move	water
knee	muscle	

1. I think I pulled a _____.

2. It hurts when I bend my _____.

3. I have a big _____ on my head.

4. My wrist is _____ because I fell on it while I was playing soccer.

5. You need to drink several glasses of _____ every day.

6. You need to eat _____ dairy products.

7. You need to _____ regularly.

B. Put the conversation in the correct order (1–7).

_____ Rest it?

___1___ What seems to be the problem?

_____ I see. Do you have any idea what might have caused this?

_____ I want you to rest it for the next week.

_____ Yes. If you do that, you'll probably feel a lot better.

_____ Yes. I lifted a very heavy box at work, and I think I pulled a muscle in my back.

_____ My back has been hurting for more than a week.

Student's Name _____

Date _____

Medical History Form

Name _____ **Date of Birth** _____

Please check any current symptoms you have.

Whole Body	**Ears/Nose/Throat/Mouth**	**Gastrointestinal**
❏ recent fcvers	❏ difficulty hearing	❏ heartburn
❏ sudden weight loss	❏ allergies	❏ nausea/vomiting
❏ sudden weight gain	❏ stuffy nose	❏ diarrhea
❏ tiredness/weakness	❏ trouble swallowing	❏ pain in abdomen
Eyes	**Cardiovascular**	**Respiratory**
❏ change in vision	❏ chest pains	❏ coughing frequently
	❏ short of breath	❏ coughing up blood
Musculoskeletal	**Skin**	**Neurological**
❏ muscle pain	❏ rash	❏ headaches
❏ joint pain	❏ new or change in mole	❏ memory loss
❏ recent back pain		❏ fainting

Please check if you have had any of the following health problems.

___ chicken pox	___ diabetes	___ high blood pressure
___ measles	___ tuberculosis	___ pneumonia
___ mumps	___ cancer	___ liver disease (hepatitis)
___ asthma	___ AIDS	___ influenza
___ heart disease	___ kidney disease	

Please check if anyone in your family (parents, siblings, grandparents, children) has had any of the following illnesses.

___ asthma	___ diabetes	___ AIDS
___ heart disease	___ tuberculosis	___ kidney disease
___ high blood pressure	___ cancer	___ liver disease

List the medications you are now taking. Include non-prescription drugs and vitamins.

_____

List any allergies you have to drugs, food, or other items.

_____

Student's Name _____

Date _____

Nutrition and Food Labels

Countryside Plain Non-Fat Yogurt

Nutrition Facts
Serving Size: 1 cup
Servings Per Container: 1

Calories 110	Calories from Fat 0

	% Daily Value
Total Fat 0g	0%
Saturated Fat 0g	0%
Trans Fat 0g	
Cholesterol 3mg	1%
Sodium 160mg	7%
Total Carbohydrate 15g	5%
Dietary Fiber 0g	
Sugars 0g	
Protein 13g	

Vitamin A	0%	Vitamin C	4%
Calcium	45%	Vitamin D	0%

1. How many servings are there in this container of yogurt? _____

2. How many calories are there in a serving? _____

3. How many calories are there in a half a cup of yogurt? _____

4. What nutrients are in the yogurt?

   _____

5. What vitamins and minerals are there in this yogurt?

   _____

6. How much protein is there in a serving of this yogurt? _____

7. How much fiber is there in a serving of this yogurt? _____

8. Is this yogurt good for you? Explain your answer.

   _____

   _____

Student's Name _____

Date _____

Reading a Medicine Label

Read the label and circle T for *True* or F for *False*.

Extra-Strength Pain Reliever

Active Ingredient: Acetaminophen 500 mg

Uses: Temporarily relieves the aches and pains due to
- headache
- backache
- the common cold
- toothache
- arthritis
- reduces fever

Directions
- Adults and children 12 years and over: Take 2 caplets every 6 hours.
- Do not take more than 8 caplets in 24 hours.
- Children under 12: Do not use this Extra-Strength product.

Alcohol Warning
If you consume 3 or more alcoholic drinks a day, ask your doctor if you should take acetaminophen. It may cause liver damage.

Stop Use If
- redness and swelling is present.
- fever gets worse or lasts for more than 3 days.
- pain gets worse or lasts for more than 10 days.

Inactive Ingredients: carnauba wax, croscarmellose sodium, starch, stearic acid   **Expiration date:** 11/2012

---

1. Take this medicine if you have a fever.   T   F

2. Take this medicine if you have a stomachache.   T   F

3. Don't take this medicine if you drink three alcoholic drinks a day.   T   F

4. Children under 12 should not take this medicine.   T   F

5. 10 caplets in 24 hours is an overdose.   T   F

6. If the pain gets worse, stop taking this medicine.   T   F

7. Starch and stearic acid are active ingredients.   T   F

8. You should throw this medicine out in December 2012.   T   F

9. If you have a fever for three or more days, you should take three   T   F
   caplets every six hours.

Work Safety

Write the words under the safety signs.

biohazard	first-aid kit	no drinks allowed	safety glasses
combustible materials	flammable materials	no food allowed	safety gloves
corrosive materials	helmet	poison	
fire extinguisher	high voltage	respirator	

1. _____

2. _____

3. _____

4. _____

5. _____

6. _____

7. _____

8. _____

9. _____

10. _____

11. _____

12. _____

13. _____

14. _____

An Accident Report at Work

Complete the accident report form.

EMPLOYEE ACCIDENT REPORT

Name of injured
employee: _____ Date of report: _____

SS#: _____ Sex: ___ M ___ F Date of birth: _____

Home address of employee: _____

Job title: _____ Department: _____

Date and time of accident: _____

Location of accident: _____
(BUILDING AREA: HALLWAY, OFFICE, ETC.)

Describe in detail how the accident occurred: _____

_____

_____

_____

_____

What safety equipment, if any, did the employee use? _____

_____

Part of body injured: _____
(BE SPECIFIC—EXAMPLE: RIGHT INDEX FINGER, LEFT ANKLE, UPPER BACK)

Type of injury: _____
(EXAMPLE: SPRAIN, BURN, BROKEN BONE)

Was medical treatment sought? If so: _____
NAME OF MEDICAL PROVIDER   PHONE NUMBER

Name of witness: _____ Phone no.: _____

Name of witness: _____ Phone no.: _____

Name of witness: _____ Phone no.: _____

No. of days missed from work: _____

Return to work date (as stated by physician): _____

Supervisor signature: _____ Date: _____

Employee signature: _____ Date: _____

Student's Name _____

Date _____

Reading an Evacuation Map

Read the evacuation map and answer the questions.

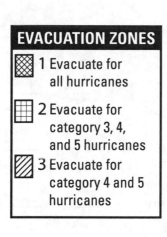

EVACUATION ZONES

⊠ **1** Evacuate for all hurricanes

▦ **2** Evacuate for category 3, 4, and 5 hurricanes

▨ **3** Evacuate for category 4 and 5 hurricanes

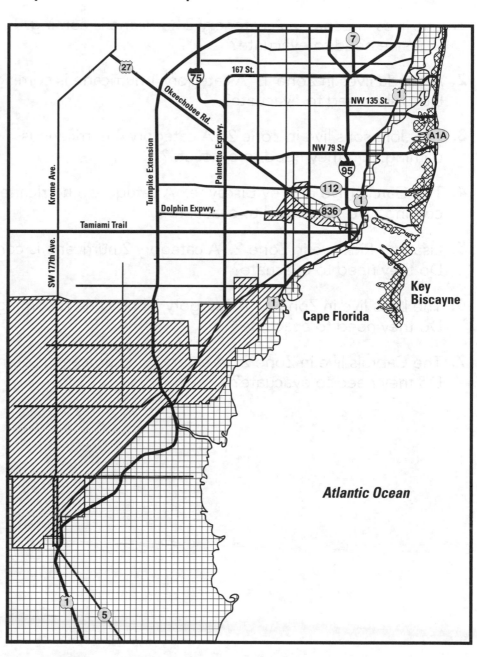

This is an evacuation map for residents of Miami-Dade County in Florida. If a hurricane comes to the area, residents might be told to leave their homes (evacuate) and travel to a shelter. Evacuation orders depend on the intensity of the hurricane and the location of the home.

Reading an Evacuation Map (continued)

	Yes	No
1. Eric lives in Zone 3. A category 2 hurricane is coming. Does he need to evacuate?	____	____
2. Amanda lives in Zone 1. A category 1 hurricane is coming. Does she need to evacuate?	____	____
3. The Johnsons live in Zone 2. A category 4 hurricane is coming. Do they need to evacuate?	____	____
4. The Garcias live on Key Biscayne. A category 3 hurricane is coming. Do they need to evacuate?	____	____
5. Lisa and Rick live in Zone 2. A category 2 hurricane is coming. Do they need to evacuate?	____	____
6. The Lees live in Zone 3. A category 5 hurricane is coming. Do they need to evacuate?	____	____
7. The Cabrals live in Zone 2. A category 3 hurricane is coming. Do they need to evacuate?	____	____

Job Interview Vocabulary

Complete the sentences with the appropriate words. There are two extra words.

attitude	familiar	promotion
communicator	get along	skills
employed	goals	specific
enthusiastic	position	weakness

A. What are your greatest strengths?

B. I'm a good _____¹, and I _____² well with

  people. I have a positive _____³, and I try to improve my

  _____⁴.

A. Do you know what we do here?

B. Yes. I'm _____⁵ with your work because my friend Ruth Gomez

  has been _____⁶ here for two years.

A. Do you have any questions for me?

B. Yes. Can you tell me more about the _____⁷ job
  responsibilities?

A. Certainly. You will greet patients, answer the telephone, schedule
  appointments, find medical records, and communicate with insurance
  companies.

B. Are there opportunities for _____⁸ and advancement?

A. Yes. You can move up to the position of office supervisor.   What are your

  long-term _____⁹?

B. I would like to become a medical office administrator.

A. I see.

B. When do you plan to fill the _____¹⁰?

A. The job starts October 4th.

Help Wanted Ads

A. Write the full words next to the abbreviations.

assistant	certified	driver's license	experience	previous
available	company	equivalent	office	references
benefits	diploma	excellent	opportunity	required

1. excel. _____

2. asst. _____

3. co. _____

4. refs. _____

5. driv. lic. _____

6. exp. _____

7. req'd. _____

8. cert. _____

9. ofc. _____

10. bnfts. _____

11. equiv. _____

12. avail. _____

13. dipl. _____

14. oppt. _____

15. prev. _____

B. Read the help wanted ads. Choose the correct answer.

Secretary	Home Health Aide
Ofc. asst. 2 years. prev. exp req'd. High School dipl. or equiv. Excel bnfts. Oppt. for promotion. Fax resume to 209-555-3656.	Need cert. home aides. Co. car avail. Must have driv. lic., refs. 1 year prev. exper. Weekend and evening hours. Call Maxim at 209-555-7412.

1. Both positions require _____.
   a. a driver's license
   b. a high school diploma
   c. references
   d. previous experience

2. Neither ad includes information on _____.
   a. the benefits
   b. the name of the person to call
   c. the pay
   d. the work days

3. The home health aide must _____.
   a. drive
   b. work weekends
   c. provide references
   d. do all the above

4. The secretary job doesn't require _____.
   a. a high school diploma
   b. a promotion
   c. experience
   d. a resume

Job Application

Complete the job application. (Use any information you wish.)

PERSONAL DATA

Name: _____
           LAST   FIRST   MIDDLE

Home Address: _____ _____
                        NUMBER   STREET   APT #

_____ _____ _____
           CITY   STATE   ZIP CODE

Social Security Number: _____

Home Number: _____ Cell Phone Number: _____

EMPLOYMENT DESIRED

Position you are applying for: _____

Date available for work: _____ Total hours available per week: _____

What type of work are you looking for?   ☐ PART-TIME   ☐ FULL-TIME   ☐ TEMPORARY

Please list all the times you are available to work (From 6 AM to 12 AM):

Sun _____ M _____ T _____ W _____ Th _____ F _____ Sat _____

EXPERIENCE (List most recent first)

Employer Name: _____ Phone Number: _____

Address: _____

Supervisor's Name: _____ Dates Worked: FROM _____ TO _____

Position: _____ Salary: _____

Duties: _____

Reason for Leaving: _____

Employer Name: _____ Phone Number: _____

Address: _____

Supervisor's Name: _____ Dates Worked: FROM _____ TO _____

Position: _____ Salary: _____

Duties: _____

Reason for Leaving: _____

EXPERIENCE (Continued)

Employer Name: _____ Phone Number: _____

Address: _____

Supervisor's Name: _____ Date Worked: FROM _____ TO _____

Position: _____ Salary: _____

Duties: _____

Reason for Leaving: _____

EDUCATION HISTORY

High School: _____
                NAME   CITY   STATE

Diploma or GED Received: Yes _____ No _____ Date: _____

College	Location	Field of Study	Degree/Certification

SKILLS (Please check all that apply.)

☐ Bookkeeping ☐ Customer Service ☐ Inventory Clerk ☐ Payroll ☐ Switchboard

☐ Calculator ☐ Data Entry ☐ Maintenance ☐ PowerPoint ☐ Typing

☐ Cashier ☐ Excel ☐ Packer ☐ Stock Room ☐ Word

Typing Speed: _____ wpm

List any special training, experience, or skills you have that are relevant to the position you are applying for.

_____

_____

_____

_____

REFERENCES (No relatives please)

      Name   Relationship   Telephone Number

1. _____

2. _____

3. _____

My signature certifies that what I have written is true.

Signature: _____ Date: _____

Student's Name _____

Date _____

Work and Education Experience Timeline

A. Brainstorming. Think about your work experience and skills. Read the questions below.

> When did you graduate from school?
> When did you start working? What was your job? What were your job duties?
> When did you get your second job? What was your job? What were your job duties?
> Have you ever received a pay raise or a job promotion? When?
> Have you ever taken an interesting class or learned a special skill in a training program? What was it? When was it?
> When did you start studying English?

B. Writing. Write a timeline of important work and education experiences and their dates. Start with your most recent experiences.

Month/Year	Work or Education Experience

105

Student's Name _____

Date _____

Write Your Resume

Look at this template. Then write your own resume on a separate piece of paper. (Use any information you wish.)

_____
(Name)

_____
(Address)

_____   _____   _____
(Home phone)   (Cell phone)   (E-mail)

OBJECTIVE: A position in _____

EDUCATION: School, city, state
Degree or certification, year

School, city, state
Degree or certification, year

EXPERIENCE: (list most recent first)

Dates   Position, Place of Employment, City, State

Description of job duties _____

_____

Dates   Position, Place of Employment, City, State

Description of job duties _____

_____

Dates   Position, Place of Employment, City, State

Description of job duties _____

_____

SKILLS: (List special skills here—for example: languages you speak, typing or
computer skills, machine operating skills, any special license you have to
drive or operate equipment, certifications, etc.)

OTHER ACTIVITIES: (List other interests here—for example: community service, volunteer
positions, hobbies)

References Available Upon Request

Student's Name _____

Date _____

A Cover Letter

A. Read the cover letter and circle T for *True* or F for *False*.

15 Vista Road
San Antonio, TX 78238

April 17, 2010

Sandra Miller
Tech Specialties
6700 Old Highway
San Antonio, TX 78227

Dear Ms. Miller:

I would like to apply for the position of office manager at Tech Specialties. I saw your advertisement in the *San Antonio Globe* newspaper.

As you can see from my attached resume, my skills and experience are a good match for the position. I have worked for years as an administrative assistant and secretary. I have also taken courses in technology and software development. As an office manager at Tech Specialties, I would be able to combine my interest in technology and my skills as an experienced office administrator.

If I can provide you with any further information on my background and qualifications, please let me know. I look forward to hearing from you. Thank you for your consideration.

Respectfully yours,

Alice Gatano

Alice Gatano

1. This letter was sent with a resume.   T   F

2. Ms. Gatano has many years of work experience in technology.   T   F

3. Ms. Gatano found out about the job from a local newspaper.   T   F

4. In paragraph 2, Ms. Gatano explains why she is writing to Ms. Miller.   T   F

5. In paragraph 1, she thanks Ms. Miller for reading her letter and resume.   T   F

6. In paragraph 2, she explains why she would be a good office manager at Tech Specialties.   T   F

B. Write your own cover letter on a separate piece of paper.

Asking for & Responding to Feedback

Complete the conversations with the correct words. There is one extra word.

connect	filling out	procedure
copier	labeling	supposed
correctly	list	telling
excuse	original	

A. Am I doing this _____[1]?

B. No, you aren't. You should _____[2] the printer to the computer.

A. Am I _____[3] the cans correctly?

B. No. You're _____[4] to put the label on the top of the can.

A. Am I _____[5] the timesheet correctly?

B. No. You should _____[6] the hours separately.

A. _____[7] me. Am I using the _____[8] correctly?

B. No. You're supposed to put the _____[9] face up in the feeder.

A. Oh, okay. I didn't know that. Thanks for _____[10] me.

Employee Benefits Checklist

Read *The Shelby Company Employee Benefits* on student text page 144b
again. Check (✓) *True* or *False* for each statement.

		True	False
1.	Part-time employees get health insurance.	____	____
2.	Employees help pay the health insurance premium.	____	____
3.	The health insurance plan covers eyeglasses.	____	____
4.	Full-time employees can have free check-ups with their dentist.	____	____
5.	Only full-time employees are eligible for 9 paid holidays a year.	____	____
6.	For every dollar an employee saves in the 401(k) retirement plan, the Shelby Company saves a dollar for the employee, too.	____	____
7.	If an employee doesn't use all four personal days, the employee can save them for the following year.	____	____
8.	Employees can get free counseling.	____	____
9.	Employees can take their nine holidays any time they want to.	____	____
10.	The Shelby Company pays for its full-time employees' life insurance plan.	____	____
11.	Money in a 401(k) plan is not taxed until a person has retired.	____	____
12.	Employees get two weeks of sick days every year.	____	____
13.	Employees can save up as many vacation days as they wish and use them in the future.	____	____

Pay Stub

Look at the pay stub and complete the statements below.

Shelby Company		Erin Taylor Employee No. 2132	Pay Period Ending 04/02/09	
Earnings	**Rate**	**Hours**	**This Period**	**Year to Date**
Regular	12.00	32	384.00	5,928.00
Overtime	18.00	5	90.00	990.00
Holiday	12.00	8	96.00	192.00
		Gross Pay	570.00	7,110.00
Leave	**Earned**	**Used**	**Used–Year to Date**	**Accrued–Year to Date**
Vacation	1.6	0.0	8.0	16.8 hours
Sick Time	.75	0.0	0.0	9.75 hours
Taxes & Deductions			**This Period**	**Year to Date**
Federal Tax			58.00	735.00
State Tax			27.00	350.00
FICA/Medicare			45.00	550.00
Health Plan			40.00	520.00
401(k) (co. match 100%)			40.00	520.00
Total			210.00	2,675.00
Net Pay			360.00	4,435.00

1. Erin worked a total of _____ regular and overtime hours during this pay period.

2. _____ was deducted from Erin's paycheck this pay period.

3. Erin took home _____ this pay period.

4. Before deductions, Erin has earned _____ this year.

5. She has taken home _____ in paychecks.

6. She paid _____ for state and federal taxes in this pay period.

7. Erin has paid _____ for state and federal taxes this calendar year.

8. Erin contributed _____ to her retirement plan this pay period.

9. The company contributed _____ to her retirement plan this pay period.

10. Erin has contributed _____ to her retirement plan this calendar year.

11. Erin's health plan costs _____ each pay period.

12. Erin has accrued _____ hours of sick time this year.

13. Erin has used _____ vacation hours this calendar year.

Student's Name _____

Date _____

Describing Your Qualities

A. Circle the words and phrases that describe you.

adaptable	a good communicator
considerate	a good team player
cooperative	a leader
dedicated	a problem solver
dependable	the first to arrive
efficient	the last to leave
flexible	
friendly	focus on the big picture
hardworking	get along with others
helpful	learn quickly
honest	try to improve all the time
industrious	see a challenge as an opportunity
punctual	
willing to work	

B. Using the words you circled, write several sentences to describe yourself.

_____

_____

_____

_____

_____

_____

Citizenship Vocabulary

Match the words on the left with their definitions on the right.

_____ **1.** income tax

_____ **2.** jury

_____ **3.** national defense

_____ **4.** natural-born citizen

_____ **5.** naturalized citizen

_____ **6.** permanent resident

_____ **7.** privilege

_____ **8.** property tax

_____ **9.** responsibilities

_____ **10.** criminal or civil offense

_____ **11.** verdict

_____ **12.** trial

a. a person who moves to the United States and then becomes a citizen

b. the military—for example the army, navy, and air force

c. duties

d. a special right or advantage a person has

e. the tax a person pays the government for the things he or she owns (for example—a house, a car, a boat)

f. the decision a jury makes about whether a person is guilty or innocent

g. a person who legally lives in the United States but is not a citizen

h. a group of 12 citizens in a court who decide if a person is guilty or innocent

i. a person who was born in the United States

j. the tax an employee pays the government for the money that person makes

k. a procedure in court to decide if someone is guilty or innocent

l. when a person is accused of breaking the law

Student's Name _____

Date _____

Legal Services Information Form

Name of Health Agency: _____

Address: _____

Phone Number: _____ Hours of Operation: _____

Services	Yes	No
Fair Housing		
housing conditions		
eviction from your home		
housing discrimination		
problems with tenant and landlord		
other:		
Family Law		
legal separation		
divorce		
child support		
counseling services		
child custody		
other:		
Immigration Services		
tourist and student visas		
changing immigration status		
work permits		
naturalization		
legal residency		
other:		
Language Services*		
interpreters on phone		
interpreters in person		

*Languages _____

_____

113

Legal Language

A. Complete the sentences with the correct words. There is one extra word.

child support	legal	rights
civil law	low-income	tourist visa
domestic violence	naturalization	work permit

1. You need a _____ to travel to Brazil.

2. _____ is a crime.

3. Yuyan was born in China. She became a United States citizen through

_____.

4. The tenant didn't know his _____, and he allowed his landlord to evict him.

5. They don't make a lot of money. They're a _____ family.

6. He needs a _____ to have a job in this country.

7. Housing, immigration, and family law are all part of _____.

8. After the divorce, Ivan paid _____ to his wife every month.

B. Write the letter of the office each person should visit.

A Family Law	C Tenant Rights
B Domestic Violence	D Immigration Services

_____ **1.** Magda has received an eviction letter from her landlord.

_____ **2.** Kenji's visa is going to expire.

_____ **3.** Janice wants to get a divorce.

_____ **4.** Tomas wants to become naturalized.

_____ **5.** Kate's husband hurts her and the children.

_____ **6.** The superintendent still hasn't fixed the lock on the apartment door.

_____ **7.** Lydia's ex-husband wants to see the children more often.

_____ **8.** Alicia needs to get a work permit.

Side by Side Plus 4
Life Skills Worksheet Answer Key

UNIT 1

Worksheet 1:
Parent-School Communication
1. teacher
2. nurse's office
3. classroom
4. problems, class
5. homework, idea
6. playground

Worksheet 2:
School Registration Form
(Answers will vary.)

Worksheet 3:
Note to School
(Answers will vary.)

Worksheet 4:
Reasons for Notes to School
1. g
2. d
3. a
4. h
5. b
6. c
7. i
8. f
9. e

Worksheet 5:
Checklist: *Helping Your Children Succeed in School*
1. ✓
2. ___
3. ✓
4. ✓
5. ___
6. ___
7. ✓
8. ✓
9. ___
10. ✓
11. ___
12. ___
13. ✓
14. ✓

Worksheet 6:
Parent Volunteer Form
(Answers will vary.)

UNIT 2

Worksheet 7:
Giving Directions
1. straight
2. light
3. right
4. left
5. two
6. Maple
7. second
8. first
9. stop sign
10. Lawson

Worksheet 8:
Train Schedule: *Chicago*
1. 3:00 P.M.
2. 5:15 A.M.
3. 9:41 A.M.
4. 6:34 P.M.
5. 11:03 P.M.
6. Illinois, Indiana, Michigan
7. 204
8. 2 hours and 2 minutes

Worksheet 9:
Train Schedule: *Louisiana–Texas–New Mexico–Arizona*
1. 11:55 A.M.
2. 1:20 A.M.
3. 9:13 P.M.
4. 5:45 A.M.
5. 11:20 P.M.
6. 920
7. 13 hours and 25 minutes
8. 30 minutes

Worksheet 10:
Train Schedule: *Southern California*
1. 8
2. 1 hour and 2 minutes
3. 2 hours and 9 minutes
4. 95
5. 10:23 A.M.
6. Train 572 / the 11:10 A.M. train
7. Train 566 / the 9:00 A.M. train

Worksheet 11:
Train Schedule: *Florida*
1. 1:10 P.M.
2. 8:40 A.M.
3. 4:54 P.M.
4. 10:17 A.M.
5. 6:55 P.M.
6. 54
7. 3 hours and 10 minutes
8. 3 hours and 13 minutes

UNIT 2

Worksheet 12:
Train Schedule: *Northeast*
1. 8:18 A.M.
2. 9:45 A.M.
3. 15 minutes
4. 6 hours and 40 minutes
5. 7 hours and 55 minutes
6. Saturday and Sunday
7. Monday through Friday
8. Massachusetts, Rhode Island, Connecticut, New York, New Jersey, Pennsylvania, Delaware, Maryland

Worksheet 13:
Train Schedule: *Sacramento–San Jose*
1. 7
2. 1 hour and 17 minutes
3. 2 hours and 10 minutes
4. 133
5. 4:08 P.M.
6. 6:38 P.M.
7. Train 547 / the 5:55 P.M. train
8. Train 551 / the 9:12 P.M. train

Worksheet 14:
Plan a Trip
1. 75
2. 27
3. 4
4. 95
5. 464
6. 75
7. 50
You Decide: (Answers will vary.)

Worksheet 15:
Movie Listings
1. 10
2. 5
3. 11:00 P.M., Cinema Plex 1
4. Baby Bonzo
5. 6:50, Royal Theater
6. 3:35, Cinema Plex 1
7. 6:45, Royal Theater

Worksheet 16:
Traffic Accident Report Form
(Answers will vary.)

Worksheet 17:
Application for a Driver's License
(Answers will vary.)

UNIT 3

Worksheet 18:
Key Words: *World War I–World War II*
A.

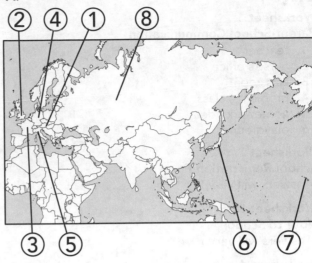

B.
1. World War I
2. World War II
3. Allies
4. Adolf Hitler
5. Franklin D. Roosevelt
6. Great Depression
7. Holocaust
8. New Deal
9. Pearl Harbor

Worksheet 19:
Key Words: *The United Nations–The Civil Rights Movement*
A.

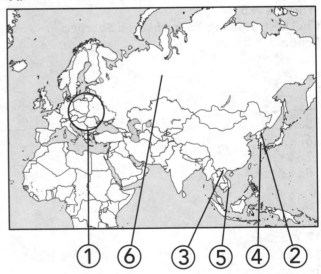

B.
1. United Nations
2. superpowers
3. Cold War
4. Korean War
5. Vietnam War
6. Martin Luther King, Jr.

Worksheet 20:
Key Words: *September 11, 2001–The War in Iraq*
A.

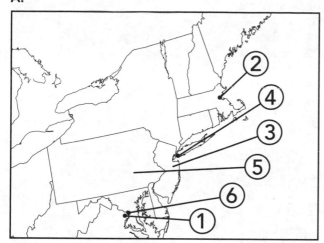

B.
1. Saddam Hussein
2. George W. Bush
3. Afghanistan
4. Pentagon
5. weapon of mass destruction

Worksheet 21:
U.S. History Timeline
1914 World War I began.
1917 The United States entered World War I.
1929 The U.S. stock market collapsed.
1932 Franklin D. Roosevelt became President of the United States.
1939 World War II began.
1941 The United States entered World War II.
1945 Two atomic bombs were dropped on Japan.
1945 World War II ended.
1945 The United Nations was formed.
1963 Martin Luther King, Jr. gave his famous "I Have a Dream" speech.

Worksheet 22:
Life and Work History Timeline
(Answers will vary.)

UNIT 4
Worksheet 23:
Explaining Problems with Products
A.

1. broken	5. charge
2. problem	6. repair
3. stuck	7. warranty
4. receipt	8. less

B.

1. May	4. work
2. return	5. exchange
3. matter	6. refund

Worksheet 24:
Number Practice: *Estimating Costs*
1. a
2. b
3. c
4. b
5. c
6. a

Worksheet 25:
Warranty Vocabulary
A.

1. j	6. h
2. a	7. c
3. e	8. g
4. i	9. d
5. f	10. b

B.
1. dealer
2. guaranteed
3. shipped
4. workmanship
5. defect
6. bill of sale
7. exchange
8. charge
9. warranty

Worksheet 26:
Number Practice: *Interpreting Charts and Prices*

1. c	3. b
2. a	4. a

Worksheet 27:
Warranty Card
(Answers will vary.)

Worksheet 28:
Consumer Complaint Form
(Answers will vary.)

UNIT 5

Worksheet 29:
CPR Instructions
(For student reference.)

Worksheet 30:
The Heimlich Maneuver
A.

1. True	5. False
2. False	6. True
3. True	7. True
4. False	

B.

4
2
5
3
6
1

Worksheet 31:
Your Escape Plan
(Answers will vary.)

Worksheet 32:
Home Fire Safety Checklist
(Answers will vary.)

Worksheet 33:
Reading a Smoke Detector Diagram

1. b	3. b	5. b
2. c	4. c	

Worksheet 34:
Reading Apartment Ads
A.

1. bedroom	11. transportation
2. washer and dryer	12. heat
3. air conditioning	13. included
4. eat-in kitchen	14. hot water
5. dining room	15. immediately
6. living room	16. near
7. bathroom	17. basement
8. elevator	18. large
9. building	19. available
10. parking	20. utilities

B.

1. C	5. A	8. B
2. A	6. B	9. B
3. B	7. C	10. C
4. A		

Worksheet 35:
Reading a Rental Agreement

1. F	5. F
2. F	6. T
3. T	7. F
4. F	

UNIT 6

Worksheet 36:
Bank Services
A.

1. make	6. savings
2. order	7. sign
3. certified	8. deposit
4. withdrawal	9. account
5. send	

B.

11
5
7
1
9
3
10
6
8
2
4

Worksheet 37:
Number Practice: *Money*

1. $2,175	7. $6.50
2. $1,895	8. $16.95
3. $645	9. $33.05
4. $639.40	10. No
5. $869.40	11. $0.98
6. Yes	

Worksheet 38:
Bank Account Vocabulary

1. e	6. g
2. i	7. a
3. h	8. j
4. b	9. f
5. c	10. d

Worksheet 39:
Bank Account Application
(Answers will vary.)

Worksheet 40:
Budgeting Worksheet
(Answers will vary.)

Worksheet 41:
Number Practice: *Utility Bills*

1. May 14	7. $.20 / 20¢
2. $57.49	8. $86.28
3. $53.71	9. 6/27/09
4. 263	10. $79.93
5. $29.38	11. $49.99, $19.95
6. $24.33	12. $2.20

UNIT 7

Worksheet 42:
Community Health Provider Information Form
(Answers will vary.)

Worksheet 43:
Symptoms and Medical Advice
A.

1. muscle
2. knee
3. bump
4. swollen
5. water
6. low-fat
7. exercise

B.

6
1
3
5
7
4
2

Worksheet 44:
Medical History Form
(Answers will vary.)

Worksheet 45:
Nutrition and Food Labels

1. one
2. 110
3. 55
4. Cholesterol, Sodium, Carbohydrates, Protein
5. Vitamin C, calcium
6. 13 grams
7. 0 grams
8. (Answers will vary. Possible answer: "Yes. This yogurt is very healthy. It doesn't have very many calories. It has a lot of protein, and it's low in fat, cholesterol, sodium, and carbohydrates.")

Worksheet 46:
Reading a Medicine Label

1. T
2. F
3. T
4. T
5. T
6. T
7. F
8. T
9. F

Worksheet 47:
Work Safety

1. corrosive materials
2. poison
3. high voltage
4. biohazard
5. combustible materials
6. flammable materials
7. safety gloves
8. no drinks allowed
9. safety glasses
10. helmet
11. first-aid kit
12. fire extinguisher
13. respirator
14. no food allowed

Worksheet 48:
An Accident Report at Work
(Answers will vary.)

Worksheet 49:
Reading an Evacuation Map

	Yes	No
1.		✓
2.	✓	
3.	✓	
4.	✓	
5.		✓
6.	✓	
7.	✓	

UNIT 8

Worksheet 50:
Job Interview Vocabulary
A.

1. communicator
2. get along
3. attitude
4. skills
5. familiar
6. employed
7. specific
8. promotion
9. goals
10. position

UNIT 8

Worksheet 51:
Help Wanted Ads
A.
1. excellent
2. assistant
3. company
4. references
5. driver's license
6. experience
7. required
8. certified
9. office
10. benefits
11. equivalent
12. available
13. diploma
14. opportunity
15. previous

B.
1. d
2. c
3. d
4. b

Worksheet 52:
Job Application
(Answers will vary.)

Worksheet 53:
Work and Education Experience Timeline
(Answers will vary.)

Worksheet 54:
Write Your Resume
(Answers will vary.)

Worksheet 55:
A Cover Letter
A.

1. T		4. F	
2. F		5. F	
3. T		6. T	

B. (Answers will vary.)

UNIT 9

Worksheet 56:
Asking for & Responding to Feedback
1. correctly
2. connect
3. labeling
4. supposed
5. filling out
6. list
7. Excuse
8. copier
9. original
10. telling

Worksheet 57:
Employee Benefits Checklist

	True	False
1.		✓
2.	✓	
3.	✓	
4.	✓	
5.		✓
6.	✓	
7.		✓
8.	✓	
9.		✓
10.	✓	
11.	✓	
12.		✓
13.		✓

Worksheet 58:
Pay Stub
1. 45
2. $210.00
3. $360.00
4. $7,110.00
5. $4,435.00
6. $85.00
7. $1,085.00
8. $40.00
9. $40.00
10. $520.00
11. $40.00
12. 9.75
13. 8

Worksheet 59:
Describing Your Qualities
(Answers will vary.)

UNIT 10

Worksheet 60:
Citizenship Vocabulary
1. j
2. h
3. b
4. i
5. a
6. g
7. d
8. e
9. c
10. l
11. f
12. k

Worksheet 61:
Legal Services Information Form
(Answers will vary.)

Worksheet 62:
Legal Language
A.
1. tourist visa
2. Domestic violence
3. naturalization
4. rights
5. low-income
6. work permit
7. civil law
8. child support

B.
1. C
2. D
3. A
4. D
5. B
6. C
7. A
8. D

Side by Side Plus 4
Activity Masters

The activity masters include ready-to-use word cards, graphics, charts, and activity sheets for the multilevel activities and games suggested throughout the *Side by Side Plus 4* Teacher's Guide.

has – having – my – in – any – daughter – been – problems – school – ?

here – I'm – volunteer – to – classroom – my – in – child's – .

may – I – you – how – help – ?

idea – no – had – I – .

talk – it – to – I'll – him – about – .

in – she's – her – to – been – forgetting – homework – hand – .

very – helpful – be – would – that – .

son – my – here – to – up – I'm – pick – .

my – meet – to – here – teacher – with – son's – I'm – .

the – fights – getting – he's – playground – been – on – into – .

class – falling – she's – asleep – been – during – .

School Notes A

November 3, 2010

Dear Mr. Wilson,

   My daughter will be absent next Monday because it is a religious holiday. Please excuse her absence. Thank you.

           Sincerely,

           Salwa Hassan

_____

_____,

_____

_____

_____

_____,

           Lisa Smith

School Notes B

_____

_____,

_____

_____

_____

_____,

           Salwa Hassan

December 12, 2010

Dear Ms. Taylor,

   I give my son permission to go home with his friend Jack Chang after school today. Mrs. Chang will pick him up.

           Very truly yours,

           Lisa Smith

Topic: Make sure your children have the energy they need to pay attention in class.	Make sure your children have a good night's sleep.
Topic: Show your children that you value learning.	Make sure your children eat a healthy breakfast.
Topic: Encourage your children to read.	Take an interest in what your children are learning in school.
Topic: Make sure your children can concentrate on their homework.	Show your children how to connect their school learning to the world around them.
Topic: Keep the lines of communication open with your children's teachers.	Show your children that you enjoy learning.
Keep books, magazines, and newspapers around the home.	Give your children a quiet place to study at home with good lighting.
Read to your children often.	Have your children do their homework at the same time every day.
Attend parent-teacher conferences.	Make sure your children don't talk to their friends while they're doing their homework.
Contact teachers whenever you have a question or concern.	Participate in school activities or events.
Volunteer in your children's classrooms.	Join the Parent-Teacher Association at your children's school.

he – speak – Arabic – since – move to Saudi Arabia

by the time – she – cooked dinner – the kids – already – fall asleep

they – live – in Rome – before – move to Singapore

he – live – in Florida – since – he – retire

I – deliver – 25 packages – since – this morning

he – deliver – packages – since – 8:00 this morning

she – already – give blood – the week before

by the time – we – get – to the plane – it – already – take off

she – take pictures – since – 6 A.M.

they – already – go – to the library – the evening before

she – have trouble – with her classmates – recently

- Put your markers on *Start*.
- Take turns tossing the die (or flipping a coin) to move your marker around the board.
- Follow the instructions in each space.

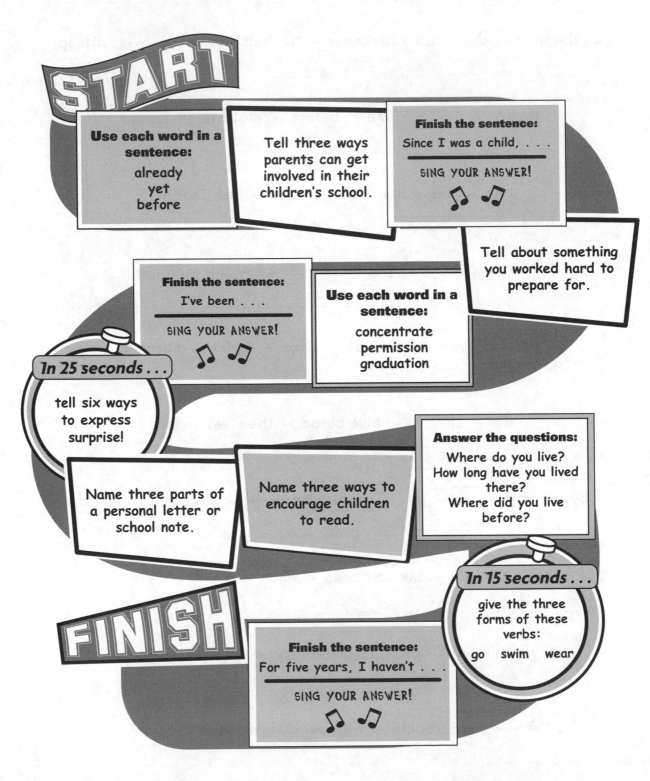

START

Use each word in a sentence:
already
yet
before

Tell three ways parents can get involved in their children's school.

Finish the sentence:
Since I was a child, . . .
SING YOUR ANSWER!

Tell about something you worked hard to prepare for.

Finish the sentence:
I've been . . .
SING YOUR ANSWER!

Use each word in a sentence:
concentrate
permission
graduation

In 25 seconds . . .
tell six ways to express surprise!

Name three parts of a personal letter or school note.

Name three ways to encourage children to read.

Answer the questions:
Where do you live?
How long have you lived there?
Where did you live before?

In 15 seconds . . .
give the three forms of these verbs:
go   swim   wear

FINISH

Finish the sentence:
For five years, I haven't . . .
SING YOUR ANSWER!

AR	AZ	CA
FL	GA	IL
MD	MO	NC
NJ	NY	SC
TX	VA	
Arkansas	Arizona	California
Florida	Georgia	Illinois
Maryland	Missouri	North Carolina
New Jersey	New York	South Carolina
Texas	Virginia	

Train Schedule A

Caltrain Southbound Service

Caltrain Southbound Service

Train No.	206	208	210
San Francisco	6:11		6:44
22nd Street	6:16	6:29	6:49
Millbrae	6:29		7:01
Burlingame		6:52	—
San Mateo	6:36	6:55	
Hillsdale	6:40	7:01	—
San Carlos	6:44		7:13
Redwood City		7:12	7:18
Menlo Park	6:54	—	
Palo Alto	6:57	7:18	7:26
Mountain View		—	7:38
Lawrence	7:12	—	7:49
Santa Clara	—	7:34	
San Jose	7:24		8:06

What time does Train Number __206__
get to __Burlingame__?

Which is the longest train ride between
San Francisco and San Jose?
Which is the shortest?

Train Schedule B

Caltrain Southbound Service

Caltrain Southbound Service

Train No.	206	208	210
San Francisco	6:11	6:24	
22nd Street		6:29	6:49
Millbrae	6:29	6:48	7:01
Burlingame	6:33		—
San Mateo	6:36	6:55	7:07
Hillsdale		7:01	—
San Carlos	6:44	7:07	7:13
Redwood City	6:49	7:12	
Menlo Park	6:54	—	7:23
Palo Alto	6:57		7:26
Mountain View	7:07	—	
Lawrence		—	7:49
Santa Clara	—		7:56
San Jose		7:43	8:06

What time does Train Number __206__
get to __22nd Street__?

Which is the longest train ride between
San Francisco and San Jose?
Which is the shortest?

Traveling by Bus

Advantages (+)	Disadvantages (–)

Traveling by Train

Advantages (+)	Disadvantages (–)

Traveling by Airplane

Advantages (+)	Disadvantages (–)

- Put your markers on *Start*.
- Take turns tossing the die (or flipping a coin) to move your marker around the board.
- Follow the instructions in each space.

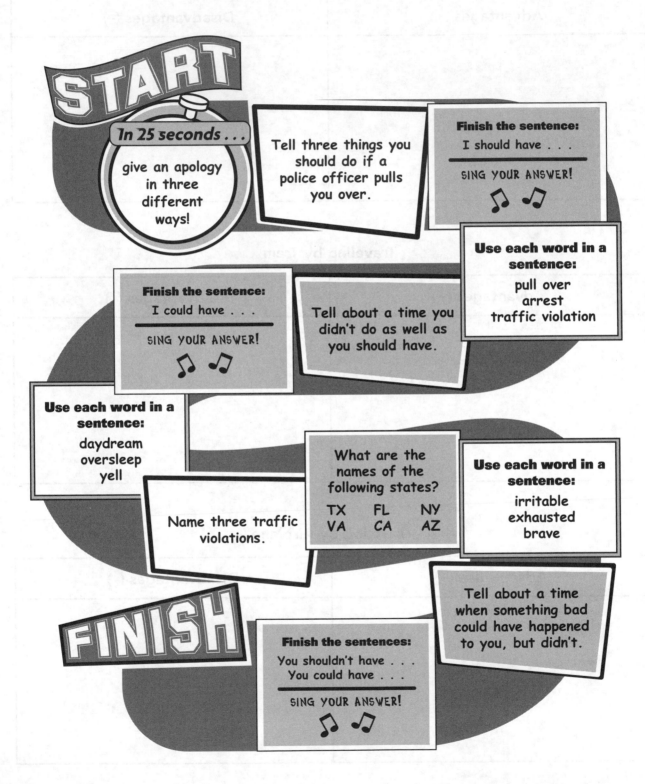

START

In 25 seconds . . . give an apology in three different ways!

Tell three things you should do if a police officer pulls you over.

Finish the sentence:
I should have . . .
SING YOUR ANSWER!

Use each word in a sentence:
pull over
arrest
traffic violation

Finish the sentence:
I could have . . .
SING YOUR ANSWER!

Tell about a time you didn't do as well as you should have.

Use each word in a sentence:
daydream
oversleep
yell

Name three traffic violations.

What are the names of the following states?
TX   FL   NY
VA   CA   AZ

Use each word in a sentence:
irritable
exhausted
brave

Tell about a time when something bad could have happened to you, but didn't.

FINISH

Finish the sentences:
You shouldn't have . . .
You could have . . .
SING YOUR ANSWER!

When did World War I occur?	From 1914 to 1918.
When did World War II occur?	From 1939 to 1945.
When did the Korean war occur?	From 1950 to 1953.
When did the Vietnam War occur?	From 1964 to 1973.
When did the Iraq War begin?	In 2003.
Why did President Roosevelt start the New Deal?	To give people jobs and benefits.
Which two wars were part of the Cold War?	The Korean War and the Vietnam War.
What did people in the civil rights movement work for?	The end of discrimination against African-Americans.
Whose life is remembered on the third Monday of every January?	Dr. Martin Luther King, Jr.'s life.
How did terrorists attack the World Trade Center in New York City?	They hijacked airplanes and flew them into the buildings.
Why did President Bush send troops to Afghanistan?	To fight the terrorist organization responsible for the attacks on 9/11.

airplane	bed	bicyclist
birthday present	building	cartoon
casserole	computer	courier
decoration	dinosaur skeleton	electric light
flowerpot	identification card	monkey
mural	poodle	portrait
puddle	soldier	trash
uniform	wedding cake	windowsill

computer – be repaired – now – .

he – be hurt – in a game – four times this year – .

many cities – be destroyed – in World War I – .

millions of people – be killed – World War II – .

the decorations – already – be hung – .

the mail carrier – be bitten – two times this year – .

the meeting room – be set up – yet – ?

the packages – already – be sent – .

the poodle – be clipped – yet – ?

the United Nations – be established – in 1945 – .

yesterday – his wallet – be stolen – by a pickpocket – .

- Put your markers on *Start*.
- Take turns tossing the die (or flipping a coin) to move your marker around the board.
- Follow the instructions in each space.

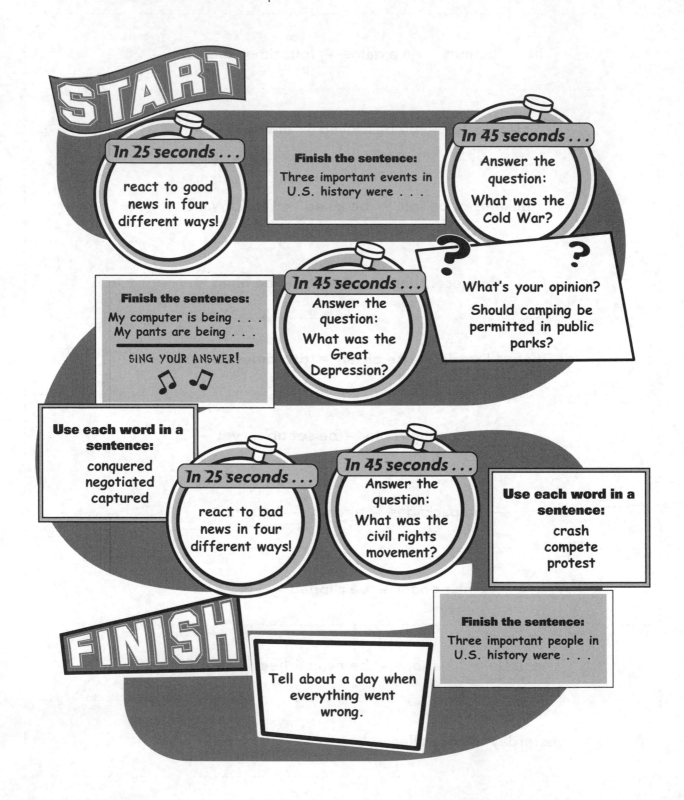

START

In 25 seconds . . .
react to good news in four different ways!

Finish the sentence:
Three important events in U.S. history were . . .

In 45 seconds . . .
Answer the question:
What was the Cold War?

Finish the sentences:
My computer is being . . .
My pants are being . . .
SING YOUR ANSWER!

In 45 seconds . . .
Answer the question:
What was the Great Depression?

What's your opinion?
Should camping be permitted in public parks?

Use each word in a sentence:
conquered
negotiated
captured

In 25 seconds . . .
react to bad news in four different ways!

In 45 seconds . . .
Answer the question:
What was the civil rights movement?

Use each word in a sentence:
crash
compete
protest

FINISH

Finish the sentence:
Three important people in U.S. history were . . .

Tell about a day when everything went wrong.

134

Can you tell me . . . ?

"Where do I return this?"

Do you know . . . ?

"Where is the service center?"

Do you have any idea . . . ?

"How much does the vacuum cleaner cost?"

Do you by any chance know . . . ?

"When does the warranty expire?"

Could you possibly tell me . . . ?

"Why won't they repair it?"

Could you please tell me . . . ?

"What is the return policy?"

Can anybody tell me . . . ?

"Who do I call if I have a problem?"

Do you remember . . . ?

"How long is the return period?"

Does anyone know . . . ?

"Do they guarantee the workmanship?"

Who can tell me . . . ?

"Can I get a replacement?"

135

- Put your markers on *Start*.
- Take turns tossing the die (or flipping a coin) to move your marker around the board.
- Follow the instructions in each space.

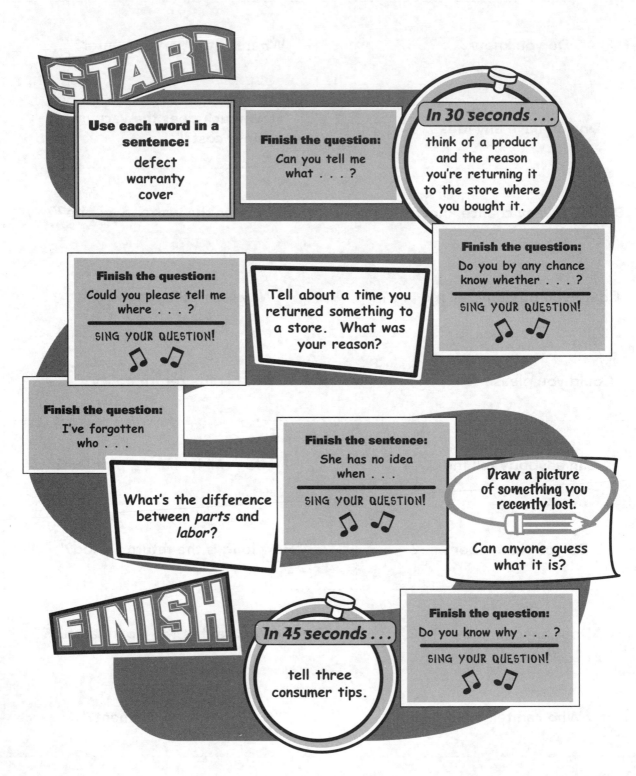

START

Use each word in a sentence:
defect
warranty
cover

Finish the question:
Can you tell me what . . . ?

In 30 seconds . . .
think of a product and the reason you're returning it to the store where you bought it.

Finish the question:
Could you please tell me where . . . ?
SING YOUR QUESTION!

Tell about a time you returned something to a store. What was your reason?

Finish the question:
Do you by any chance know whether . . . ?
SING YOUR QUESTION!

Finish the question:
I've forgotten who . . .

What's the difference between *parts* and *labor*?

Finish the sentence:
She has no idea when . . .
SING YOUR QUESTION!

Draw a picture of something you recently lost.
Can anyone guess what it is?

FINISH

In 45 seconds . . .
tell three consumer tips.

Finish the question:
Do you know why . . . ?
SING YOUR QUESTION!

136

	Yes	No	N/A*
1. Do you keep a fire extinguisher in your kitchen?	____	____	____
2. Do you keep flammable products away from heat?	____	____	____
3. Do you change batteries in your smoke detector twice a year?	____	____	____
4. Do you have an emergency escape plan?	____	____	____
5. Do you keep space heaters away from flammable material?	____	____	____
6. Do you know how to escape from every room in your home?	____	____	____
7. _____	____	____	____
8. _____	____	____	____

* Not applicable to my situation.

If he studied more,	he'd get better grades.
If there's a fire,	we'll meet at our neighbor's house.
If she stays up late,	she'll be tired in the morning.
If he marries Irene,	he'll regret it the rest of his life.
If the batteries get low,	the smoke detector will chirp.
If the economy gets worse,	I'll have to get a second job.
If she were stronger,	she'd be able to lift weights.
If he exercised more,	he'd be healthier.
If they didn't have an exam today,	they wouldn't be so nervous.
If she weren't allergic to cats,	she wouldn't be sneezing so much.
If he starts to choke,	I'll perform the Heimlich maneuver.

- Put your markers on *Start*.
- Take turns tossing the die (or flipping a coin) to move your marker around the board.
- Follow the instructions in each space.

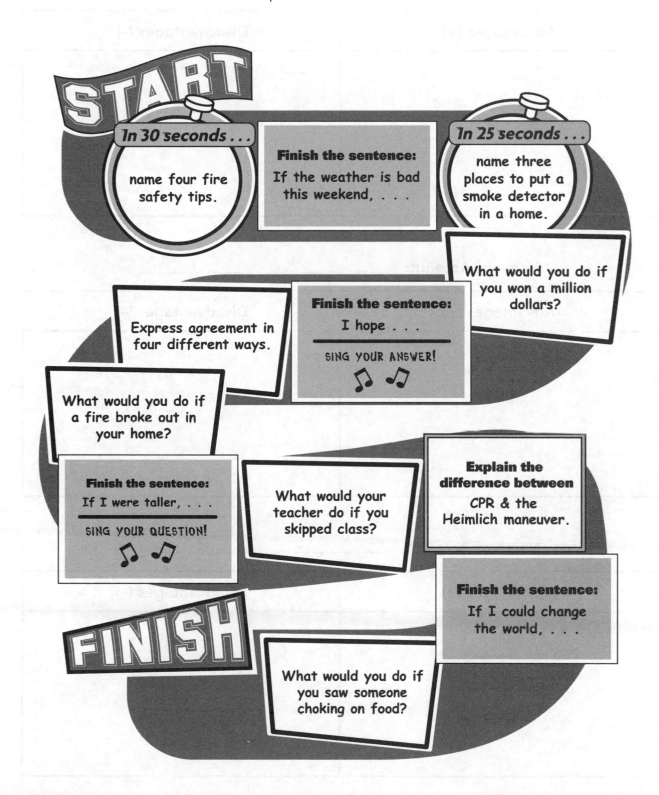

START

In 30 seconds . . . name four fire safety tips.

Finish the sentence: If the weather is bad this weekend, . . .

In 25 seconds . . . name three places to put a smoke detector in a home.

What would you do if you won a million dollars?

Express agreement in four different ways.

Finish the sentence: I hope . . . SING YOUR ANSWER!

What would you do if a fire broke out in your home?

Finish the sentence: If I were taller, . . . SING YOUR QUESTION!

What would your teacher do if you skipped class?

Explain the difference between CPR & the Heimlich maneuver.

Finish the sentence: If I could change the world, . . .

FINISH

What would you do if you saw someone choking on food?

Name of Account: _____

Advantages (+)	Disadvantages (−)

Name of Account: _____

Advantages (+)	Disadvantages (−)

Name of Account: _____

Advantages (+)	Disadvantages (−)

Role Play 1—Student A

You're a Midtown Bank customer. You want to open a checking account. Ask the bank officer about choosing a Midtown Bank account. You write about 12 checks a month. Your usual bank account balance is between $800 and $1,200. You have direct deposit from your employer.

Role Play 1—Student B

You're a Midtown Bank officer. You're helping a customer choose the best checking account. Ask the customer about the number of checks he or she writes a month, the usual balance in the account, and whether that person has direct deposit.

Role Play 2—Student A

You're a Midtown Bank customer. You want to open up a savings account for your daughter. She has $200 in savings to deposit. Ask the bank officer for the best account for your daughter. She can deposit about $25 a month.

Role Play 2—Student B

You're a Midtown Bank officer. You're helping a customer choose the best savings account for his or her daughter. Ask the customer about the amount of the opening deposit and how much the daughter plans to save.

	Yes	No
1. Do you record your expenses?	____	____
2. Do you have a budget?	____	____
3. Do you use coupons?	____	____
4. Do you buy food in wholesale stores?	____	____
5. Do you shop for things on sale?	____	____
6. Do you bring your own lunch or snack to work?	____	____
7. _____	____	____
8. _____	____	____
9. _____	____	____

- Put your markers on *Start*.
- Take turns tossing the die (or flipping a coin) to move your marker around the board.
- Follow the instructions in each space.

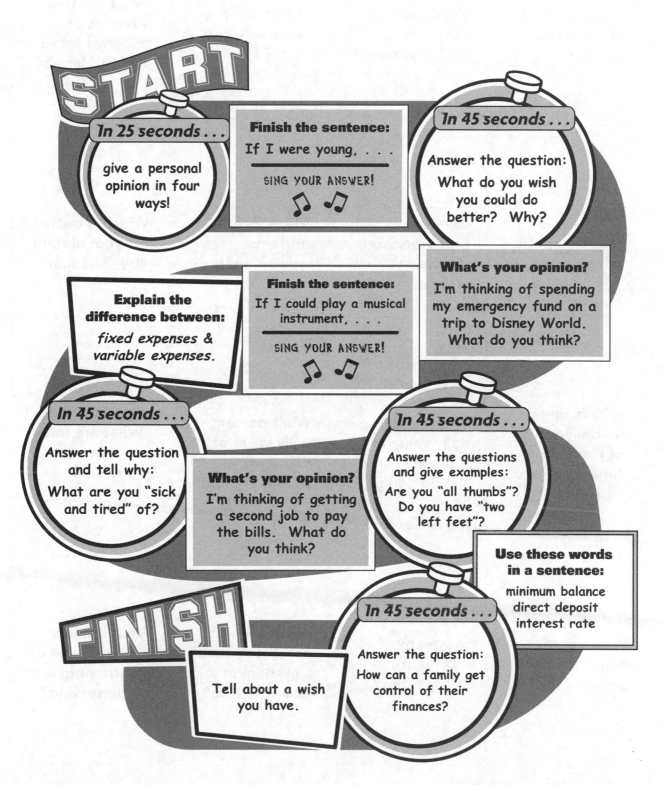

What are two different kinds of fats?	What are two nutrients in carbohydrates?	What are two nutrients you should limit?	What are two vitamins or minerals listed on food labels?
What do calories measure?	Which nutrients can lead to high blood pressure and heart disease?	Which three nutrients provide energy?	Which is better for you: dietary fiber or sugar?
Why is there no daily value of protein on American food labels?	What percent daily value of Vitamin C should you get?	What percent daily value of dietary fiber should you get?	What are four nutrients in a food?
Which nutrients help prevent disease?	How many calories are in the average diet?	What is a high percent value of a nutrient in a single serving?	What is a low percent value of a nutrient in a single serving?

Nutrition Facts A

2% Reduced Fat Milk
Nutrition Facts
Serving Size: ____ cup
Servings Per Container: 16

Calories ____   Calories from Fat 45

	% Daily Value
Total Fat ____g	8%
Saturated Fat 3g	0%
Trans Fat 0g	
Cholesterol 20mg	7%
Sodium ____mg	5%
Total Carbohydrate 12g	4%
Dietary Fiber 0g	0%
Sugars 11g	
Protein ____g	

Vitamin A   10%   Vitamin C ____%
Calcium ____%   Vitamin D 25%

Non-Fat Milk
Nutrition Facts
Serving Size: 1 cup
Servings Per Container: ____

Calories 80   Calories from Fat ____

	% Daily Value
Total Fat 0g	0%
Saturated Fat 0g	0%
Trans Fat 0g	
Cholesterol ____mg	0%
Sodium 120mg	5%
Total Carbohydrate 11g	4%
Dietary Fiber 0g	0%
Sugars 11g	
Protein 9g	

Vitamin A ____%   Vitamin C 4%
Calcium   30%   Vitamin D ____%

Nutrition Facts B

2% Reduced Fat Milk
Nutrition Facts
Serving Size: 1 cup
Servings Per Container: ____

Calories 120   Calories from Fat ____

	% Daily Value
Total Fat 8g	8%
Saturated Fat 3g	0%
Trans Fat 0g	
Cholesterol ____mg	7%
Sodium 120mg	5%
Total Carbohydrate ____g	4%
Dietary Fiber 0g	0%
Sugars 11g	
Protein 9g	

Vitamin A ____%   Vitamin C 4%
Calcium   30%   Vitamin D ____%

Non-Fat Milk
Nutrition Facts
Serving Size: ____ cup
Servings Per Container: 16

Calories ____   Calories from Fat 0

	% Daily Value
Total Fat ____g	0%
Saturated Fat 0g	0%
Trans Fat 0g	
Cholesterol 0mg	0%
Sodium ____mg	5%
Total Carbohydrate 11g	4%
Dietary Fiber 0g	0%
Sugars 11g	
Protein ____g	

Vitamin A   10%   Vitamin C ____%
Calcium ____%   Vitamin D 25%

145

1. What is the name of the medicine?

   _____

2. What is the dosage for an adult?

   _____

3. What is the dosage for a child under 12?

   _____

4. What are the active ingredients?

   _____

5. What are the inactive ingredients?

   _____

6. What are the side effects?

   _____

7. Who should not use this medicine?

   _____

8. When should a person stop using this medicine?

   _____

What are active ingredients?	What are inactive ingredients?	What should you do if your symptoms don't go away after taking the medicine?	What are three examples of side effects?
What are over-the-counter medicines?	What should you use to measure the dosage of liquid medicine?	What are two examples of inactive ingredients?	How do you know when medicine is too old to take?
What kinds of drugs do some teens abuse?	Why is it important to check inactive ingredients if you have allergies?	What should you always do before you take medicine?	Why is it important to check the active ingredients if you're taking several medications at the same time?
What does the warning on the label tell you?	What is one way to find out if teenagers in your house are abusing over-the-counter drugs?	Is it possible to overdose on over-the-counter medicines?	Do all people react to medicine in the same way?

Use machine guards when	you operate a machine.
Shut down your machine when	you leave work.
Clean up promptly when	there is a spill.
Know the two exits	closest to your work area.
Know where to meet outside	if there's an evacuation.
Know where to find	fire extinguishers and first-aid kits.
Wear your safety equipment, such as	your helmet and your respirator.
Don't eat or drink	in your work area.
Read and obey	all safety signs and warnings.
Report injuries and accidents	to your supervisor.

- Put your markers on *Start*.
- Take turns tossing the die (or flipping a coin) to move your marker around the board.
- Follow the instructions in each space.

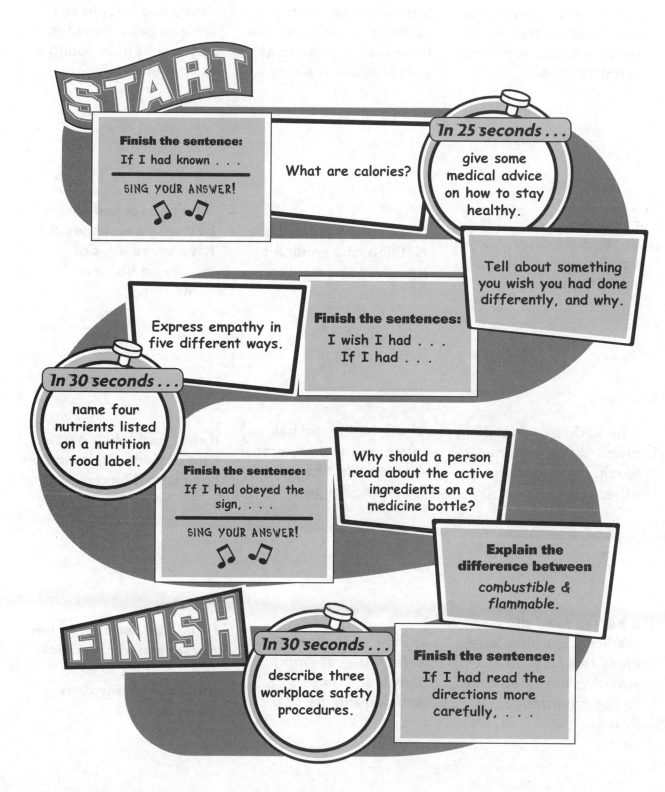

START

Finish the sentence:
If I had known . . .
SING YOUR ANSWER!

What are calories?

In 25 seconds . . .
give some medical advice on how to stay healthy.

Tell about something you wish you had done differently, and why.

Express empathy in five different ways.

Finish the sentences:
I wish I had . . .
If I had . . .

In 30 seconds . . .
name four nutrients listed on a nutrition food label.

Finish the sentence:
If I had obeyed the sign, . . .
SING YOUR ANSWER!

Why should a person read about the active ingredients on a medicine bottle?

Explain the difference between *combustible & flammable.*

FINISH

In 30 seconds . . .
describe three workplace safety procedures.

Finish the sentence:
If I had read the directions more carefully, . . .

If he hadn't fallen in last night's basketball game, he wouldn't have missed tonight's game.

If they had evacuated earlier, there would have been plenty of room at the hurricane shelter.

If they had bought the airplane tickets sooner, they would have found a less expensive flight.

If they had watered their plants more often, they would have had a beautiful garden.

If she hadn't worn loose clothing, she wouldn't have had the accident.

If he had looked for better prices, he would have saved a lot of money on his new computer.

If he hadn't been talking on his cell phone, he would have seen the other car.

If she had saved her work on the computer, she wouldn't have had to work all night.

If they had taken better care of their car, it would have lasted longer.

If he had read the medicine warning label more carefully, he wouldn't have had to go to the Emergency Room.

If they had followed the safety rules at work, they would have avoided the fire.

If she had listened to her doctor's medical advice, she wouldn't have missed so many days at work.

refs.	grad.	incl.	temp.
cert.	mgmt.	w/	prev.
dept.	bnfts.	wpm	min.
references	graduate	including	temporary
certified	management	with	previous
department	benefits	words per minute	minimum

Administrative Asst. PT. Must have gd. comp. skills and HS dipl.	Administrative Assistant. Part-time. Must have good computer skills and a high school diploma.
Administrative Asst. FT. Must have gd. comp. skills and HS dipl.	Administrative Assistant. Full-time. Must have good computer skills and a high school diploma.
FT driver needed. 1 yr. exp. req. Co. car provided. Must be avail. wknds.	Full-time driver needed. One year experience required. Company car provided. Must be available weekends.
FT driver needed. No exp. req. Co. car provided. Must be avail. wknds.	Full-time driver needed. No experience required. Company car provided. Must be available weekends.
PT Dental Asst. Grad. of approved program w/ 2 yrs. exp. Refs req'd.	Part-time dental assistant. Graduate of an approved program with two years experience. References required.
PT Dental Asst. Grad. of approved program w/ 2 yrs. exp. Cert req'd.	Part-time dental assistant. Graduate of an approved program with two years experience. Certification required.
FT Bilingual Secy. 60 wpm min. Oppty. for advancement. Excel. bnfts incl. health and dental ins.	Full-time bilingual secretary. 60 words per minute minimum. Opportunity for advancement. Excellent benefits including health and dental insurance.
FT Bilingual Secy. 50 wpm min. Oppty. for advancement. Excel. bnfts incl. health and dental ins.	Full-time bilingual secretary. 50 words per minute minimum. Opportunity for advancement. Excellent benefits including health and dental insurance.
Maintenance position avail. Plumbing and elec. exp. req'd. Temp. Start immed.	Maintenance position available. Plumbing and electrical experience required. Temporary job. Start immediately.
Maintenance position avail. Plumbing and elec. exp. req'd. Temp. Start next mo.	Maintenance position available. Plumbing and electrical experience required. Temporary job. Start next month.

152

Help Wanted Bingo

Associate's degree	employer	position
Bachelor of Science	full-time	reference
benefits	hire	skills
diploma	part-time	words per minute

September 2007–present: Supervisor Computer Services

June 2007–August 2007: Computer Specialist

July 2004–June 2007: Student at Community College

December 2002–April 2004: Maintenance worker

February 2002–October 2002: Painter and maintenance worker

April 2001–November 2001: Painter

May 2000–March 2001: Driver

154

She asked, "What are your strengths?"

He said, "I'm dependable and hardworking."

She asked, "Where did you go to school?"

He said, "I went to Stratford Community College."

She asked, "Have you had special training?"

He said, "I studied computer engineering."

She asked, "Can you work overtime and on the weekends?"

He said, "I'm available most evenings and weekends."

She asked, "Why do you want to work here?"

He said, "I want to work in a fast-paced and exciting workplace."

She said, "Please send us your references."

He said, "I'll get them to you tomorrow."

She asked, "Do you have any questions for me?"

He said, "I have one question. When will you make your decision?"

- Put your markers on *Start*.
- Take turns tossing the die (or flipping a coin) to move your marker around the board.
- Follow the instructions in each space.

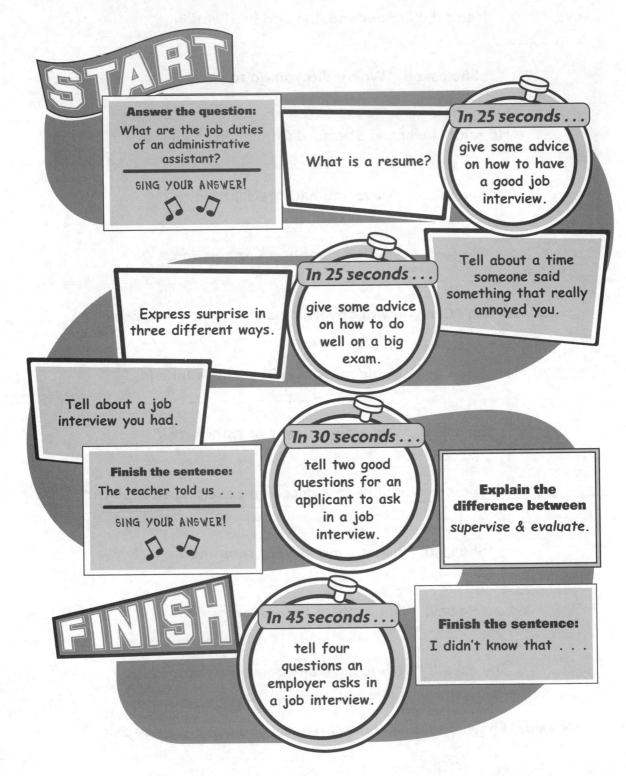

START

Answer the question:
What are the job duties of an administrative assistant?
_____
SING YOUR ANSWER!
♪ ♪

What is a resume?

In 25 seconds...
give some advice on how to have a good job interview.

Tell about a time someone said something that really annoyed you.

Express surprise in three different ways.

In 25 seconds...
give some advice on how to do well on a big exam.

Tell about a job interview you had.

Finish the sentence:
The teacher told us . . .
_____
SING YOUR ANSWER!
♫ ♫

In 30 seconds...
tell two good questions for an applicant to ask in a job interview.

Explain the difference between *supervise & evaluate.*

FINISH

In 45 seconds...
tell four questions an employer asks in a job interview.

Finish the sentence:
I didn't know that . . .

accrue	insurance premium	personal day
calendar year	life insurance	savings plan
defer	medical plan	sick time
dental plan	paid holiday	401(k) plan

We've learned a lot of English this year.	They make a nice couple.
He's getting quite a few gray hairs.	The milk tastes sour.
The new air conditioner is noisy.	We don't get much vacation time.
Our insurance doesn't cover eyeglasses.	He gets along with everyone.
That was a very generous pay raise.	The color red looks good on her.
She's a problem solver.	He performs many different tasks.
He didn't do a very good job.	She gave an excellent presentation.
Our teacher gives us a lot of homework.	Kids watch too much TV these days.
They've been online for more than an hour.	We were very late for the party.
They won't miss the city.	She'll get a promotion soon.
We've already seen this movie.	They haven't called us in a long time.
They made a lot of mistakes.	You're supposed to put the label on the top.

This is the train to the beach, . . .	I can eat food at my desk, . . .
You work in the marketing department, . . .	You aren't allergic to eggs, . . .
The alarm isn't on, . . .	He didn't work late yesterday, . . .
They were very helpful, . . .	They contribute to your retirement plan, . . .
We can accrue sick days, . . .	This is the way to the mall, . . .
She's a full-time employee, . . .	I'm filling out my timesheet correctly, . . .
You turned off the oven, . . .	We've met them before, . . .
This apartment has air conditioning, . . .	We don't have to dress up, . . .
I wasn't speeding, . . .	I didn't make too many mistakes, . . .
We haven't arrived too late, . . .	I'm not late, . . .
These dresses are on sale, . . .	You didn't eat the last cookie, . . .
You won't be late, . . .	She got the job, . . .

- Put your markers on *Start*.
- Take turns tossing the die (or flipping a coin) to move your marker around the board.
- Follow the instructions in each space.

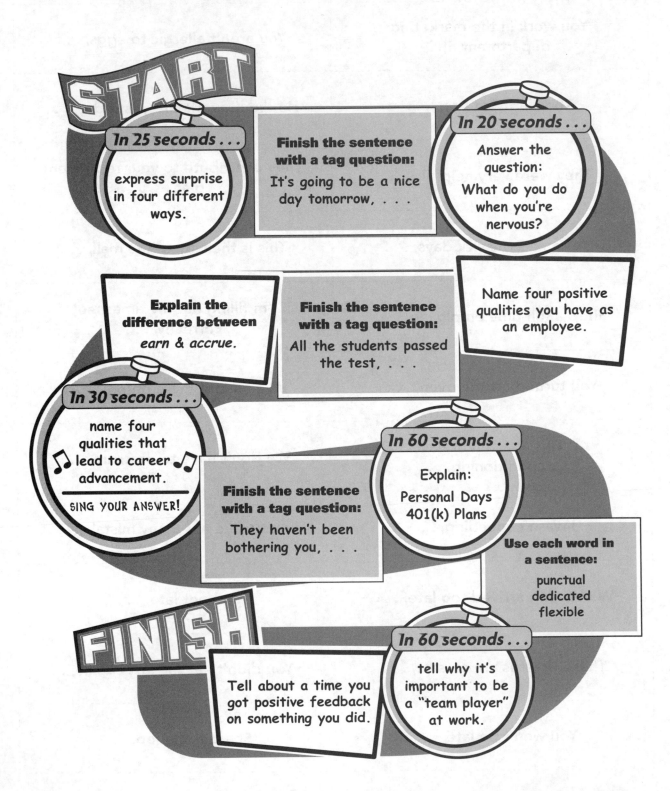

START

In 25 seconds . . .
express surprise in four different ways.

Finish the sentence with a tag question:
It's going to be a nice day tomorrow, . . .

In 20 seconds . . .
Answer the question:
What do you do when you're nervous?

Explain the difference between *earn & accrue.*

Finish the sentence with a tag question:
All the students passed the test, . . .

Name four positive qualities you have as an employee.

In 30 seconds . . .
name four qualities that lead to career advancement.
SING YOUR ANSWER!

Finish the sentence with a tag question:
They haven't been bothering you, . . .

In 60 seconds . . .
Explain:
Personal Days
401(k) Plans

Use each word in a sentence:
punctual
dedicated
flexible

FINISH

Tell about a time you got positive feedback on something you did.

In 60 seconds . . .
tell why it's important to be a "team player" at work.

a parent and a child	a supervisor and an employee
a teacher and a student	a bride and a groom
two neighbors	a taxi driver and a passenger
a police officer and a driver	a journalist and a politician
a waiter or waitress and a customer	a landlord and a tenant
a job interviewer and a job applicant	a husband and wife

161

federal government	natural-born citizen	property tax
income tax	naturalized citizen	responsibilities
jury	permanent resident	trial
national defense	privilege	verdict

How informed and involved are you?   Yes   No

1. Do you read the newspaper?   ____ ____

2. Do you watch the news?   ____ ____

3. Do you talk with your neighbors?   ____ ____

4. Do you attend school meetings?   ____ ____

5. Do you attend neighborhood meetings?   ____ ____

6. Do you attend city or town council meetings? ____ ____

7. Do you vote?   ____ ____

8. Have you ever served on a jury?   ____ ____

9. _____   ____ ____

Tenant Rights Office	problems with housing conditions
Family Law Office	problems with a landlord
Domestic Violence Office	rent problems
Immigration Services	eviction
divorce	problems with an apartment building superintendent
legal separation	tourist visas
problems with child support	emotional abuse
physical abuse	sexual abuse
adjustment of immigration status	legal residency
naturalization	work permits

air conditioner	bathtub	bookcase
button on a phone	cat	cell phone
chicken pox	cockroach	computer
computer key on a keyboard	elevator	garbage
hamster	leg in a cast	lock on a door
piano	picnic	pillow
satellite dish	ski slope	umbrella
video	wallpaper	wisdom tooth

- Put your markers on *Start*.
- Take turns tossing the die (or flipping a coin) to move your marker around the board.
- Follow the instructions in each space.

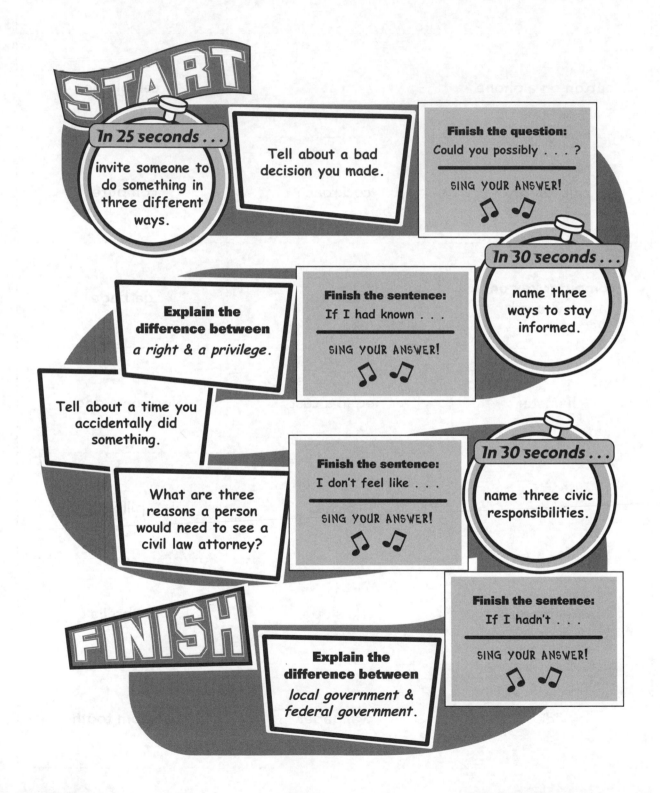

Side by Side Plus 4
Activity Masters Answer Key

UNIT 1

Activity Master 1:
Scrambled Sentence Prompts

Has my daughter been having any problems in school?
I'm here to volunteer in my child's classroom.
How may I help you?
I had no idea.
I'll talk to him about it.
She's been forgetting to hand in her homework./
    She's been forgetting to hand her homework in.
That would be very helpful.
I'm here to pick up my son./I'm here to pick my son up.
I'm here to meet with my son's teacher.
He's been getting into fights on the playground.
She's been falling asleep during class.

Activity Master 3:
Success-in-School Matching Game

Topic: Make sure your children have the energy they need to pay attention in class.
    Make sure your children have a good night's sleep.
    Make sure your children eat a healthy breakfast.

Topic: Show your children that you value learning.
    Take an interest in what your children are learning in school.
    Show your children how to connect their school learning to the world around them.
    Show your children that you enjoy learning.

Topic: Encourage your children to read.
    Keep books, magazines, and newspapers around the home.
    Read to your children often.

Topic: Make sure your children can concentrate on their homework.
    Give your children a quiet place to study at home with good lighting.
    Have your children do their homework at the same time every day.
    Make sure your children don't talk to their friends while they're doing their homework.

Topic: Keep the lines of communication open with your children's teachers.
    Attend parent-teacher conferences.
    Contact teachers whenever you have a question or concern.
    Participate in school activities or events.
    Volunteer in your children's classrooms.
    Join the Parent-Teacher Association at your children's school.

Activity Master 4:
Sentence Prompts

He's been speaking Arabic since he moved to Saudi Arabia./He's spoken Arabic since he moved to Saudi Arabia.
By the time she cooked dinner, the kids had already fallen asleep.
They lived in Rome before they moved to Singapore.
He's been living in Florida since he retired./He's lived in Florida since he retired.
I've delivered 25 packages since this morning.
He's been delivering packages since 8:00 this morning.
She had already given blood the week before.
By the time we got to the plane, it had already taken off.
She's been taking pictures since 6 A.M.
They had already gone to the library the evening before.
She's been having trouble with her classmates recently.

UNIT 3

Activity Master 12:
Passive Voice Sentence Prompts

The computer is being repaired now.
He's been hurt in a game four times this year.
Many cities were destroyed in World War I.
Millions of people were killed in World War II.
The decorations have already been hung.
The mail carrier has been bitten two times this year.
Has the meeting room been set up yet?
The packages have already been sent.
Has the poodle been clipped yet?
The United Nations was established in 1945.
Yesterday his wallet was stolen by a pickpocket.

UNIT 10

Activity Master 43:
Legal Issues Matching Game

Tenant Rights Office:
    problems with housing conditions
    problems with a landlord
    rent problems
    eviction
    problems with an apartment building superintendent

Family Law Office:
    divorce
    legal separation
    problems with child support

Domestic Violence Office:
   emotional abuse
   physical abuse
   sexual abuse

Immigration Services:
   tourist visas
   adjustment of immigration status
   legal residency
   naturalization
   work permits

Side by Side Plus 4
Unit Achievement Tests & Assessment Resources
Teacher Notes

The *Side by Side Plus 4* Multilevel Activity and Achievement Test Book and CD-ROM offers the following reproducible resources for student assessment and record-keeping:

- Ten reproducible Unit Achievement Tests— one for each unit

- A Listening Script for the listening activities in the unit achievement tests

- An Answer Sheet for use with all tests

- An Answer Key

- Learner Assessment Records for evaluating and documenting each student's test performance and progress, including easy-to-use scoring rubrics for assessing writing and speaking skills

- A Learner Progress Chart for students to use to record their test scores and to chart their progress

GOAL OF THE UNIT ACHIEVEMENT TESTS

The unit achievement tests are designed to assess student progress and prepare students for the types of standardized tests and performance assessments used by many instructional programs. Such tests have become common tools for assessing students' educational advancement and for evaluating programs' effectiveness in meeting outcome-based performance standards.

TEST CONTENT

The tests include multiple-choice questions that assess vocabulary, grammar, reading, listening skills, life-skill competencies, and document literacy tasks, such as reading a school announcement, bus and train schedules, community information flyers, consumer protection information, news articles, a fire safety notice, a chart comparing bank account features, a bank statement, nutrition facts on food labels, medicine labels, help wanted ads, a resume, an employee benefits manual, an employee newsletter, and authentic academic material such as civics textbook lessons. Writing assessment tasks include filling out a warranty registration form, a bank account application, a medical history form, and a voter registration form, writing a note to school to explain a child's absence, a letter giving directions to the student's home, a personal timeline, a resume, and instructions for

a procedure, and drawing a fire escape plan and writing instructions for evacuating a building. Speaking performance assessments are designed to stimulate face-to-face interactions between students, for evaluation by the teacher using a standardized scoring rubric, or for self-evaluation by students. The writing assessments can also be evaluated with a standardized scoring rubric and be collected in portfolios of students' work.

Students can record their answers to each test's multiple-choice questions in two ways. They can "bubble in" their answers directly on the test page, or they can use the Answer Sheet for useful and realistic practice placing answers on a separate sheet rather than in a test booklet. Students can answer the other questions by writing directly on the test page.

USING THE TESTS

You can use the tests in a variety of ways to carefully develop students' test-taking skills. For the first test, it may be helpful to do each section of the test separately. Go over each section as a class, and then have students try to answer the questions in that section. Make sure students understand the question format and any example that is provided. For the second test, you may want to preview all the sections at once, make sure students understand all the formats, and then have them take the test in its entirety. For the remaining tests (or for all of them, if appropriate), in order to simulate a real test-taking situation, have students answer all the questions without any preview of the material.

Over time, you can modify other aspects of the test-taking experience to develop students' skills. For example, for the first test, you might allow students to ask for help when they have difficulty understanding a question format. For the remaining tests, it will be better not to allow students to ask for help. Also, you may want to have students do a few tests on an untimed basis, allowing them as much time as they need to answer all the questions. Eventually, though, it is good practice for students to take the tests on a timed basis, especially if they will experience timed tests in your program. (When you use timed tests, let students complete the unfinished items later in class or at home so they benefit from the practice.)

STRATEGIES FOR USING THE TEST FORMATS

We encourage you to use the unit achievement tests in the way that is most appropriate given the needs and abilities of your students as well as your teaching style, classroom situation, and the assessment requirements of your program. Here are some strategies for using the different test formats:

MULTIPLE-CHOICE QUESTIONS

Each test includes 40 multiple-choice questions. Have students indicate their answers by bubbling in the correct letter in the answer grid at the bottom of the test page or on the separate reproducible answer sheet. In this way, students practice the coordination skills involved in matching questions in a test booklet with their corresponding answer lines on a separate answer sheet.

The different sets of multiple-choice questions in each test cover a range of topics and language skills:

> LIFESKILL COMPETENCY questions focus on relevant topics and vocabulary.

> GRAMMAR IN CONTEXT sections help students practice functional language and grammar through contextualized conversations. (After the test, students will benefit from practicing these conversations in pairs or as a class.)

> READING COMPREHENSION sections include authentic life-skill reading material such as a school event announcement, parents' notes to school, bus and train schedules, a community information flyer, consumer protection information, news articles, a newspaper advice column, an apartment building fire safety notice, a chart comparing bank account features, a bank statement, nutrition facts on food labels, medicine labels, help wanted ads, a resume, an employee benefits manual, an employee newsletter, a brochure describing community health, legal, and human services, and authentic academic material such as civics textbook lessons.

> CLOZE READING sections develop students' ability to use their knowledge of vocabulary and grammar to select the correct words to complete a narrative passage or a life-skill document, such as a letter to parents from a school principal, an e-mail with directions to a place, a history textbook lesson, a product complaint letter, workplace safety notices, a cover letter, a magazine article, and a voter registration information flyer.

LISTENING ASSESSMENT sections evaluate listening comprehension skills. The Listening Script contains the exercise instructions, the questions, and the listening passage. Have students read along silently as you read the exercise instructions and the questions one or more times. In this way, students know what information to listen for when they hear the listening passage. Then read the listening passage one or more times and have students answer the questions.

WRITING ASSESSMENTS

Writing tasks include filling out a warranty registration form, a bank account application, a medical history form, and a voter registration form, writing a note to school to explain a child's absence, a letter giving directions to the student's home, a personal timeline, a resume, and instructions for a procedure, and drawing a fire escape plan and writing instructions for evacuating a building. Have students write their answers on the test page. These writing assessments can be evaluated using the scoring rubrics provided on the Learner Assessment Record sheets and can be collected in portfolios of students' work.

SPEAKING ASSESSMENTS

The speaking assessment section at the end of each test provides a checklist of questions designed to stimulate brief, face-to-face conversations between students. First, preview the questions to make sure students understand the vocabulary. Then have students practice the questions in one or more of the following ways:

> PAIR PRACTICE: Have students work in pairs, taking turns asking and answering the questions.

> LINE CONVERSATIONS: Have students stand in two lines facing each other. Each pair of facing students should take turns asking and answering a question (or two or more questions if you prefer). After sufficient time for this practice, say "Move," and have one line of students move down one position while the other line remains in place. (The student at the end of the line moves to the beginning of the line.) In this way, new pairs are created and students can practice with another partner. Continue the line conversations until students have practiced asking and answering all the questions.

> "ROUND ROBIN": Have students circulate around the room and ask each other the questions. Students should move on to another person after they have taken turns asking and answering a question.

To evaluate students, you can observe them as they practice asking and answering the questions during the above activities. Or, have pairs of students present some of the questions and answers to the entire class or just for you. Score each student separately using the scoring rubrics provided on the Learner Assessment Record sheets.

(**CLASSROOM MANAGEMENT TIP:** To save time, you might begin the test-taking practice by previewing the Speaking Assessment questions and having students practice them using one or more of the suggestions above. Then have students take the written test in class. While they are occupied, call out students in pairs to present to you some of the Speaking Assessment questions and answers, perhaps in the hallway or in an adjacent room, so the rest of the class is not disturbed.)

USING THE LEARNER ASSESSMENT RECORDS

A reproducible Learner Assessment Record for each unit achievement test is designed for easy scoring of a student's performance. It provides specific scoring rubrics for all multiple-choice questions, writing assessments, and speaking assessments. Each test is scored on a 100-point scale, providing a consistent means to evaluate student achievement of topics, vocabulary, grammar, and listening, speaking, reading, and writing skills. The Learner Assessment Records can serve as documentation of students' progress during the course of the instructional program.

TEST-TAKING STRATEGIES FOR STUDENTS

As students work with the tests, focus on strategies that students need to develop in order to perform well on authentic tests. Work on these strategies at a pace and intensity that are appropriate for the needs and abilities of your students.

BUBBLING IN THE BUBBLES

Make sure students know how to use a pencil to fill in a bubble completely on an answer grid so that the answer is recorded. Explain if necessary how the answer sheet on a standardized test is scored by a machine. (You may want to have a supply of Number 2 pencils available for test-taking practice.)

ERASURES AND STRAY MARKS

Students should be sure to erase completely any bubbled-in answer that they wish to change. They should also be sure to erase any stray marks they may have accidentally made on a page.

BUBBLING IN ON THE CORRECT LINE OF THE ANSWER SHEET

Make sure students avoid some common mistakes when recording their answers on the answer

sheet. They shouldn't put the answer to a sample question as the first answer on the answer sheet. If they skip a question, they need to be sure to skip the corresponding line on the answer sheet as well. (Encourage students to make a mark on the test page next to any question they have skipped so they can locate these questions quickly when they come back to them.)

FOLLOWING DIRECTIONS

Students should always look at the instructions and any example carefully so that they know what to do with each set of questions. (For example, a common mistake is for students to fill out a form that might appear on a test page rather than to follow the instructions to answer questions *about* the form.)

MULTIPLE-CHOICE STRATEGIES

When students don't know the answer to a multiple-choice question, they should learn to eliminate the choice or choices that they know are incorrect. By doing this, they might arrive at the correct answer, or they may narrow down the number of possible answers and then guess. (If you wish, have students actually cross out on the test page the letters of answer choices they can eliminate so that they can focus on a narrower set of choices.)

MULTIPLE-CHOICE "TRAPS"

After students have taken a test, go over the multiple-choice questions and point out the *distractors* (the wrong choices). Have students notice the distractors that are "traps"—choices that are tricky for one or more reasons. For example, a choice might have correct information but incorrect grammar, or correct grammar but incorrect information, or information that is somewhat related to the question but doesn't answer it.

ANSWERING EASY QUESTIONS FIRST

Students should understand that tests are often arranged so that within each set of questions, easier items come before more difficult ones. Especially when students begin practicing the tests on a timed basis, they should be careful not to spend too much time dwelling on difficult questions. Encourage them to keep moving by answering the easier questions first and then going back to the more difficult ones. Make sure that if they skip a question, they also skip the corresponding line on the answer sheet. (Suggest that students make a mark on the test page next to any question they have skipped so they can quickly locate these questions later.)

PACING

Prepare students to take tests on a timed basis. Have them look briefly at a test before taking it in order to identify the number and types of questions in each section and to decide approximately how much time they should plan to spend on each section. Then have them take the test and keep track of their pacing and progress. If they are falling behind, they should not dwell on the most difficult questions, but instead move on to other test sections and then go back later to the difficult items. Make sure students allow enough time after their first pass through a test to go back to unanswered questions and then to check their work.

COMPLETING WRITING ASSESSMENTS APPROPRIATELY

Students should be sure they understand what is expected in each writing assessment, and they should be sure to do the task completely and correctly. Some writing assessments involve filling out a form, while others require students to write a list of procedures or a letter. Point out to students that they will be evaluated on the appropriateness of their answers, spelling, punctuation and capitalization, and when applicable, grammar and completeness of sentences. For the letter-writing tasks, students will be evaluated on both the content of their writing and how well they follow the standard format for the parts of a letter.

CHECKING ANSWERS

Make sure students allow enough time to go over their work before handing in a test. They should first try to answer any questions they have skipped and then go over their work to check it. Caution students that they shouldn't change an answer unless they know it is incorrect. If they have guessed an answer and they are still not sure of the correct choice, their first guess is more likely to be the accurate one.

OTHER FORMS OF ASSESSMENT

In addition to using the unit achievement tests, you should plan to use a variety of other forms of assessment with your students. Alternative assessment activities that involve students performing classroom or real-life tasks, playing games, or participating in role plays, simulations, and other performance-based activities should be part of a well-rounded assessment program. Using portfolio assessment strategies to keep files of student work (for example, homework, in-class writing, creative projects, teacher evaluations, and student self-evaluations) creates a much more comprehensive picture of student achievement and progress than that represented by a set of test scores.

LEARNER PROGRESS CHART

The reproducible Learner Progress Chart enables students to record their test scores and chart their progress. You may want to keep the charts in a folder and have students update them as each test is completed.

INTEGRATING SCANS SKILLS

For programs that integrate the objectives of the Secretary's Commission on Achieving Necessary Skills (SCANS), it is very appropriate to give students responsibility for the day-to-day management of classroom logistics, such as recording attendance, obtaining supplies and equipment, or making copies of lesson handouts. Students can also take responsibility for aspects of their assessment, including scoring the Unit Achievement Tests, copying blank answer sheets, graphing their performance on their Learner Progress Chart, and maintaining their student portfolios.

A PARENT/SCHOOL COMMUNICATION; HELPING CHILDREN SUCCEED IN SCHOOL

Example:

Sam has to _____ his son at school.
- Ⓐ worry
- Ⓑ volunteer
- ● pick up
- Ⓓ pay attention

1. He's gotten behind in class because he was _____ for three days.
   - Ⓐ absent
   - Ⓑ appointment
   - Ⓒ absence
   - Ⓓ afraid

2. Parents should _____ the teacher about bullying.
   - Ⓐ discuss
   - Ⓑ tease
   - Ⓒ compliment
   - Ⓓ speak with

3. Parents have to sign _____ form for the class trip.
   - Ⓐ a concern
   - Ⓑ an absence
   - Ⓒ a permission
   - Ⓓ an appointment

4. If you are worried about your child's progress in school, it's a good idea to _____.
   - Ⓐ apologize to the teacher
   - Ⓑ contact the teacher
   - Ⓒ call the school nurse
   - Ⓓ excuse the teacher

5. Talking with children about what they are learning at school shows that you _____ their education.
   - Ⓐ pay attention
   - Ⓑ succeed
   - Ⓒ value
   - Ⓓ don't care about

6. Children should _____ while doing their homework.
   - Ⓐ watch TV
   - Ⓑ talk to friends online
   - Ⓒ talk to friends on the telephone
   - Ⓓ study in a quiet place

7. Pay attention to any social problems your child talks about, such as _____.
   - Ⓐ fights or teasing
   - Ⓑ parties or games
   - Ⓒ grades or tests
   - Ⓓ lunches or snacks

8. A breakfast that is _____ will give students energy for the school day.
   - Ⓐ quick and strong
   - Ⓑ high in sugar
   - Ⓒ low in protein
   - Ⓓ nutritious

9. A _____ is a good way to find out about your child's progress in school.
   - Ⓐ school health meeting
   - Ⓑ parent-teacher conference
   - Ⓒ school volunteer meeting
   - Ⓓ class field trip

....

1 Ⓐ Ⓑ Ⓒ Ⓓ   4 Ⓐ Ⓑ Ⓒ Ⓓ   7 Ⓐ Ⓑ Ⓒ Ⓓ

2 Ⓐ Ⓑ Ⓒ Ⓓ   5 Ⓐ Ⓑ Ⓒ Ⓓ   8 Ⓐ Ⓑ Ⓒ Ⓓ

3 Ⓐ Ⓑ Ⓒ Ⓓ   6 Ⓐ Ⓑ Ⓒ Ⓓ   9 Ⓐ Ⓑ Ⓒ Ⓓ

Go to the next page →

Example:

Grant School. How
_____ help you?
- Ⓐ I can
- Ⓑ may
- Ⓒ I may
- ⬤ may I

10. This is Mary Chan. My
son Tim _____ very sick.
He won't be at school
today. His teacher is Ms.
Clark.
- Ⓐ will be
- Ⓑ has been
- Ⓒ been
- Ⓓ isn't

11. Okay. I'll let Ms. Clark
know that Tim _____ today.
- Ⓐ absence
- Ⓑ absent
- Ⓒ will be absent
- Ⓓ reports his absence

12. Thank you. I think
_____ better tomorrow.
- Ⓐ he'll
- Ⓑ he was
- Ⓒ he'll be
- Ⓓ he's been

13. I'm your daughter's
teacher. I'm calling
because I'm _____ her
progress at school.
- Ⓐ worried about
- Ⓑ afraid of
- Ⓒ helpful
- Ⓓ pleased to meet

14. Oh, really? _____
problems lately?
- Ⓐ Does she have
- Ⓑ Will she be having
- Ⓒ Did she used to have
- Ⓓ Has she been having

15. Yes. She seems very
tired, and _____ trouble
concentrating in class.
- Ⓐ she had
- Ⓑ she's having
- Ⓒ she'll have
- Ⓓ she's going to have

16. Thanks for telling me.
She usually _____ to bed
at midnight.
- Ⓐ goes
- Ⓑ going
- Ⓒ had gone
- Ⓓ will have gone

17. That's very late. I think
she needs _____.
- Ⓐ she's sleeping
- Ⓑ help her sleep
- Ⓒ a good night's sleep
- Ⓓ good night

18. I understand. I'll make
sure _____.
- Ⓐ she gets up earlier
- Ⓑ she goes to bed earlier
- Ⓒ she is awake in the
   morning
- Ⓓ she has breakfast

---

10 Ⓐ Ⓑ Ⓒ Ⓓ   **13** Ⓐ Ⓑ Ⓒ Ⓓ   **15** Ⓐ Ⓑ Ⓒ Ⓓ   **17** Ⓐ Ⓑ Ⓒ Ⓓ

11 Ⓐ Ⓑ Ⓒ Ⓓ   **14** Ⓐ Ⓑ Ⓒ Ⓓ   **16** Ⓐ Ⓑ Ⓒ Ⓓ   **18** Ⓐ Ⓑ Ⓒ Ⓓ

12 Ⓐ Ⓑ Ⓒ Ⓓ

Go to the next page ⟶

Look at this school announcement. Then do Numbers 19 through 24.

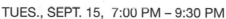

Mark your calendar!

Save the date!

BACK-TO-SCHOOL NIGHT
GRANT MIDDLE SCHOOL
TUES., SEPT. 15, 7:00 PM – 9:30 PM

Parents: *You're invited to our first school event of the year. Come meet your child's teachers, the school staff, and the principal!*

Schedule

7:00 – 7:10 **Principal Sandra Lopez** (Greeting and opening message)
Auditorium

7:15 – 7:25 **Homeroom visits** (Visit the homeroom class where your child begins the day. This is Period 1.)

7:30 – 8:40 **Subject classroom visits** (Follow your child's schedule.)
7:30–7:40 Period 2   8:00–8:10 Period 4   8:30–8:40 Period 6
7:45–7:55 Period 3   8:15–8:25 Period 5

8:45 – 9:00 **Talk with subject teachers** (Talk with your child's subject teachers and sign up for October Parent-Teacher Conferences.)
Gym

9:00 – 9:30 **Visit information tables** (Learn more about the Parent-Teacher Association, After-school programs, Sports, Counseling, and Volunteer opportunities.)
Library

---

19. The homeroom is _____.
- Ⓐ where students register
- Ⓑ where students do homework
- Ⓒ where students have their first class
- Ⓓ where students have all of their classes

20. To find out about athletic programs, parents should go to _____.
- Ⓐ the gym
- Ⓑ the library
- Ⓒ the auditorium
- Ⓓ the homeroom

21. Parent-Teacher conferences are held in _____.
- Ⓐ the gym
- Ⓑ the library
- Ⓒ September
- Ⓓ October

22. Each subject classroom visit lasts for _____ minutes.
- Ⓐ 5
- Ⓑ 10
- Ⓒ 30
- Ⓓ 60

23. The first place parents should go on Back-to-School night is the _____.
- Ⓐ homeroom
- Ⓑ gym
- Ⓒ library
- Ⓓ auditorium

24. We can infer that _____ will be at the event.
- Ⓐ all of the teachers
- Ⓑ only homeroom teachers
- Ⓒ only subject teachers
- Ⓓ only parents

....

19 Ⓐ Ⓑ Ⓒ Ⓓ   **21** Ⓐ Ⓑ Ⓒ Ⓓ   **23** Ⓐ Ⓑ Ⓒ Ⓓ

20 Ⓐ Ⓑ Ⓒ Ⓓ   **22** Ⓐ Ⓑ Ⓒ Ⓓ   **24** Ⓐ Ⓑ Ⓒ Ⓓ

Go to the next page ⇨

Read the notes from parents. Then do Numbers 25 through 28.

Oct. 17, 2009

Dear Mr. Vega,

My son, Mark, will be absent from school on Friday next week. He has a dentist appointment and will not be able to return to school. He's going to have a tooth pulled. Please excuse his absence. Also, he will ask you for any assignments on Thursday.

Sincerely,
Paul Chase
379-1287

October 16, 2009

Dear Mr. Vega,

My daughter, Rachel, has been very upset about school lately. She says that other girls are teasing her during recess. They've been making fun of her clothing and her hair. Rachel has been crying every day after school.

Could you kindly call me this week to talk about this problem? The best time to call is between 6 p.m. and 9 p.m. Thank you.

Yours truly,
Roberta Smith
379-5670

Subject:	**Kim Wong**
Date:	Monday, October 17, 2009 7:59 PM
From:	Peter Wong <peter.wong@mrn.com>
To:	Daniel Vega <dvega@dps.k12.org>

Dear Mr. Vega:

I'm writing you about my daughter, Kim Wong. She's been having trouble seeing the blackboard from her seat at the back of the classroom. We have scheduled an appointment with the eye doctor for Saturday to see if she needs glasses. In the meantime, could you please move her seat assignment to the front row so she can see the board? Thank you for your help.

Sincerely,
Peter Wong

25. Kim has a doctor's appointment _____.
   Ⓐ on Saturday
   Ⓑ on Friday
   Ⓒ next week
   Ⓓ on October 17

26. Ms. Smith wrote to Mr. Vega because her daughter _____.
   Ⓐ was absent
   Ⓑ is teasing other girls
   Ⓒ has been upset
   Ⓓ doesn't like her clothing

27. Currently, Kim sits _____.
   Ⓐ in back of the blackboard
   Ⓑ far from the blackboard
   Ⓒ in front of the class
   Ⓓ behind Rachel

28. Mark will be absent _____.
   Ⓐ for a week
   Ⓑ on Thursday
   Ⓒ on Thursday and Friday
   Ⓓ for one day next week

25 Ⓐ Ⓑ Ⓒ Ⓓ   26 Ⓐ Ⓑ Ⓒ Ⓓ   27 Ⓐ Ⓑ Ⓒ Ⓓ   28 Ⓐ Ⓑ Ⓒ Ⓓ

Go to the next page ➤

CLOZE READING: A Letter from the Principal

Choose the correct answers to complete the letter.

CHAVEZ
High School

Dear Parents,

Welcome to Chavez High School! We know you want your child to **support succeed increase** ,
(A)   ●   (C)

so here are some homework **tips questions chores** ²⁹ for parents.
(A)   (B)   (C)

• Make sure your child has a **big quiet cheap** ³⁰ place to do homework.
(A)   (B)   (C)

• Be positive about homework. Your **sign problem attitude** ³¹ should show that
(A)   (B)   (C)

you value education. Ask questions and show you are **interested energetic specific** ³².
(A)   (B)   (C)

• Many students need help to manage and **organize research behave** ³³ their study time.
(A)   (B)   (C)

Help your child **show schedule cancel** ³⁴ a daily time for homework.
(A)   (B)   (C)

• Make sure your child understands each **test attention assignment** ³⁵. If something is not
(A)   (B)   (C)

clear, your child can call a classmate or **contact come up limit** ³⁶ the teacher by e-mail.
(A)   (B)   (C)

• If you have any questions or **examples opportunities concerns** ³⁷, get in touch with your
(A)   (B)   (C)

child's teacher by phone or e-mail.

Sincerely,
Janet Morris
Janet Morris, Principal

LISTENING ASSESSMENT: Reporting an Absence

Read and listen to the questions. Then listen to the parent's message and answer the questions.

38. Who is leaving a
message?
Ⓐ The student.
Ⓑ The mother.
Ⓒ The secretary.
Ⓓ The principal.

39. What grade is the
student in?
Ⓐ Ninth.
Ⓑ Tenth.
Ⓒ Eleventh.
Ⓓ Twelfth.

40. Why is the student absent?
Ⓐ He has a baseball game.
Ⓑ He is sick.
Ⓒ He broke his leg.
Ⓓ He hurt his ankle.

---

29 Ⓐ Ⓑ Ⓒ Ⓓ   32 Ⓐ Ⓑ Ⓒ Ⓓ   35 Ⓐ Ⓑ Ⓒ Ⓓ   38 Ⓐ Ⓑ Ⓒ Ⓓ

30 Ⓐ Ⓑ Ⓒ Ⓓ   33 Ⓐ Ⓑ Ⓒ Ⓓ   36 Ⓐ Ⓑ Ⓒ Ⓓ   39 Ⓐ Ⓑ Ⓒ Ⓓ

31 Ⓐ Ⓑ Ⓒ Ⓓ   34 Ⓐ Ⓑ Ⓒ Ⓓ   37 Ⓐ Ⓑ Ⓒ Ⓓ   40 Ⓐ Ⓑ Ⓒ Ⓓ

WRITING ASSESSMENT: A Note to School

Duc Vu needs to write a note to Mrs. Roke, his son's teacher. His son's name is Tom Vu. Tom was absent on Wednesday and Thursday because he was sick. He had a bad stomachache and a fever. Today is Friday, May 1. Tom is at school today. He needs the assignments from Wednesday and Thursday. On Monday morning, May 4, Tom has a doctor's appointment. He will arrive at school after the appointment at about 11:00 A.M. Write a letter to the teacher.

_____

(today's date)

_____

(salutation)

_____

_____

_____

_____

_____

_____

_____

_____

_____

_____

(closing)

_____

(signature)

H **SPEAKING ASSESSMENT**

I can ask and answer these questions:

Ask Answer
☐ ☐ How long have you lived here?
☐ ☐ Where did you live before?
☐ ☐ How long did you live there?
☐ ☐ How long have you been going to this school?

Ask Answer
☐ ☐ Have you ever been absent from class? When? Why?
☐ ☐ Where do you usually do your homework?
☐ ☐ How can parents help children succeed in school?

STOP

Look at the bus and train schedules. Then do Numbers 19 through 22.

Greyhound Bus		Bus 1431
Location	**Arrives**	**Departs**
Seattle, WA		1:35 PM
Tacoma, WA	2:20 PM	2:25 PM
Olympia, WA	3:05 PM	3:10 PM
Longview, WA	4:35 PM	4:35 PM
Vancouver, WA	5:25 PM	5:25 PM
Portland, OR	5:50 PM	6:55 PM
Salem, OR	7:55 PM	8:05 PM
Eugene, OR	9:25 PM	9:40 PM
Grants Pass, OR	12:15 AM	12:20 AM
Medford, OR	1:20 AM	1:30 AM
Redding, CA	4:30 AM	4:50 AM
Sacramento, CA	7:30 AM	

Greyhound Bus		Bus 1436
Location	**Arrives**	**Departs**
Sacramento, CA		6:00 PM
Chico, CA	8:15 PM	8:20 PM
Red Bluff, CA	9:10 PM	9:10 PM
Redding, CA	9:50 PM	10:20 PM
Medford, OR	1:20 AM	1:35 AM
Eugene, OR	4:35 AM	4:45 AM
Salem, OR	6:05 AM	6:10 AM
Portland, OR	7:10 AM	8:00 AM
Olympia, WA	10:00 AM	10:05 AM
Tacoma, WA	10:45 AM	10:55 AM
Seattle, WA	11:40 AM	

COAST STARLIGHT

Seattle • Vancouver • Portland • Eugene
Redding • Chico • Sacramento

11		Train Number		11
Daily		Days of Operation		Daily
Read Down				Read Up
9 45A	Dp	Seattle, WA	Ar	8 45P
10 31A		Tacoma, WA		7 11P
11 21A		Olympia-Lacey, WA		6 22P
12 29P		Kelso-Longview, WA		5 14P
1 08P		Vancouver, WA		4 36P
1 50P	Ar	Portland, OR	Dp	4 20P
2 25P	Dp		Ar	3 40P
3 37P		Salem, OR		2 03P
4 10P		Albany, OR		1 30P
5 10P		Eugene-Springfield,		12 44P
8 05P		Chemult, OR		9 40A
10 00P		Klamath Falls, OR		8 25A
12 35A		Dunsmuir, CA		5 04A
2 21A		Redding, CA		3 14A
3 50A		Chico, CA		1 55A
6 35A	Ar	Sacramento, CA		11 59P

19. How long does it take to go by bus from Tacoma, WA, to Sacramento, CA?
ⓐ 13 hours
ⓑ 13 hours and 15 minutes
ⓒ 17 hours
ⓓ 17 hours and 5 minutes

20. How long does Bus 1436 stop in Portland, OR?
ⓐ 10 minutes
ⓑ 15 minutes
ⓒ 50 minutes
ⓓ 1 hour and 5 minutes

21. What time does the train depa[rt] Vancouver, WA, for Seattle, WA[?]
ⓐ 9:45 AM
ⓑ 1:08 PM
ⓒ 4:36 PM
ⓓ 8:45 PM

22. On Train 14, how long does it tak[e] to travel from Chico, CA, to Portland[,] OR?
ⓐ 13 hours and 15 minutes
ⓑ 13 hours and 45 minutes
ⓒ 14 hours
ⓓ 14 hours and 35 minutes

19 ⓐ ⓑ ⓒ ⓓ   20 ⓐ ⓑ ⓒ ⓓ   21 ⓐ ⓑ ⓒ ⓓ   22 ⓐ ⓑ ⓒ ⓓ

Read the flyer. Then do Numbers 23 though 28.

Neighborhood Watch

What is Neighborhood Watch?

The NEIGHBORHOOD WATCH program works to bring communities together with the police to achieve the common goal of preventing crime. NEIGHBORHOOD WATCH informs residents about how to discourage and prevent crimes such as burglary, auto theft, and car break-ins. Issues such as vandalism, graffiti, drug dealing, and gang activity are also discussed when necessary.

How can a meeting be arranged?

To request a NEIGHBORHOOD WATCH, call Crime Prevention at (321) 223-4567. The Crime Specialist will work with you to schedule the meeting date. Invitation notices will be sent to you to distribute to your neighbors.

NEIGHBORHOOD WATCH meetings are held on Monday, Tuesday, Wednesday, or Thursday evenings at 7:00 P.M. and last approximately two hours. At least TEN homes must be represented in order for the meeting to take place. Most meetings are held in your home or at a neighborhood center.

What happens at the meeting?

At a NEIGHBORHOOD WATCH meeting, you will meet a representative of your police department and discuss how to solve problems in your community or to keep the problems from starting in the first place!

Through this program, you will learn facts about:
- Police districts
- Duties of local officers
- Crime trends in your area
- How to react to suspicious or criminal activity
- How our city's 911 system works
- How to make your home safer with special locks, alarms, and lighting

Residents at the meeting will receive a NEIGHBORHOOD WATCH window sign and other materials.

If at least 80% of the homes on your block come to the meeting, metal NEIGHBORHOOD WATCH signs will be installed on the streetlight poles on your block.

> YOUR CITY'S POLICE DEPARTMENT wants to work with you to reduce crime!

23. The goal of a Neighborhood Watch program is to help residents _____.
   - Ⓐ meet their neighbors
   - Ⓑ have neighborhood meetings
   - Ⓒ prevent crime
   - Ⓓ call the police

24. To schedule a meeting, a resident _____.
   - Ⓐ calls the police department
   - Ⓑ calls the Crime Prevention unit
   - Ⓒ calls at 7 PM
   - Ⓓ writes a letter

25. At least _____ residents need to attend a meeting.
   - Ⓐ ten
   - Ⓑ two
   - Ⓒ eighty percent of the
   - Ⓓ one hundred percent of the

26. _____ would NOT be a topic of discussion at a Neighborhood Watch meeting.
   - Ⓐ Gang activity
   - Ⓑ Security systems
   - Ⓒ Car insurance
   - Ⓓ Suspicious activity

27. A Neighborhood Watch meeting usually lasts _____.
   - Ⓐ one hour
   - Ⓑ two hours
   - Ⓒ three hours
   - Ⓓ four hours

28. All residents who attend a meeting will receive _____.
   - Ⓐ a certificate
   - Ⓑ an alarm
   - Ⓒ a street sign
   - Ⓓ a window sign

23 Ⓐ Ⓑ Ⓒ Ⓓ   25 Ⓐ Ⓑ Ⓒ Ⓓ   27 Ⓐ Ⓑ Ⓒ Ⓓ
24 Ⓐ Ⓑ Ⓒ Ⓓ   26 Ⓐ Ⓑ Ⓒ Ⓓ   28 Ⓐ Ⓑ Ⓒ Ⓓ

Go to the next page

Choose the correct answers to complete the e-mail.

From: Ted Pran
To: Felipe Santos
Date: Tuesday, November 15, 11:45 AM
Subject: Your visit

Hi, Felipe. Here are the instructions directions maps to my apartment. If you're driving from
                                (A)   ●(B)   (C)

the school, go straight direct down 29 on Hamilton Avenue. Then drive five block blocks stops 30.
                (A)   (B)   (C)   (A)   (B)   (C)

Don't speed drive run 31 because that part of the street is in a school exit entrance zone 32.
       (A)   (B)   (C)   (A)   (B)   (C)

At the second stop street sign vehicle 33, turn left on Williams Street. Then make turn get 34
                    (A)   (B)   (C)   (A)   (B)   (C)

your second left. That's Rose Street. It's a one-way only-way three-way 35 Street. My address is
                                              (A)   (B)   (C)

217 Rose Street, Apartment 3C. By bus, take Bus number 39 on Hamilton Avenue.

Get on off in 36 at Williams Street. Walk illegal straight fast 37 on Williams and take
     (A) (B) (C)   (A)   (B)   (C)

the second left. That's Rose Street. My apartment is on the left.
See you soon!
Ted

Read and listen to the questions. Then listen to the recording and answer the questions.

38. Why did the person call?
    (A) To ask questions about an account.
    (B) To get directions to the store.
    (C) To talk with the customer service department.
    (D) To find out store hours.

39. Which directions does the recording give?
    (A) Only walking.
    (B) By car and walking.
    (C) By car and by bus.
    (D) Only by car.

40. Which buses stop at the mall?
    (A) 880 and 17.
    (B) 19 and Stevens Avenue.
    (C) 9 and 21.
    (D) 19 and 21.

29 (A) (B) (C) (D)   32 (A) (B) (C) (D)   35 (A) (B) (C) (D)   38 (A) (B) (C) (D)

30 (A) (B) (C) (D)   33 (A) (B) (C) (D)   36 (A) (B) (C) (D)   39 (A) (B) (C) (D)

31 (A) (B) (C) (D)   34 (A) (B) (C) (D)   37 (A) (B) (C) (D)   40 (A) (B) (C) (D)

Side by Side Plus Book 4
Unit 2 Achievement Test (Page 5 of 6)
183
© 2009 Pearson Education, Inc.
Duplication for classroom use is permitted.
Go to the next page ⟶

G WRITING ASSESSMENT: A Personal Letter with Directions

A classmate is going to visit you at your home. Write a personal letter with directions from the school to your home. You can give the directions for public transportation, walking, or driving. Number each part of the directions.

_____
(today's date)

_____
(salutation)

_____

_____

_____

_____

_____

_____

_____

_____

_____

_____

_____
(closing)

_____
(signature)

H SPEAKING ASSESSMENT

I can ask and answer these questions:

Ask Answer

☐ ☐ Can you tell me how to get to the nearest supermarket?

☐ ☐ Can you tell me how to get to the nearest police station?

☐ ☐ If a bus is late, what might have happened?

☐ ☐ Have you ever been pulled over for a traffic violation? What happened? What should you have done differently?

☐ ☐ Have you apologized to someone recently? Why? What should you have done differently?

☐ ☐ How can residents work with the police department to improve their city?

STOP

A UNITED STATES HISTORY

Example:

The United Nations was formed to _____ between countries.
- Ⓐ promote war
- Ⓑ increase trade
- ● keep peace
- Ⓓ develop communication

1. The United Nations provides economic _____ to many countries.
   - Ⓐ protests
   - Ⓑ forces
   - Ⓒ aid
   - Ⓓ welfare

2. During the _____, many banks and businesses closed.
   - Ⓐ Depression
   - Ⓑ economy
   - Ⓒ stock market
   - Ⓓ history

3. The stock market _____ on October 29, 1929.
   - Ⓐ controlled
   - Ⓑ gained
   - Ⓒ collapsed
   - Ⓓ lasted

4. The Social Security system was _____ during the New Deal.
   - Ⓐ established
   - Ⓑ revised
   - Ⓒ unemployed
   - Ⓓ invested

5. During World War II, Germany, _____, and Japan fought against the Allies.
   - Ⓐ Spain
   - Ⓑ Italy
   - Ⓒ China
   - Ⓓ Russia

6. The United States dropped the first atomic _____ during World War II.
   - Ⓐ attack
   - Ⓑ plane
   - Ⓒ collapse
   - Ⓓ bomb

7. On September 11, 2001, terrorists _____ four planes.
   - Ⓐ bombed
   - Ⓑ hijacked
   - Ⓒ bought
   - Ⓓ conquered

8. During the Cold War, the U.S. fought against _____ forces.
   - Ⓐ Communist
   - Ⓑ democratic
   - Ⓒ Allied
   - Ⓓ United Nations

9. Reverend Martin Luther King, Jr., was a leader of the _____ movement.
   - Ⓐ civics
   - Ⓑ civil rights
   - Ⓒ holiday
   - Ⓓ discrimination

1 Ⓐ Ⓑ Ⓒ Ⓓ   4 Ⓐ Ⓑ Ⓒ Ⓓ   7 Ⓐ Ⓑ Ⓒ Ⓓ

2 Ⓐ Ⓑ Ⓒ Ⓓ   5 Ⓐ Ⓑ Ⓒ Ⓓ   8 Ⓐ Ⓑ Ⓒ Ⓓ

3 Ⓐ Ⓑ Ⓒ Ⓓ   6 Ⓐ Ⓑ Ⓒ Ⓓ   9 Ⓐ Ⓑ Ⓒ Ⓓ

Example:

Do you _____ any questions about today's history lesson?
- Ⓐ had
- ● have
- Ⓒ having
- Ⓓ have had

11. Who knows the answer? _____ did the Depression happen?
- Ⓐ Which
- Ⓑ When
- Ⓒ Why
- Ⓓ What

10. Yes. I have a question. What _____ the Great Depression?
- Ⓐ caused
- Ⓑ did cause
- Ⓒ has caused
- Ⓓ should cause

12. I know. Americans _____ money and invested in companies, and then the value of the companies _____ suddenly.
- Ⓐ borrow . . . fell
- Ⓑ borrowed . . . fell
- Ⓒ borrow . . . fall
- Ⓓ borrowed . . . fall

13. Which president _____ laws that helped the economy?
- Ⓐ introduce
- Ⓑ introducing
- Ⓒ introduced
- Ⓓ was introduced

14. Franklin D. Roosevelt. His plan _____ the New Deal.
- Ⓐ called
- Ⓑ has called
- Ⓒ calling
- Ⓓ was called

15. What important event _____ in 1939?
- Ⓐ should occur
- Ⓑ occurred
- Ⓒ what happened
- Ⓓ didn't happen

16. World War II _____. The Allies _____ against Germany, Italy, and Japan.
- Ⓐ has begun . . . fight
- Ⓑ began . . . fight
- Ⓒ begins . . . fought
- Ⓓ began . . . fought

17. When did the U.S. _____ World War II?
- Ⓐ enter
- Ⓑ entered
- Ⓒ was entered
- Ⓓ should have entered

18. In 1941. Pearl Harbor _____ by Japan, and then the U.S. _____ war.
- Ⓐ attacked . . . declared
- Ⓑ attacked . . . was declared
- Ⓒ was attacked . . . declared
- Ⓓ was attacked . . . was declared

....

10 Ⓐ Ⓑ Ⓒ Ⓓ   13 Ⓐ Ⓑ Ⓒ Ⓓ   16 Ⓐ Ⓑ Ⓒ Ⓓ

11 Ⓐ Ⓑ Ⓒ Ⓓ   14 Ⓐ Ⓑ Ⓒ Ⓓ   17 Ⓐ Ⓑ Ⓒ Ⓓ

12 Ⓐ Ⓑ Ⓒ Ⓓ   15 Ⓐ Ⓑ Ⓒ Ⓓ   18 Ⓐ Ⓑ Ⓒ Ⓓ

186

Go to the next page ⟩

Read the civics textbook lesson. Then do Numbers 19 through 24.

GEORGE H.W. BUSH   1989-1993

George Bush had been the vice president during the presidency of Ronald Reagan. During Bush's term, the Cold War came to an end. In 1989, the Berlin Wall was destroyed. It had separated West Berlin from communist East Germany. In 1990, Iraqi leader Saddam Hussein invaded Kuwait. Bush sent military troops into Iraq in 1991 for a short and successful war. This was called the Gulf War. During Bush's four years in office, the economy slowed more and more.

WILLIAM J. (BILL) CLINTON   1993–2001

Clinton worked to improve the economy. He increased taxes, cut government spending, and increased federal money for schools and police departments. Under Clinton, the North American Free Trade Agreement (NAFTA) was signed in 1994. NAFTA removed restrictions on commerce and investment with Mexico and Canada.

Clinton worked to keep peace in the Middle East, Eastern Europe, and Africa. Clinton was accused of an improper relationship with a female employee. The House of Representatives tried to remove him from office, but the Senate did not approve. Clinton was president for eight years.

GEORGE W. BUSH   2001–2009

George W. Bush is the son of the former President Bush. On September 11, 2001, international terrorists crashed planes into the World Trade Center in New York City, the Pentagon in Washington, D.C., and in Pennsylvania. Bush ordered attacks on terrorists in Afghanistan. In 2003, he ordered troops into Iraq to destroy the government of the dictator Saddam Hussein. Under Bush, the economy in the U.S. became very weak.

19. _____ was president before George H.W. Bush.
   Ⓐ William J. Clinton
   Ⓑ George W. Bush
   Ⓒ Ronald Reagan
   Ⓓ Barack Obama

20. The _____ took place during the early 1990s.
   Ⓐ Gulf War
   Ⓑ Cold War
   Ⓒ Iraq War
   Ⓓ Afghanistan War

21. Clinton and George W. Bush both _____.
   Ⓐ sent troops to Iraq
   Ⓑ tried to bring peace to the Middle East
   Ⓒ were sons of presidents
   Ⓓ were in office for 8 years

22. You can infer that _____ was an important part of the end of the Cold War.
   Ⓐ George Bush
   Ⓑ the fall of the Berlin Wall
   Ⓒ the year 1990
   Ⓓ East Germany

23. George W. Bush ordered troops into Afghanistan after _____.
   Ⓐ the attacks on September 11, 2001
   Ⓑ sending troops to Iraq
   Ⓒ NAFTA
   Ⓓ they fought in Kuwait

24. You can infer that the economy got better under _____.
   Ⓐ Ronald Reagan
   Ⓑ George H.W. Bush
   Ⓒ George W. Bush
   Ⓓ William J. Clinton

19 Ⓐ Ⓑ Ⓒ Ⓓ   21 Ⓐ Ⓑ Ⓒ Ⓓ   23 Ⓐ Ⓑ Ⓒ Ⓓ

20 Ⓐ Ⓑ Ⓒ Ⓓ   22 Ⓐ Ⓑ Ⓒ Ⓓ   24 Ⓐ Ⓑ Ⓒ Ⓓ

Go to the next page ⟩

Read the civics textbook lesson. Then do Numbers 25 though 28.

Dr. Martin Luther King, Jr.

Martin Luther King, Jr., was born on January 15, 1929 in Atlanta, Georgia. His father was the minister of a church. His mother and father taught him to respect all people, but King saw that black people were not respected. In many states, discrimination against blacks was legal.

He married Coretta Scott in 1953, and the next year they moved to Montgomery, Alabama, where he was the minister of a church.

King became active in the civil rights movement in Montgomery. By state law, African-Americans had to sit in the back of the bus. In December of 1955, the African-American community organized an action against the city bus company in Montgomery. No African-Americans rode the bus for almost 11 months. Finally, the United States Supreme Court said that the laws were illegal.

Dr. King became one of the most famous leaders of the civil rights movement. He traveled to many cities and towns in the southern U.S., giving speeches and helping to organize efforts to end discrimination.

In 1960, Dr. King returned to Atlanta, Georgia, and became a minister in his father's church. Dr. King became more and more active in the growing civil rights movement. There were many demonstrations and confrontations with the police. The civil rights movement was growing stronger, but many people were against it. In 1963, King led the March on Washington with 200,000 demonstrators.

In 1964, President Johnson signed into law the Civil Rights Act. That same year, King won the Nobel Peace Prize. He continued working for the civil rights of all Americans. In addition, he protested the Vietnam War. On April 4, 1968, he was assassinated.

Martin Luther King, Jr., was one of the most important leaders of the American civil rights movement of the 1950s and 1960s. Although he died more than 40 years ago, his life influences and educates people all over the world.

25. The civil rights movement in the U.S. started in _____.
    Ⓐ 1963
    Ⓑ 1964
    Ⓒ the 1950s
    Ⓓ the 1960s

26. King was _____ years old when he was assassinated.
    Ⓐ 29
    Ⓑ 39
    Ⓒ 40
    Ⓓ 49

27. King was _____ the Vietnam War.
    Ⓐ a soldier in
    Ⓑ jobless during
    Ⓒ a supplier for
    Ⓓ against

28. You can infer that African-Americans protested the bus laws in Montgomery because _____.
    Ⓐ they weren't allowed on the buses
    Ⓑ there was discrimination on the buses
    Ⓒ buses didn't go to their neighborhoods
    Ⓓ bus tickets were too expensive

25 Ⓐ Ⓑ Ⓒ Ⓓ   27 Ⓐ Ⓑ Ⓒ Ⓓ

26 Ⓐ Ⓑ Ⓒ Ⓓ   28 Ⓐ Ⓑ Ⓒ Ⓓ

Go to the next page ⇨

Choose the correct answers to complete the reading.

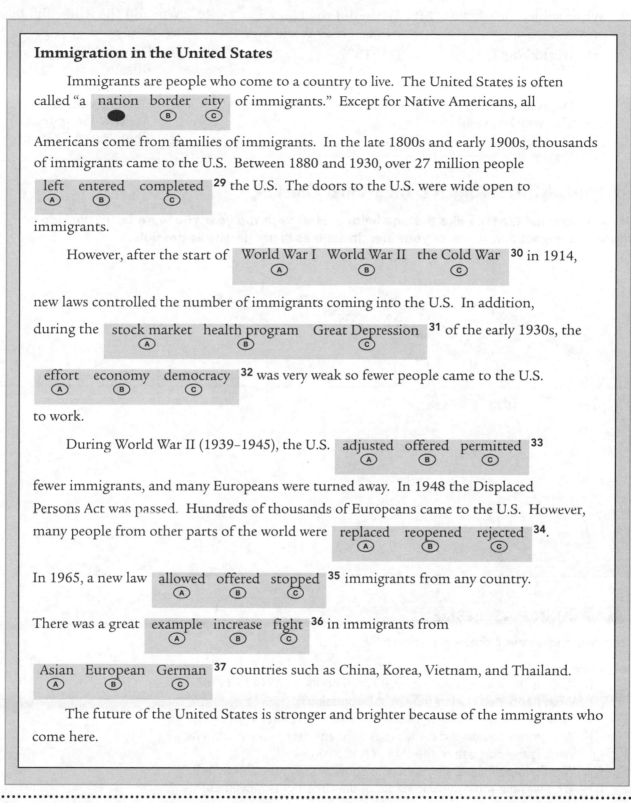

Immigration in the United States

Immigrants are people who come to a country to live. The United States is often called "a nation border city of immigrants." Except for Native Americans, all Americans come from families of immigrants. In the late 1800s and early 1900s, thousands of immigrants came to the U.S. Between 1880 and 1930, over 27 million people left entered completed [29] the U.S. The doors to the U.S. were wide open to immigrants.

However, after the start of World War I World War II the Cold War [30] in 1914, new laws controlled the number of immigrants coming into the U.S. In addition, during the stock market health program Great Depression [31] of the early 1930s, the effort economy democracy [32] was very weak so fewer people came to the U.S. to work.

During World War II (1939–1945), the U.S. adjusted offered permitted [33] fewer immigrants, and many Europeans were turned away. In 1948 the Displaced Persons Act was passed. Hundreds of thousands of Europeans came to the U.S. However, many people from other parts of the world were replaced reopened rejected [34].

In 1965, a new law allowed offered stopped [35] immigrants from any country.

There was a great example increase fight [36] in immigrants from Asian European German [37] countries such as China, Korea, Vietnam, and Thailand.

The future of the United States is stronger and brighter because of the immigrants who come here.

29 Ⓐ Ⓑ Ⓒ Ⓓ	32 Ⓐ Ⓑ Ⓒ Ⓓ	35 Ⓐ Ⓑ Ⓒ Ⓓ
30 Ⓐ Ⓑ Ⓒ Ⓓ	33 Ⓐ Ⓑ Ⓒ Ⓓ	36 Ⓐ Ⓑ Ⓒ Ⓓ
31 Ⓐ Ⓑ Ⓒ Ⓓ	34 Ⓐ Ⓑ Ⓒ Ⓓ	37 Ⓐ Ⓑ Ⓒ Ⓓ

Go to the next page ⟩

F · LISTENING ASSESSMENT: Classroom Discussion

Read and listen to the questions. Then listen to the conversation and answer the questions.

38. What subject WON'T be on the test?
- Ⓐ World War I
- Ⓑ World War II
- Ⓒ The Great Depression
- Ⓓ The war between the U.S. and England

39. When did the United States enter World War I?
- Ⓐ 1907.
- Ⓑ 1917.
- Ⓒ 1918.
- Ⓓ 1929.

40. Who did the Allies fight against?
- Ⓐ England, France, and Russia.
- Ⓑ Germany.
- Ⓒ Germany and Austria-Hungary.
- Ⓓ The United States.

G · WRITING ASSESSMENT: A Personal Timeline

Draw a personal timeline like the one below. Start with the year you were born. Include important events and dates in your life. Include as many details as possible.

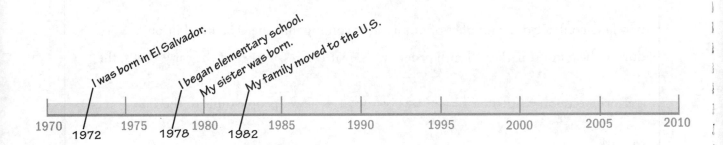

H · SPEAKING ASSESSMENT

I can ask and answer these questions:

Ask Answer
- ☐ ☐ What is the name of the war that happened from 1914 to 1918?
- ☐ ☐ What happened during the Great Depression?
- ☐ ☐ How did the New Deal help the U.S. after the Great Depression?
- ☐ ☐ What three countries did the Allies fight against during World War II?
- ☐ ☐ What is the purpose of the United Nations?
- ☐ ☐ What two political systems were in conflict during the Cold War?
- ☐ ☐ Who was the most famous leader of the Civil Rights Movement?
- ☐ ☐ What happened on September 11, 2001?

....

38 Ⓐ Ⓑ Ⓒ Ⓓ   **39** Ⓐ Ⓑ Ⓒ Ⓓ   **40** Ⓐ Ⓑ Ⓒ Ⓓ

© 2009 Pearson Education, Inc.
Duplication for classroom use is permitted.

A CONSUMER COMPLAINTS AND WARRANTIES

Example:

I need to return this because it is
_____.
- Ⓐ breaking
- Ⓑ breaks
- ● broken
- Ⓓ break

1. Would you like to _____ this iron for a new one?
   - Ⓐ return
   - Ⓑ exchange
   - Ⓒ repair
   - Ⓓ receipt

2. The warranty doesn't _____ water damage.
   - Ⓐ insist
   - Ⓑ deduct
   - Ⓒ obtain
   - Ⓓ cover

3. The store _____ is to accept returns that are made within 30 days.
   - Ⓐ privacy
   - Ⓑ policy
   - Ⓒ exchange
   - Ⓓ refund

4. Unfortunately, the warranty on my computer _____ last month.
   - Ⓐ expired
   - Ⓑ broke
   - Ⓒ dropped
   - Ⓓ started

5. Sam wrote a letter of _____ to the company.
   - Ⓐ consumer
   - Ⓑ complaining
   - Ⓒ complaint
   - Ⓓ exchange

6. To get a refund, you have to mail in your proof of _____.
   - Ⓐ receipt
   - Ⓑ refund
   - Ⓒ defect
   - Ⓓ purchase

7. The manager _____ my defective air conditioner with one that works.
   - Ⓐ replaced
   - Ⓑ refunded
   - Ⓒ repaired
   - Ⓓ returned

8. The _____ is good for 90 days.
   - Ⓐ bill of sale
   - Ⓑ warranty
   - Ⓒ refund
   - Ⓓ receipt

9. The new faucet must have a _____ because it is leaking.
   - Ⓐ defect
   - Ⓑ dispute
   - Ⓒ return
   - Ⓓ exchange

1 Ⓐ Ⓑ Ⓒ Ⓓ   4 Ⓐ Ⓑ Ⓒ Ⓓ   7 Ⓐ Ⓑ Ⓒ Ⓓ

2 Ⓐ Ⓑ Ⓒ Ⓓ   5 Ⓐ Ⓑ Ⓒ Ⓓ   8 Ⓐ Ⓑ Ⓒ Ⓓ

3 Ⓐ Ⓑ Ⓒ Ⓓ   6 Ⓐ Ⓑ Ⓒ Ⓓ   9 Ⓐ Ⓑ Ⓒ Ⓓ

Go to the next page ▷

Example:

I'd like _____ this printer.
- Ⓐ to returning
- Ⓑ returning
- Ⓒ return
- ● to return

10. What _____ the problem?
- Ⓐ are
- Ⓑ seem to be
- Ⓒ seems to be
- Ⓓ is the matter

11. The paper _____ every time I use the machine. Here's my receipt.
- Ⓐ jam
- Ⓑ jammed
- Ⓒ jams
- Ⓓ was jammed

12. It's still under warranty. You _____ and get a new one.
- Ⓐ will exchange me
- Ⓑ can exchange it
- Ⓒ could have exchanged
- Ⓓ exchanged it

13. I bought this coffee machine here, and _____ broken.
- Ⓐ I
- Ⓑ I'm
- Ⓒ it
- Ⓓ it's

14. Can you tell me what the problem _____?
- Ⓐ is
- Ⓑ be
- Ⓒ are
- Ⓓ will be

15. The water _____.
- Ⓐ leak
- Ⓑ leaking out
- Ⓒ leak out
- Ⓓ leaks out

16. _____ your receipt?
- Ⓐ Does it have
- Ⓑ Do you have
- Ⓒ Would you
- Ⓓ Will there be

Yes. Here you are.

17. Could you tell me _____ there will be a charge for this repair?
- Ⓐ where
- Ⓑ what
- Ⓒ whether
- Ⓓ when

18. Yes, there will. The warranty _____.
- Ⓐ has expired
- Ⓑ have expired
- Ⓒ expire
- Ⓓ expires

10	Ⓐ Ⓑ Ⓒ Ⓓ		13	Ⓐ Ⓑ Ⓒ Ⓓ		16	Ⓐ Ⓑ Ⓒ Ⓓ
11	Ⓐ Ⓑ Ⓒ Ⓓ		14	Ⓐ Ⓑ Ⓒ Ⓓ		17	Ⓐ Ⓑ Ⓒ Ⓓ
12	Ⓐ Ⓑ Ⓒ Ⓓ		15	Ⓐ Ⓑ Ⓒ Ⓓ		18	Ⓐ Ⓑ Ⓒ Ⓓ

192

Go to the next page ⟩

Read the web page with consumer information. Then do Numbers 19 through 22.

Is the new car you just bought a "lemon?" Is it having many problems? Every state has a **"lemon law"** that protects consumers against problems with new products they purchase. The lemon law usually covers new cars, but in some states the law also covers used cars. The coverage considers the number of repair attempts (times the customer tried to repair the car) and how many days the car is out of service (days when the car cannot be used).

Here are some examples of lemon law coverage for cars. For more information, check with your state consumer affairs office.

Lemon Law Coverage

State	Car	Repair attempts	Lemon Law Coverage
Arizona	New and used cars	4 repair attempts or 30 days out of service	Manufacturer's warranty period, 2 years, or 24,000 miles
California	New cars only	4 repair attempts or 30 days out of service	18 months or 18,000 miles
Florida	New cars only	3 repair attempts or 30 days out of service	2 years
Illinois	New cars only	4 repair attempts or 30 days out of service	1 year or 12,000 miles
New Jersey	New and used cars	3 repair attempts or 30 days out of service	2 years or 18,000 miles
New Mexico	New and used cars	4 repair attempts or 30 days out of service	Manufacturer's warranty period or 1 year
New York	New cars only	4 repair attempts or 20 days out of service	2 years or 24,000 miles
Texas	New cars only	4 repair attempts or 30 days out of service	Manufacturer's warranty period or 1 year

19. Which states have lemon laws to cover used cars?
   - Ⓐ Arizona, Florida, and New Jersey.
   - Ⓑ New Jersey, New York, and New Mexico.
   - Ⓒ Arizona, New Jersey, and New Mexico.
   - Ⓓ Arizona, New York, and New Mexico.

20. How many states have coverage for more than 20,000 miles?
   - Ⓐ One.
   - Ⓑ Two.
   - Ⓒ Three.
   - Ⓓ Four.

21. What is the number of repair attempts required before using the lemon law in most of these states?
   - Ⓐ One.
   - Ⓑ Two.
   - Ⓒ Three.
   - Ⓓ Four.

22. Which state has the best coverage for consumers?
   - Ⓐ Arizona.
   - Ⓑ California.
   - Ⓒ Texas.
   - Ⓓ Illinois.

19 Ⓐ Ⓑ Ⓒ Ⓓ   20 Ⓐ Ⓑ Ⓒ Ⓓ   21 Ⓐ Ⓑ Ⓒ Ⓓ   22 Ⓐ Ⓑ Ⓒ Ⓓ

Go to the next page ⇨

Look at the newspaper advice column. Then do Numbers 23 through 28.

CONSUMER ACTION MAILBAG—SEND US YOUR QUESTIONS

Dear Consumer Action,
I bought a sofa from Sofas & More. In the store, I checked the sofa that I bought, and it looked fine. The sofa was delivered 3 days later. It was wrapped in plastic for protection. It looked like the right sofa, so I signed the receipt saying that I had received the sofa in good condition. Later, when I took off the plastic, I saw that the sofa color was wrong. I called the store, and the salesperson said it was the last one so I couldn't exchange it. I had signed the delivery receipt, so I can't get a refund. The store is going out of business in one week. What can I do?
Sorry in San Jose

Dear Sorry in San Jose,
    You took the first step to take care of your problem—you called the store. However, you didn't take the next step—you needed to talk with the manager. If you have a problem, always ask to speak with the manager or supervisor. I called the manager at Sofas & More, and he apologized for the problems. The manager said that he would refund the amount you paid to your credit card when the sofa is returned. Please call him to schedule a pick-up!
Consumer Action

Dear Consumer Action,
I have a serious problem with the person I hired to paint my house. I thought I was hiring a company, A-1 Painters. I discovered that this is not a real company, just a man with a business card. I hired this man because he gave me a low price and because he seemed very experienced. When we agreed on the job, he asked me for $300.00 in cash to buy the paint. I gave him the money. That was two weeks ago. He doesn't return my phone calls and the phone number for his company doesn't work. Help!
Paintless in Piedmont

Dear Paintless in Piedmont,
    I'm sorry to tell you that you have lost $300.00, but you have learned an important lesson: Always find out about a company, and never pay in cash. I called the Better Business Bureau (BBB). They said that they have received many complaints about this company. Unfortunately, the BBB said that it would be hard to get your money back since you paid in cash. However, if you write to the BBB and explain your problem, they will try to help you.
Consumer Action

23. The person who bought the sofa _____.
  Ⓐ will get the sofa she wanted
  Ⓑ will get a cash refund
  Ⓒ will keep the sofa that was delivered
  Ⓓ will get a refund to her credit card

24. Sorry in San Jose should have _____.
  Ⓐ paid by check
  Ⓑ spoken with the truck driver
  Ⓒ checked the sofa before accepting it
  Ⓓ called the salesperson again

25. The manager of Sofas & More _____.
  Ⓐ apologized
  Ⓑ offered to give a cash refund
  Ⓒ refused to take back the sofa
  Ⓓ offered to exchange the sofa

26. Paintless in Piedmont _____.
  Ⓐ paid $300 by check
  Ⓑ paid $300 in cash
  Ⓒ didn't pay for the paint
  Ⓓ received $300 in cash

27. Paintless in Piedmont _____.
  Ⓐ probably won't get the money back
  Ⓑ will get a cash refund
  Ⓒ probably had the wrong phone number
  Ⓓ should have paid $300

28. The Better Business Bureau _____.
  Ⓐ collects money for consumers
  Ⓑ can help consumers with problems
  Ⓒ had never heard of A-1 Painters
  Ⓓ only helps businesses

23 Ⓐ Ⓑ Ⓒ Ⓓ   25 Ⓐ Ⓑ Ⓒ Ⓓ   27 Ⓐ Ⓑ Ⓒ Ⓓ
24 Ⓐ Ⓑ Ⓒ Ⓓ   26 Ⓐ Ⓑ Ⓒ Ⓓ   28 Ⓐ Ⓑ Ⓒ Ⓓ

Go to the next page ⟩

E CLOZE READING: A Product Complaint Letter

Choose the correct answers to complete the letter.

Camera Warehouse, Inc.
598 South St.
Danville, NY 10019

Dear Sir or Madam:

I [replaced (A) ordered (●) returned (C)] a camera from your company on December 10, 2009,

and I [received (A) resolved (B) requested (C)] 29 the shipment on December 17. When I opened the

package, I saw that the camera was [arrived (A) disputed (B) damaged (C)] 30. I called your

[salesperson (A) customer (B) refund (C)] 31 service department, and the manager told me to return the

camera to you. I mailed it back with a note and the [receipt (A) return (B) proof (C)] 32 of purchase.

Two weeks later, I called your company. The person said that they had not received the package.

He said it must have gotten [found (A) lost (B) exchanged (C)] 33. However, the post office said that it

was [received (A) delivered (B) disputed (C)] 34 to you on December 27. I have called many times, but

the clerk says that they are still [investigating (A) complaining (B) insisting (C)] 35 the problem. Could

you please help me with this problem? How can I [expire (A) result (B) obtain (C)] 36 a replacement?

Please [call (A) come by (B) bill (C)] 37 me at 432-923-4567.

Sincerely,

Ben Vuong

Ben Vuong

F LISTENING ASSESSMENT: Calling a Store about a Problem

Read and listen to the questions. Then listen to the conversation and answer the questions.

38. Why is the customer calling the store?
    - (A) She wants to buy a refrigerator.
    - (B) She doesn't have a warranty.
    - (C) She wants to exchange her refrigerator.
    - (D) The refrigerator light doesn't work.

39. How long has she had the refrigerator?
    - (A) Two months.
    - (B) Two weeks.
    - (C) Three months.
    - (D) Three weeks.

40. What does the salesman offer to do?
    - (A) Exchange the refrigerator.
    - (B) Send a repairperson.
    - (C) Explain how to fix it.
    - (D) Give her a warranty.

....

29 (A) (B) (C) (D)   32 (A) (B) (C) (D)   35 (A) (B) (C) (D)   38 (A) (B) (C) (D)

30 (A) (B) (C) (D)   33 (A) (B) (C) (D)   36 (A) (B) (C) (D)   39 (A) (B) (C) (D)

31 (A) (B) (C) (D)   34 (A) (B) (C) (D)   37 (A) (B) (C) (D)   40 (A) (B) (C) (D)

Go to the next page ⟩

You bought a new flat-screen TV (Model XY79) this year on November 3 at Big Buy Appliance Store. The serial number of the TV is AJ-128739-CX. Fill in the form below.

SonoVision   *2-Year Warranty Registration Form*

Receive a 2-Year Warranty with the purchase of our flat-screen television models XY76, XY79, and XY83.

Please print clearly and complete all information. (No P.O. Box numbers will be accepted.)

Name _____

Address (No P.O. boxes) _____

City _____ State _____ Zip _____

Phone Number _____ E-mail Address (optional) _____

Where did you buy it? (Name of store) _____

Model Number _____ Serial Number _____

Date of Purchase _____

Signature _____ Today's Date _____

Mail your completed warranty form to: *SonoVision* 2-Year Warranty
P. O. Box 599
Memphis, TN 38101

I can ask and answer these questions:

Ask Answer
☐ ☐ What is a warranty?
☐ ☐ Are any of your appliances covered by warranties? Which ones?
☐ ☐ Have you ever returned something you purchased? What was it? Why did you return it?
☐ ☐ What is the best way to take care of a complaint in a store?
☐ ☐ Have you ever written a letter of complaint? What was the situation?
☐ ☐ What is a consumer hotline?
☐ ☐ What should you do if you receive a damaged product in the mail?

STOP

A ⬛ HOME FIRE SAFETY AND EMERGENCY PROCEDURES

Example:

Every family should have and should _____ an emergency route.
- Ⓐ replace
- ⬤ practice
- Ⓒ lock up
- Ⓓ shut off

1. The _____ in smoke detectors should be replaced every six months.
- Ⓐ batteries
- Ⓑ electricity
- Ⓒ fire extinguishers
- Ⓓ utilities

2. Newspapers, clothing, and furniture are all _____ materials.
- Ⓐ soft
- Ⓑ resistant
- Ⓒ inflammable
- Ⓓ flammable

3. Space heaters should be at least _____ away from walls and furniture.
- Ⓐ one inch
- Ⓑ three inches
- Ⓒ three feet
- Ⓓ three yards

4. Your family should have _____ in case of a fire in your home.
- Ⓐ an inside meeting place
- Ⓑ an outside meeting place
- Ⓒ a special door
- Ⓓ a neighbor's phone number

5. Don't put a _____ in the kitchen. Install a _____ instead.
- Ⓐ fire extinguisher . . . smoke detector
- Ⓑ smoke detector . . . heat detector
- Ⓒ fire extinguisher . . . utility shutoff
- Ⓓ smoke detector . . . first-aid kit

6. Smoke detectors should be installed outside each _____.
- Ⓐ sleeping area
- Ⓑ bathroom
- Ⓒ hallway
- Ⓓ house

7. If a person is _____, you must act very quickly.
- Ⓐ breathing
- Ⓑ coughing
- Ⓒ blocking
- Ⓓ choking

8. If a person's airway is blocked, the person can die _____.
- Ⓐ slowly
- Ⓑ in a few seconds
- Ⓒ in a few minutes
- Ⓓ in several hours

9. For the Heimlich maneuver, stand _____ the person, make a fist, and use your arms to thrust.
- Ⓐ next to
- Ⓑ over
- Ⓒ in front of
- Ⓓ behind

....

1 Ⓐ Ⓑ Ⓒ Ⓓ   4 Ⓐ Ⓑ Ⓒ Ⓓ   7 Ⓐ Ⓑ Ⓒ Ⓓ

2 Ⓐ Ⓑ Ⓒ Ⓓ   5 Ⓐ Ⓑ Ⓒ Ⓓ   8 Ⓐ Ⓑ Ⓒ Ⓓ

3 Ⓐ Ⓑ Ⓒ Ⓓ   6 Ⓐ Ⓑ Ⓒ Ⓓ   9 Ⓐ Ⓑ Ⓒ Ⓓ

Go to the next page ⟩

Example:

What _____ you buy
at the hardware store?
- Ⓐ are
- ● did
- Ⓒ was
- Ⓓ does

11. Why? We _____ two
detectors last year.
- Ⓐ install
- Ⓑ installed
- Ⓒ installing
- Ⓓ have installed

13. You're right. If there
were a fire at night, we
probably _____ the
detector in the hallway.
- Ⓐ will hear
- Ⓑ won't hear
- Ⓒ didn't hear
- Ⓓ wouldn't hear

10. I _____ three new smoke
detectors.
- Ⓐ buy
- Ⓑ was buying
- Ⓒ bought
- Ⓓ would buy

12. Yes, but we should _____
a detector outside each
bedroom, too.
- Ⓐ had
- Ⓑ to have
- Ⓒ have
- Ⓓ will have

14. I hope we don't ever
_____ a fire in the house.
- Ⓐ have
- Ⓑ had
- Ⓒ having
- Ⓓ would have

15. Emergency Operator.
_____ your emergency?
- Ⓐ What is
- Ⓑ How is
- Ⓒ What was
- Ⓓ Why is

17. Is he _____?
- Ⓐ breathe
- Ⓑ breathing
- Ⓒ breathed
- Ⓓ breathes

I'll send an ambulance
right away.

16. My grandfather _____
and suddenly he fell
from his chair.
- Ⓐ eat
- Ⓑ eating
- Ⓒ is eating
- Ⓓ was eating

18. Yes. And his eyes _____
open.
- Ⓐ is
- Ⓑ are
- Ⓒ will be
- Ⓓ weren't

10 Ⓐ Ⓑ Ⓒ Ⓓ	**13** Ⓐ Ⓑ Ⓒ Ⓓ	**16** Ⓐ Ⓑ Ⓒ Ⓓ	
11 Ⓐ Ⓑ Ⓒ Ⓓ	**14** Ⓐ Ⓑ Ⓒ Ⓓ	**17** Ⓐ Ⓑ Ⓒ Ⓓ	
12 Ⓐ Ⓑ Ⓒ Ⓓ	**15** Ⓐ Ⓑ Ⓒ Ⓓ	**18** Ⓐ Ⓑ Ⓒ Ⓓ	

Read the news article. Then do Numbers 19 though 22.

Boy saves mother's life with Heimlich maneuver

HARWOOD – A Harwood boy is being called an amazing nine-year-old for saving his mother's life after she choked on a grape. Jason Clark performed the Heimlich maneuver on his mother, Terry Clark, at their home on Wednesday afternoon.

Terry Clark said she choked on a grape while she was eating. She started hitting the kitchen table to get the attention of her son, who was in the living room.

"All of a sudden, he came behind me, grabbed me, and then he started squeezing me hard. He did several thrusts. At first it didn't work," she said Thursday.

"Then he grabbed me again, gave a big thrust, and suddenly the grape flew out of my mouth."

When the mother could breathe, she told her son that he had saved her life.

Where did Jason learn the Heimlich maneuver? The boy said he saw a safety demonstration at school. Later, he looked up the procedure on the Internet and

9-year-old Jason Clark performed the Heimlich maneuver on his mother.

learned it on his own.

After the emergency, Jason said, "I'm so happy that I knew how to do the Heimlich maneuver. She might have died."

On Friday night, the Clark family enjoyed a special dinner at a local restaurant.

19. The mother was _____.
   Ⓐ breathing hard
   Ⓑ swallowing a grape
   Ⓒ choking on a grape
   Ⓓ calling her son

20. Jason learned the Heimlich maneuver _____.
   Ⓐ from the Internet
   Ⓑ in a safety class
   Ⓒ from his mother
   Ⓓ at a local restaurant

21. When the boy did the Heimlich maneuver, the grape came out _____.
   Ⓐ after one thrust
   Ⓑ after several thrusts
   Ⓒ after three minutes
   Ⓓ after he hit the kitchen table

22. Jason's mother must be very _____ him.
   Ⓐ exhausted by
   Ⓑ concerned about
   Ⓒ afraid of
   Ⓓ proud of

19 Ⓐ Ⓑ Ⓒ Ⓓ   20 Ⓐ Ⓑ Ⓒ Ⓓ   21 Ⓐ Ⓑ Ⓒ Ⓓ   22 Ⓐ Ⓑ Ⓒ Ⓓ

Go to the next page ⟩

Read the announcement. Then do Numbers 23 though 28.

WESTVIEW APARTMENTS

TO: All Residents of Westview Apartments
FROM: Ron Manning, Building Manager
RE: Smoke Detectors and Fire Safety

Change your clocks!
Change your batteries!

This Sunday, we change our clocks to Standard Time. Please remember to **replace** the batteries in your smoke detectors. Please also review our fire safety procedures below. All residents should have a fire emergency plan and map. Practice your escape route. If you have any questions, please call me at 499-1222.

Fire Safety Procedures
If the fire alarm sounds, all residents must immediately leave the building. Follow these instructions:

1. Put on a coat and hard-soled shoes.
2. Take a towel with you so that you don't breathe smoke.
3. Close windows.
4. Check your doorknob and door. If they are hot, do *not* open your door. Exit through a window (if you are on the first floor) or wait for help.
5. Stay low to the floor.
6. Leave the building through the nearest exit. Always know an additional emergency exit in case your first exit is blocked.
7. *Never* use the elevators! Use the stairways to leave the building.
8. Go to the emergency meeting area 100 feet away from the building.
9. Do not re-enter the building.

Important! If you can't get out because of smoke or fire in the hallway, call 9-1-1 to report your exact location. Wait in a room with a window. Close the door and seal it with tape or towels. Stay by the window and signal to firefighters with a flashlight or cloth. *Sometimes the safest thing you can do in a tall building fire is to stay in your apartment and wait for the firefighters.*

---

23. This announcement tells residents to change smoke detector batteries and to _____.
- Ⓐ review fire safety procedures
- Ⓑ check their heat detectors
- Ⓒ participate in a fire drill
- Ⓓ listen for the fire alarm

24. All residents should practice their _____ routes.
- Ⓐ fire
- Ⓑ escape
- Ⓒ building
- Ⓓ stairway

28. To not breathe smoke, residents should _____.
- Ⓐ drink water
- Ⓑ open a window
- Ⓒ take a towel
- Ⓓ use the stairway

26. If the apartment door is very hot, _____.
- Ⓐ throw water on it
- Ⓑ you should not use the elevator
- Ⓒ you should not open the door
- Ⓓ open the door slowly

27. In a tall apartment building, if you can't get out, _____.
- Ⓐ stay in a room with a window
- Ⓑ climb out a window
- Ⓒ take the elevator
- Ⓓ call the building manager

28. You can *infer* from the notice that the apartment building _____.
- Ⓐ doesn't have elevators
- Ⓑ has many floors
- Ⓒ has one floor
- Ⓓ has many older residents

···········

23 Ⓐ Ⓑ Ⓒ Ⓓ   25 Ⓐ Ⓑ Ⓒ Ⓓ   27 Ⓐ Ⓑ Ⓒ Ⓓ
24 Ⓐ Ⓑ Ⓒ Ⓓ   26 Ⓐ Ⓑ Ⓒ Ⓓ   28 Ⓐ Ⓑ Ⓒ Ⓓ

CLOZE READING: A Workplace Fire Safety Memo

Choose the correct answers to complete the memo.

To: All Employees
From: Sam Thomas, Human Resources Manager
Date: December 1
Subject: Emergency Preparedness

PRECISION
ACCOUNTING
COMPANY

Next Tuesday, December 7, we will | practice prevent escape | our company safety
(A) (B) (C)

| detectors procedures kits | **29**. When the fire alarm sounds, the fire department will come and
(A) (B) (C)

watch as we leave the building. They will tell us how to improve our fire escape plans. Please remember:

1. When the alarm sounds, all employees must | enter return leave | **30** the building quickly.
(A) (B) (C)

2. Do not use the elevators. During a fire | choking emergency airway | **31**, you must use the
(A) (B) (C)

| storage room elevators stairways | **32**.
(A) (B) (C)

3. Know the | first-aid escape test | **33** route for your office area.
(A) (B) (C)

4. If an exit is | blocked open free | **34**, use a different exit.
(A) (B) (C)

5. When you leave the building, go to the emergency | life inside meeting | **35** place.
(A) (B) (C)

6. Follow the | instructions flames plans | **36** of the fire department.
(A) (B) (C)

Before December 7, please review these fire | detector extinguisher safety | **37** procedures
(A) (B) (C)

with other employees in your department.

LISTENING ASSESSMENT: Reporting an Emergency

Read and listen to the questions. Then listen to the conversation and answer the questions.

38. Why is the person calling 9-1-1?
  (A) For a fire emergency.
  (B) For a weather emergency.
  (C) For a car accident.
  (D) For a medical emergency.

39. What happened to the caller's husband?
  (A) He cut his arm.
  (B) He broke his ankle.
  (C) He cut his thumb.
  (D) He was choking.

40. What does the operator tell the caller to do?
  (A) Call an ambulance.
  (B) Press on the cut with a towel.
  (C) Wash the arm.
  (D) Put medicine on it.

29 (A) (B) (C) (D)   32 (A) (B) (C) (D)   35 (A) (B) (C) (D)   38 (A) (B) (C) (D)
30 (A) (B) (C) (D)   33 (A) (B) (C) (D)   36 (A) (B) (C) (D)   39 (A) (B) (C) (D)
31 (A) (B) (C) (D)   34 (A) (B) (C) (D)   37 (A) (B) (C) (D)   40 (A) (B) (C) (D)

Draw an escape plan for your classroom. Show the classroom and the floor it is on in your school building. Show the emergency exits and the escape route. Include labels such as *window*, *door*, *stairway*, and *hallway*. Then write the instructions students should follow to use the escape route if there is a fire or other emergency. (Number the instructions.)

Classroom Escape Plan and Map

Map

Escape Route Instructions

_____

_____

_____

_____

_____

_____

H **SPEAKING ASSESSMENT**

I can ask and answer these questions:

Ask Answer

☐ ☐ Have you ever had an emergency at home? What happened? What did you do?

☐ ☐ Who would you call to report an emergency at home?

☐ ☐ How many smoke detectors are there in your home?

☐ ☐ Do you have any fire extinguishers in your home? Where are they?

☐ ☐ How can you improve fire safety in your home?

☐ ☐ If there were a fire in your living room, how would you escape?

☐ ☐ Do you have an escape plan for your family?

☐ ☐ Do you know how to perform CPR? the Heimlich maneuver?

STOP

A BANK SERVICES; BUDGET PLANNING

Example:

I'd like to open a _____ account.
- Ⓐ saving
- ● savings
- Ⓒ saved
- Ⓓ save

1. My checking account balance is low. I need to make a _____ soon.
   - Ⓐ paycheck
   - Ⓑ withdrawal
   - Ⓒ deposit
   - Ⓓ check

2. My bank charges a high monthly _____ for a checking account.
   - Ⓐ fee
   - Ⓑ fine
   - Ⓒ rent
   - Ⓓ penalty

3. Most banks require a _____ deposit to open an account.
   - Ⓐ maximum
   - Ⓑ minimum
   - Ⓒ typical
   - Ⓓ monthly

4. It's convenient to use a _____ account to pay your bills.
   - Ⓐ savings
   - Ⓑ deposit
   - Ⓒ checking
   - Ⓓ money market

5. With a higher _____ rate, you will earn more money on your savings account.
   - Ⓐ interest
   - Ⓑ fee
   - Ⓒ withdrawal
   - Ⓓ penalty

6. Some ATM machines charge a $2.00 fee to _____ cash.
   - Ⓐ deposit
   - Ⓑ save
   - Ⓒ check on
   - Ⓓ withdraw

7. With _____, your paycheck is automatically put into your account.
   - Ⓐ monthly savings
   - Ⓑ variable deposit
   - Ⓒ direct withdrawal
   - Ⓓ direct deposit

8. A monthly _____ will help you keep track of your spending.
   - Ⓐ budget
   - Ⓑ deposit
   - Ⓒ financial
   - Ⓓ appointment

9. You can usually reduce your _____ expenses, such as food and gas.
   - Ⓐ fixed
   - Ⓑ variable
   - Ⓒ online
   - Ⓓ bargain

1 Ⓐ Ⓑ Ⓒ Ⓓ   4 Ⓐ Ⓑ Ⓒ Ⓓ   7 Ⓐ Ⓑ Ⓒ Ⓓ

2 Ⓐ Ⓑ Ⓒ Ⓓ   5 Ⓐ Ⓑ Ⓒ Ⓓ   8 Ⓐ Ⓑ Ⓒ Ⓓ

3 Ⓐ Ⓑ Ⓒ Ⓓ   6 Ⓐ Ⓑ Ⓒ Ⓓ   9 Ⓐ Ⓑ Ⓒ Ⓓ

Go to the next page ⟩

Example:

_____ order more checks.
- Ⓐ I'll like
- ● I'd like to
- Ⓒ I would
- Ⓓ I like

10. Okay. Please _____ this form.
- Ⓐ report
- Ⓑ write
- Ⓒ fill out
- Ⓓ cut out

11. How long _____ to get new checks?
- Ⓐ did it take
- Ⓑ would take
- Ⓒ taking
- Ⓓ will it take

12. If you order them today, you _____ them in 10 days.
- Ⓐ will get
- Ⓑ getting
- Ⓒ got
- Ⓓ have gotten

13. I'd like _____ a checking account, please.
- Ⓐ open
- Ⓑ to open
- Ⓒ opening
- Ⓓ opened

14. Certainly. The minimum opening deposit _____ $50.00.
- Ⓐ has been
- Ⓑ was
- Ⓒ will
- Ⓓ is

15. I wish we _____ keep to our monthly budget.
- Ⓐ can
- Ⓑ could
- Ⓒ do
- Ⓓ did

16. I know. We have enough money for our fixed expenses, but it's difficult to _____ our variable expenses.
- Ⓐ keep
- Ⓑ keep track
- Ⓒ keep track of
- Ⓓ keep a record

17. If you ask me, we've _____ too much money at fast-food restaurants.
- Ⓐ spend
- Ⓑ have spent
- Ⓒ spending
- Ⓓ been spending

18. I agree. If we ate at home more, we _____ about $200 a month.
- Ⓐ save
- Ⓑ saved
- Ⓒ would save
- Ⓓ will save

....

10 Ⓐ Ⓑ Ⓒ Ⓓ	**13** Ⓐ Ⓑ Ⓒ Ⓓ	**16** Ⓐ Ⓑ Ⓒ Ⓓ	
11 Ⓐ Ⓑ Ⓒ Ⓓ	**14** Ⓐ Ⓑ Ⓒ Ⓓ	**17** Ⓐ Ⓑ Ⓒ Ⓓ	
12 Ⓐ Ⓑ Ⓒ Ⓓ	**15** Ⓐ Ⓑ Ⓒ Ⓓ	**18** Ⓐ Ⓑ Ⓒ Ⓓ	

Go to the next page ➡

Look at the chart comparing checking accounts at three banks. Then do Numbers 19 through 22.

	Bank A	Bank B	Bank C
Minimum Opening Deposit	$10	$500	$1000
Monthly Fee	$20	$9	$20
No Monthly Fee	No fee when you have a minimum balance of $1,000	No fee when you have a minimum balance of $5,000	No fee when you have a minimum balance of $10,000
Check Writing	$0.15 per check	$0.15 per check	Unlimited check writing
Interest Rate	1%	3%	1%
Other Features	• First order of checks is free • No-fee ATM card • No fee for traveler's checks or money orders • Free online banking • No fee for safe deposit box	• Free checks including reorders • No-fee ATM card • No fee for traveler's checks • Free online banking	• Free checks including reorders • No-fee ATM card • No fee for traveler's checks or cashier's checks • Free online banking • 50% discount on safe deposit box

19. An interest rate of 3% is available at _____.
   Ⓐ Bank A
   Ⓑ Bank B
   Ⓒ Bank C
   Ⓓ Banks A and C

20. At all three banks, there is no monthly fee if you _____.
   Ⓐ have a minimum amount in your account
   Ⓑ budget your account
   Ⓒ pay $20
   Ⓓ don't write any checks

21. Bank C has _____ for a safe deposit box.
   Ⓐ no fee
   Ⓑ a $50 fee
   Ⓒ a half-price fee
   Ⓓ a percentage

22. If you can maintain a minimum balance of $8,000 and you rarely write checks, the best bank for you is _____.
   Ⓐ Bank A
   Ⓑ Bank B
   Ⓒ Bank C
   Ⓓ Bank A or C

19 Ⓐ Ⓑ Ⓒ Ⓓ   20 Ⓐ Ⓑ Ⓒ Ⓓ   21 Ⓐ Ⓑ Ⓒ Ⓓ   22 Ⓐ Ⓑ Ⓒ Ⓓ

    Go to the next page

Read the bank statement. Then do Numbers 23 through 28.

STATEMENT PERIOD
4/16/09 THROUGH 5/14/09

CENTRAL BANK

CHECKING ACCOUNT NUMBER **024-00543**
MARTA GONZALEZ

DEPOSITS

DATE	AMOUNT			
04/17/09	$1643.00	ELECTRONIC DEP	UNIX CORP.	PAYROLL
05/01/09	$1643.00	ELECTRONIC DEP	UNIX CORP.	PAYROLL

WITHDRAWALS

DATE	AMOUNT	
04/17/09	$200.00	CASH WD ATM
05/01/09	$150.00	CASH WD ATM

CHECKS

DATE	AMOUNT	NUMBER
04/19/09	123.55	1515
04/29/09	87.62	1516
05/01/09	583.00	1517

BEGINNING BALANCE	1520.33	**AVERAGE DAILY BALANCE**	3193.77
DEPOSITS	3286.00		
WITHDRAWALS	350.00		
CHECKS	794.17		
ENDING BALANCE	3662.16		

*MONTHLY SERVICE CHARGE OF 15.00 WAS WAIVED DUE TO AVERAGE DAILY BALANCE OVER 1000.00

23. The bank statement is for
_____.
- Ⓐ April
- Ⓑ May
- Ⓒ two weeks
- Ⓓ four weeks

24. Unix is the name of _____.
- Ⓐ Marta's bank
- Ⓑ Marta's boss
- Ⓒ the company where Marta works
- Ⓓ the building where Marta lives

25. Marta is paid _____.
- Ⓐ once a week
- Ⓑ every two weeks
- Ⓒ twice a week
- Ⓓ once a month

26. The total amount of her ATM withdrawals during this statement period was _____.
- Ⓐ $150
- Ⓑ $200
- Ⓒ $300
- Ⓓ $350

27. The total amount of money Marta spent from this account was _____.
- Ⓐ $350.00
- Ⓑ $1,796.17
- Ⓒ $1,144.17
- Ⓓ $3,286.00

28. During this statement period, Marta _____.
- Ⓐ saved more than she spent
- Ⓑ spent more than she saved
- Ⓒ paid a monthly service charge
- Ⓓ made two ATM deposits

23 Ⓐ Ⓑ Ⓒ Ⓓ   25 Ⓐ Ⓑ Ⓒ Ⓓ   27 Ⓐ Ⓑ Ⓒ Ⓓ

24 Ⓐ Ⓑ Ⓒ Ⓓ   26 Ⓐ Ⓑ Ⓒ Ⓓ   28 Ⓐ Ⓑ Ⓒ Ⓓ

Choose the correct answers to complete the article.

D₀ you [want (A) | like (B) | wish ●] you could manage your [finances (A) | balances (B) | averages (C)] ²⁹ better? It's a good idea to make a [monthly fee (A) | budget (B) | passbook (C)] ³⁰. If you don't [plan (A) | trim (B) | take (C)] ³¹ control of your spending, you will not be able to pay your bills or [save (A) | spend (B) | reduce (C)] ³² for the future. A budget will help you spend [wisely (A) | quickly (B) | frequently (C)] ³³. Here are some steps for making a personal budget.

1. Look at [daily (A) | fixed (B) | tiered (C)] ³⁴ expenses, such as rent and car payments. What are your average monthly costs for these?

2. For four weeks, keep [think (A) | write (B) | track (C)] ³⁵ of your spending for variable expenses, such as groceries, clothing, transportation, and entertainment.

3. What is your monthly take-home [deposit (A) | withdrawal (B) | pay (C)] ³⁶? Add up the monthly income for your family.

4. Keep an emergency [deposit box (A) | fund (B) | cost (C)] ³⁷. Use this for unusual expenses.

F **LISTENING ASSESSMENT: Recorded Bank Account Information**

Read and listen to the questions. Then listen to the phone call and answer the questions.

38. Why is this person calling the bank?
- (A) To make a deposit.
- (B) To make a withdrawal.
- (C) To get information about a savings account.
- (D) To get information about a checking account.

39. What number does the person give to get account information?
- (A) An account balance.
- (B) An account number.
- (C) A social security number.
- (D) A telephone number.

40. What account information does the person listen to?
- (A) The last three deposits.
- (B) The account balance.
- (C) Interest rates.
- (D) The last three withdrawals.

29 (A) (B) (C) (D)   32 (A) (B) (C) (D)   35 (A) (B) (C) (D)   38 (A) (B) (C) (D)

30 (A) (B) (C) (D)   33 (A) (B) (C) (D)   36 (A) (B) (C) (D)   39 (A) (B) (C) (D)

31 (A) (B) (C) (D)   34 (A) (B) (C) (D)   37 (A) (B) (C) (D)   40 (A) (B) (C) (D)

Fill in the application for a bank account.

North Bank
— Bank Account Application —

To open an account, simply complete this form. An asterisk (*) means the information is required. Please print clearly. As you fill out the application, please check your information carefully.

APPLICANT

Prefix: ☐ Miss: ☐ Mr. ☐ Mrs. ☐ Ms.

*First Name   Middle Initial *Last Name

*Home phone   Cell phone   Email

CURRENT HOME ADDRESS

*Address (P.O. Box not allowed)

*City   *State   *Zip Code

*At this address for: ☐ less than 1 year   ☐ 1–3 years   ☐ 4–8 years   ☐ more than 8 years

IDENTITY INFORMATION

*Social Security Number   *Date of Birth
                                                              mm   dd   yyyy

*Mother's Maiden Name

*Identification: ☐ U.S. driver's license   ☐ State photo ID   ☐ Passport with photo

*Identification Number: State of Issue:

*Expiration Date:
                  mm   dd   yyyy

*Employment Status: ☐ Employed   ☐ Unemployed   ☐ Retired   ☐ Student

TYPE OF ACCOUNT

☐ Checking account   ☐ Savings account   ☐ Online account

*Signature   *Date

I can ask and answer these questions:

Ask Answer

☐ ☐ What kind of bank account do you have?

☐ ☐ Do you use an ATM card? How often?

☐ ☐ Do you have a budget? Why or why not?

☐ ☐ What is your biggest fixed expense each month?

☐ ☐ What variable expenses can you reduce to save money?

☐ ☐ Do you sometimes shop at a wholesale store? What's the name of it? What do you buy there?

☐ ☐ Do you have an emergency fund? Why or why not?

☐ ☐ Are you saving for something special in the future? What?

STOP

A HEALTH CARE; NUTRITION; SAFETY

Example:

Lisa called the nurse to get _____.
- Ⓐ nutrition
- Ⓑ symptoms
- ● advice
- Ⓓ calories

1. At the clinic, Mark described his _____ to the doctor.
   - Ⓐ causes
   - Ⓑ nutrients
   - Ⓒ servings
   - Ⓓ symptoms

2. The doctor asked what had _____ the accident.
   - Ⓐ warned
   - Ⓑ exercised
   - Ⓒ caused
   - Ⓓ resulted

3. If you consume more _____ than you need every day, you will gain weight.
   - Ⓐ minerals
   - Ⓑ calories
   - Ⓒ energy
   - Ⓓ sodium

4. Calcium and iron are examples of _____.
   - Ⓐ carbohydrates
   - Ⓑ vitamins
   - Ⓒ calories
   - Ⓓ minerals

5. To know what is in a serving of food, read the _____ label.
   - Ⓐ nutrition
   - Ⓑ fiber
   - Ⓒ warning
   - Ⓓ medical

6. Choose your foods wisely and avoid foods that are high in _____.
   - Ⓐ vitamins
   - Ⓑ protein
   - Ⓒ iron
   - Ⓓ sodium

7. A medicine label will tell you the correct _____ for an adult and for a child.
   - Ⓐ dose
   - Ⓑ side effect
   - Ⓒ warning
   - Ⓓ number

8. Medication should be used before the _____ date printed on the bottle.
   - Ⓐ end
   - Ⓑ explanation
   - Ⓒ expiration
   - Ⓓ reservation

9. A _____ material such as gasoline can catch fire easily.
   - Ⓐ flame
   - Ⓑ combustible
   - Ⓒ voltage
   - Ⓓ explosion

1 Ⓐ Ⓑ Ⓒ Ⓓ   4 Ⓐ Ⓑ Ⓒ Ⓓ   7 Ⓐ Ⓑ Ⓒ Ⓓ

2 Ⓐ Ⓑ Ⓒ Ⓓ   5 Ⓐ Ⓑ Ⓒ Ⓓ   8 Ⓐ Ⓑ Ⓒ Ⓓ

3 Ⓐ Ⓑ Ⓒ Ⓓ   6 Ⓐ Ⓑ Ⓒ Ⓓ   9 Ⓐ Ⓑ Ⓒ Ⓓ

Go to the next page ➤

Example:

What _____ to be the problem?
- ● seems
- Ⓑ is
- Ⓒ feels
- Ⓓ was

10. I've _____ Cold-Ex for a cold, but I feel dizzy when I take it and I can't sleep at night.
- Ⓐ take
- Ⓑ took
- Ⓒ been taking
- Ⓓ taking

11. I see. _____ possible side effects of Cold-Ex.
- Ⓐ You are
- Ⓑ It is
- Ⓒ That is
- Ⓓ Those are

12. What medication _____ recommend?
- Ⓐ would
- Ⓑ would you
- Ⓒ would you have
- Ⓓ have you

13. Try using Relief. If you take it tonight, you _____ able to sleep.
- Ⓐ are
- Ⓑ would
- Ⓒ will be
- Ⓓ will

14. Thanks. I'll call back if the new medication _____.
- Ⓐ wouldn't help
- Ⓑ doesn't help
- Ⓒ don't help
- Ⓓ wouldn't have helped

15. My back _____ hurting for two weeks.
- Ⓐ is
- Ⓑ will be
- Ⓒ has been
- Ⓓ had been

16. Do you know what _____ caused this?
- Ⓐ did
- Ⓑ have
- Ⓒ might
- Ⓓ might have

17. I think I _____ a muscle while I was lifting boxes at work.
- Ⓐ was pulling
- Ⓑ pulled
- Ⓒ have been pulling
- Ⓓ had pulled

18. _____ taking a pain reliever or other over-the-counter medication?
- Ⓐ Have you been
- Ⓑ Have you
- Ⓒ Would you
- Ⓓ Did you

No, I haven't.

10 Ⓐ Ⓑ Ⓒ Ⓓ   13 Ⓐ Ⓑ Ⓒ Ⓓ   15 Ⓐ Ⓑ Ⓒ Ⓓ   17 Ⓐ Ⓑ Ⓒ Ⓓ

11 Ⓐ Ⓑ Ⓒ Ⓓ   14 Ⓐ Ⓑ Ⓒ Ⓓ   16 Ⓐ Ⓑ Ⓒ Ⓓ   18 Ⓐ Ⓑ Ⓒ Ⓓ

12 Ⓐ Ⓑ Ⓒ Ⓓ

Read the food labels. Then do Numbers 19 through 22.

Low Sodium Crackers
Nutrition Facts
Serving Size 15 crackers (31g)
Servings per Container about 9

Amount per Serving	
Calories 150	Calories from Fat 50
	% Daily Value
Total Fat 6g	9%
Saturated Fat 1g	5%
Trans Fat 0g	0%
Cholesterol 0mg	0%
Sodium 80 mg	3%
Total Carbohydrate 22g	7%
Dietary Fiber 1	4%
Sugars 4g	
Protein 2g	

Vitamin A 0%		Vitamin C	0%
Calcium 0%	•	Iron	6%

Cheese Crackers
Nutrition Facts
Serving Size 13 crackers (29g)
Servings per Container about 10

Amount per Serving	
Calories 150	Calories from Fat 72
	% Daily Value
Total Fat 8g	12%
Saturated Fat 1.5g	8%
Trans Fat 0g	0%
Cholesterol 0mg	0%
Sodium 230 mg	10%
Total Carbohydrate 16g	5%
Dietary Fiber 0g	0%
Sugars 0g	
Protein 4g	

Vitamin A 0%		Vitamin C	0%
Calcium 2%	•	Iron	6%

19. One serving of Low Sodium Crackers has 1 gram of _____.
   Ⓐ sugar
   Ⓑ total fat
   Ⓒ dietary fiber
   Ⓓ protein

20. One serving of Low Sodium Crackers has _____ fewer calories from fat than Cheese Crackers.
   Ⓐ 22
   Ⓑ 50
   Ⓒ 72
   Ⓓ 122

21. The Cheese Crackers have 230 _____ of sodium.
   Ⓐ grams
   Ⓑ milligrams
   Ⓒ spoons
   Ⓓ calories

22. The Cheese Crackers have more _____ than the Low Sodium Crackers.
   Ⓐ iron
   Ⓑ sugar
   Ⓒ trans fat
   Ⓓ saturated fat

19 Ⓐ Ⓑ Ⓒ Ⓓ   21 Ⓐ Ⓑ Ⓒ Ⓓ

20 Ⓐ Ⓑ Ⓒ Ⓓ   22 Ⓐ Ⓑ Ⓒ Ⓓ

Read the medicine labels. Then do Numbers 23 through 28.

Night Time Cold Relief

Warnings: Do not use

- If you drink 3 or more alcoholic beverages every day
- If sore throat is severe and is accompanied or followed by fever, rash, or nausea
- With other medicines containing acetaminophen

Ask a doctor before use if you have

- Heart disease
- Diabetes
- High blood pressure

When using this product

- Drowsiness may occur
- Avoid alcoholic drinks
- Be careful when driving or operating machinery

Stop use and ask a doctor if

- Symptoms do not get better within 7 days
- You get nervous, dizzy, or sleepless
- Fever gets worse or lasts more than 3 days

Keep out of reach of children. In case of overdose get medical help or call a Poison Control Center right away.

Sinus Clear Allergy and Cold Medicine

Warnings: Do not use

- If you consume 3 or more alcoholic drinks every day
- With any other product containing diphenhydramine

Ask a doctor before use if you have

- High blood pressure
- Heart disease
- Diabetes
- or if you are pregnant or breastfeeding

When using this product

- avoid alcoholic drinks
- alcohol, sedatives, and tranquilizers may increase drowsiness
- excitability may occur, especially in children

Stop use and ask a doctor if

- sore throat is severe
- you get nervous, dizzy, or sleepless
- new symptoms occur
- fever gets worse or lasts more than 3 days
- sore throat lasts more than 2 days

Keep out of reach of children.
In case of overdose, get medical help or contact a Poison Control Center right away.

---

23. When using Night Time Cold Relief, you may have _____.
- Ⓐ heart disease
- Ⓑ a fever
- Ⓒ drowsiness
- Ⓓ high blood pressure

24. When you are taking Sinus Clear, you should call your doctor if _____.
- Ⓐ you have fewer symptoms
- Ⓑ you have a cough
- Ⓒ your fever gets worse
- Ⓓ you have a headache

25. Women who are _____ should check with a doctor before using Sinus Clear.
- Ⓐ pregnant
- Ⓑ coughing
- Ⓒ mothers
- Ⓓ taking acetaminophen

26. You can infer that *overdose* means _____.
- Ⓐ the dosage small children take
- Ⓑ taking much more than the recommended amount
- Ⓒ taking a small dose
- Ⓓ side effects

27. Stop taking Sinus Clear if you _____.
- Ⓐ have drowsiness
- Ⓑ feel dizzy
- Ⓒ have a headache
- Ⓓ drink an alcoholic beverage

28. You can infer that Night Time Cold Relief contains _____.
- Ⓐ alcohol
- Ⓑ poison
- Ⓒ diphenhydramine
- Ⓓ acetaminophen

....

23 Ⓐ Ⓑ Ⓒ Ⓓ   25 Ⓐ Ⓑ Ⓒ Ⓓ   27 Ⓐ Ⓑ Ⓒ Ⓓ

24 Ⓐ Ⓑ Ⓒ Ⓓ   26 Ⓐ Ⓑ Ⓒ Ⓓ   28 Ⓐ Ⓑ Ⓒ Ⓓ

Choose the correct answers to complete the notice.

To: All Manufacturing Supervisors
From: Carla Ortiz, Safety [Manager ● Managing Ⓑ Manages Ⓒ]

For our monthly **Focus on Safety** exercise, we will be having a fire safety practice. Please be sure to review the [hazard Ⓐ evacuation Ⓑ explosion Ⓒ] ²⁹ plans and the outside meeting place with your team. This is also a good time to review basic safety procedures.

1. Keep floors clean and dry. Clean up [spills Ⓐ machinery Ⓑ bathrooms Ⓒ] ³⁰ immediately.

2. When mixing powder, use a [spoon Ⓐ glove Ⓑ respirator Ⓒ] ³¹ so that you do not [inhale Ⓐ exit Ⓑ assemble Ⓒ] ³² dust.

3. When using machinery, make sure all machine [signs Ⓐ guards Ⓑ items Ⓒ] ³³ are in place.

4. Use required [safety Ⓐ fire Ⓑ poisonous Ⓒ] ³⁴ glasses and other protective equipment.

5. All [loose Ⓐ machinery Ⓑ combustible Ⓒ] ³⁵ materials should be stored away from any fire hazards.

6. Use caution around high [injury Ⓐ safety Ⓑ voltage Ⓒ] ³⁶ areas to avoid the risk of electric shock.

7. In [place Ⓐ case Ⓑ contact Ⓒ] ³⁷ of an injury, call the safety office immediately.

Read and listen to the questions. Then listen to the phone call and answer the questions.

38. How did the woman hurt herself?
    Ⓐ She dropped a box.
    Ⓑ She lifted a box.
    Ⓒ She pulled a box.
    Ⓓ She put an ice pack on her back.

39. What DOESN'T the nurse tell her to do?
    Ⓐ Use an ice pack.
    Ⓑ Rest.
    Ⓒ Take pain reliever medication.
    Ⓓ Put a pillow on your head.

40. What should the woman do if her back isn't better in a few days?
    Ⓐ Go to the hospital.
    Ⓑ Take more medication.
    Ⓒ Make an appointment with the doctor.
    Ⓓ Stay home for a few more days.

29 Ⓐ Ⓑ Ⓒ Ⓓ   32 Ⓐ Ⓑ Ⓒ Ⓓ   35 Ⓐ Ⓑ Ⓒ Ⓓ   38 Ⓐ Ⓑ Ⓒ Ⓓ
30 Ⓐ Ⓑ Ⓒ Ⓓ   33 Ⓐ Ⓑ Ⓒ Ⓓ   36 Ⓐ Ⓑ Ⓒ Ⓓ   39 Ⓐ Ⓑ Ⓒ Ⓓ
31 Ⓐ Ⓑ Ⓒ Ⓓ   34 Ⓐ Ⓑ Ⓒ Ⓓ   37 Ⓐ Ⓑ Ⓒ Ⓓ   40 Ⓐ Ⓑ Ⓒ Ⓓ

Fill out the form.

MEDICAL HISTORY FORM

Age _____ How would you rate your general health? ☐ Excellent ☐ Good ☐ Fair ☐ Poor

REVIEW OF SYMPTOMS: Please check (✓) any current symptoms that you have.

General
_____ Recent fevers
_____ Unexplained weight loss
_____ Unexplained tiredness/weakness

Respiratory
_____ Coughing
_____ Coughing up blood

Skin
_____ Rash
_____ New mole

Eyes
_____ Change in vision

Gastrointestinal
_____ Heartburn
_____ Nausea/vomiting
_____ Diarrhea
_____ Abdominal pain

Neurological
_____ Headaches
_____ Memory loss
_____ Fainting

Cardiovascular
_____ Chest pains/discomfort
_____ Short of breath

Ears/Nose/Throat/Mouth
_____ Difficulty hearing
_____ Allergies
_____ Trouble swallowing

Musculoskeletal
_____ Joint pain
_____ Back pain

Psychiatric
_____ Anxiety/stress
_____ Sleep problems

Recently, have you had little interest or pleasure in doing things, or have you felt down, depressed, or hopeless? ☐ Yes ☐ No

MEDICATIONS: List all prescription and non-prescription medicines, vitamins, etc. Note the dosage that you take.

FAMILY HISTORY

Please write family members (parent, brother, sister, grandparent, aunt, or uncle) with any of the following conditions:

Alcoholism _____ High blood pressure _____
Asthma _____ Heart disease _____
Stroke _____ Diabetes _____

H **SPEAKING ASSESSMENT**

I can ask and answer these questions:

Ask Answer
☐ ☐ What advice would you give someone to lose weight?
☐ ☐ What foods do you eat that are high in fat? in sodium?
☐ ☐ What foods do you like that are high in fiber?
☐ ☐ If you wanted to reduce the number of calories you consume every day, what would you do?
☐ ☐ Why is it important to read over-the-counter medicine labels carefully?
☐ ☐ To prevent injuries or fire, what safety procedures should you follow in your kitchen?
☐ ☐ Have you ever been injured at work? at home? What happened? What do you wish you had done differently?

214

STOP

A JOB INTERVIEWS; CAREER ADVANCEMENT

Example:

Be sure to arrive _____ for an interview.
- (A) overtime
- ● on time
- (C) timely
- (D) exact

1. Before an interview, learn about the company so you are _____ with the company's work.
   - (A) confident
   - (B) dependable
   - (C) familiar
   - (D) positive

2. Be prepared for questions about your strengths and your _____.
   - (A) weaknesses
   - (B) abilities
   - (C) characteristics
   - (D) absences

3. The new job _____ was never advertised in the want ads.
   - (A) profession
   - (B) entry
   - (C) interviewer
   - (D) opening

4. You should be able to explain to the interviewer your _____ goals and your plans for the future.
   - (A) past
   - (B) long-term
   - (C) familiar
   - (D) financial

5. Most young people start their careers in _____ position.
   - (A) a qualified
   - (B) an administrative
   - (C) a managerial
   - (D) an entry-level

6. If a position is _____, it is no longer open.
   - (A) filled
   - (B) posted
   - (C) applied
   - (D) advertised

7. Employers look for applicants who are _____.
   - (A) annoyed
   - (B) enthusiastic
   - (C) provided
   - (D) supervised

8. You may want to ask if there are opportunities for _____.
   - (A) raises
   - (B) professions
   - (C) advancement
   - (D) goals

9. A positive _____ is an important ingredient for success in a job.
   - (A) training
   - (B) resume
   - (C) message
   - (D) attitude

1 (A) (B) (C) (D)   4 (A) (B) (C) (D)   7 (A) (B) (C) (D)

2 (A) (B) (C) (D)   5 (A) (B) (C) (D)   8 (A) (B) (C) (D)

3 (A) (B) (C) (D)   6 (A) (B) (C) (D)   9 (A) (B) (C) (D)

Go to the next page ⟩

Example:

How _____ your interview?

was
- (B) is
- (C) has been
- (D) would have been

11. Did he ask you _____ your career goals were?
- (A) if
- (B) whether
- (C) where
- (D) what

13. And did he ask you what your weaknesses _____?
- (A) was
- (B) were
- (C) have been
- (D) might have been

10. Good. The interviewer said I _____ qualified for the job.
- (A) will be
- (B) was
- (C) would have been
- (D) had been

12. Yes. I told him that I _____ to become a store manager.
- (A) am wanting
- (B) was wanting
- (C) wanted
- (D) had wanted

14. Yes. I told him that I _____ to improve my accounting skills.
- (A) will
- (B) would
- (C) had needed
- (D) needed

15. Did the interviewer _____ you any difficult questions?
- (A) ask
- (B) advise
- (C) tell
- (D) say

17. What _____?
- (A) do you say
- (B) do you tell her
- (C) did you say
- (D) did you tell

16. Yes. She asked whether I _____ to another city if the job required it.
- (A) moved
- (B) am moving
- (C) had moved
- (D) would move

18. I told her that I _____ sure and I would have to think about it carefully.
- (A) wasn't
- (B) was
- (C) am
- (D) would be

10 (A) (B) (C) (D)   13 (A) (B) (C) (D)   16 (A) (B) (C) (D)

11 (A) (B) (C) (D)   14 (A) (B) (C) (D)   17 (A) (B) (C) (D)

12 (A) (B) (C) (D)   15 (A) (B) (C) (D)   18 (A) (B) (C) (D)

Look at the help wanted ads. Then do Numbers 19 through 22.

LANDSCAPE MANAGER for Mid-State Landscape Co. Estimate costs & time for large jobs. Supervise workers. Min. 3 yrs. exp. Strong math skills. Medical bnfts & 401(k). Fax resume to 605-423-4567 or email to admin@landscape.com.

MACHINIST Light manufacturing company. Mill & lathe work, incl. programming machinery, job setup, quality inspection. 5 year min. exp. All shifts. Call 408-572-4567.

SUMMER JOBS w/ environmental group. **$10-15/hr.** Stop global warming! Work w/great people! Career opportunities & bnfts. No exp. req. Call Kit at 605-423-9090.

HEAD NURSE M-F in busy downtown clinic. Great compensation & benefits. Only experienced nurses need apply. Contact ABC Health Services at 415-987-6543.

DRIVER NEEDED FOR WAREHOUSE Clean DMV record, 1 yr. exp., pass drug screening, physical exam, background check. HS dipl. or GED. Must be avail. nights and weekends. Excel. communication skills. Call 605-567-8912.

SALES Cable TV. 3 FT positions avail. Salary & commission & gas allowance. Will train. Must have HS dipl or GED. Call 408-234-5678.

ADMINISTRATIVE ASSISTANT Exp. w/Word & Excel. Gd w/ details & computers. Min. 5 yr. exp. in office. Bnfts. Fax 408-333-6789. Email: frank@A1_jobs.com.

RESTAURANT MANAGER 3-5 yrs exp. in fine dining. Excel. communication w/employees & customers; strong knowledge of restaurant business. Email resume to employment@jobs.com.

CUSTOMER SALES/SERVICE Summer work, $17.00 starting salary. All ages 17+ PT/FT, flexible hours. No exp. req. Call 800-525-4212.

DENTAL ASSISTANT FT. 3 yrs exp. req. Some nights. Front desk duties. Fax resume to 605-567-8900.

DRY CLEANER Pressers and counter clerks needed. PT or FT. Will train. 456-7890.

19. A person with no job experience could apply for the position _____.
   Ⓐ as a driver
   Ⓑ in cable TV sales
   Ⓒ as an administrative assistant
   Ⓓ as a machinist

20. The _____ position requires 5 years of experience.
   Ⓐ landscape manager
   Ⓑ dental assistant
   Ⓒ head nurse
   Ⓓ administrative assistant

21. The warehouse driver needs to be available to work _____.
   Ⓐ part time
   Ⓑ full time
   Ⓒ nights and weekends
   Ⓓ Monday through Friday

22. Rob has several years of experience with a tree service company, driving the truck and supervising workers. Previously, he was a gardener. He wants more responsibility. He could apply for the _____ position.
   Ⓐ landscape manager
   Ⓑ machinist
   Ⓒ restaurant manager
   Ⓓ warehouse driver

19 Ⓐ Ⓑ Ⓒ Ⓓ   20 Ⓐ Ⓑ Ⓒ Ⓓ   21 Ⓐ Ⓑ Ⓒ Ⓓ   22 Ⓐ Ⓑ Ⓒ Ⓓ

Go to the next page

Read the resume. Then do Numbers 23 through 28.

KEN PHAM

95 California St.   Cell phone: 408-555-7654
San Jose, CA 95118   Home phone: 408-555-2793
                                                    Email: kenpham@usa.com

---

OBJECTIVE
A physical therapist position in a clinic

EXPERIENCE
Staff Physical Therapist   2006–present
   Valley Clinic, San Jose, CA
   Treated patients of all ages. Supervised two physical therapy assistants.
   Assisted in training new therapists.

Staff Physical Therapist   2004–2006
   Therapy Services, San Jose, CA
   Treated patients after injuries. Assisted in training with new office software.

Staff Physical Therapist   2000–2003
   West Health Clinic, San Ramon, CA
   Treated patients after injuries. Developed bilingual information brochures and exercise sheets.

EDUCATION
Bachelor of Science in Physical Therapy   1994–1999
   San Jose State University

SKILLS AND TRAINING
   Certificate for Documentation Specialist (2005). Proficient in Word, Excel. Fluent in Vietnamese.

OTHER WORK EXPERIENCE
   Senior Center Activities Assistant, Senior Day Center, San Jose, CA   1994–1997

REFERENCES
   Upon request

---

23. Ken has had _____ positions as a physical therapist.
- Ⓐ two
- Ⓑ three
- Ⓒ four
- Ⓓ five

24. In 2005, Ken was working at _____.
- Ⓐ Senior Day Center
- Ⓑ Therapy Services
- Ⓒ West Health Clinic
- Ⓓ Valley Clinic

25. Ken worked in San Ramon for _____ years.
- Ⓐ two
- Ⓑ three
- Ⓒ four
- Ⓓ five

26. You can infer that a physical therapist treats patients _____.
- Ⓐ who are only in the hospital
- Ⓑ who need counseling
- Ⓒ who have physical problems
- Ⓓ who are adults

27. Ken must have _____ while he was in college.
- Ⓐ been employed
- Ⓑ studied accounting
- Ⓒ received certification
- Ⓓ learned Spanish

28. Ken has _____ other employees.
- Ⓐ provided
- Ⓑ worked
- Ⓒ treated
- Ⓓ supervised

....

23 Ⓐ Ⓑ Ⓒ Ⓓ   25 Ⓐ Ⓑ Ⓒ Ⓓ   27 Ⓐ Ⓑ Ⓒ Ⓓ

24 Ⓐ Ⓑ Ⓒ Ⓓ   26 Ⓐ Ⓑ Ⓒ Ⓓ   28 Ⓐ Ⓑ Ⓒ Ⓓ

Choose the correct answers to complete the letter.

Susan Thomas
Director of Human   Healthcare   Candidates   Resources
(A)   (B)   ●

West Health Clinic
San Ramon, CA 94583

Dear Ms. Thomas:

I am writing in response to your ad in the newspaper for a senior physical therapist. You may

remember that I worked at West Health Clinic for four years, from 2000 to 2003. Since that time,

I have been employed at clinics in San Jose. I am   seeking   advising   preventing [29] a position at
(A)   (B)   (C)

West Health because I would like more opportunities for   associates   vitals   advancement [30].
(A)   (B)   (C)

Also, I am interested in using my   consultant   bilingual   web-based [31] language skills.
(A)   (B)   (C)

As you can see from my   resume   e-mail   objective [32], I have learned many skills in the
(A)   (B)   (C)

past years. In my present position, I   cancel   oversee   escape [33] physical therapy assistants
(A)   (B)   (C)

and train new therapists. I am very   engaged   proficient   willing [34] with computers and
(A)   (B)   (C)

goal   field   data [35] entry. I am   fast-paced   enthusiastic   certified [36] about my profession
(A)   (B)   (C)   (A)   (B)   (C)

and I enjoy working with patients. I can give you references upon   request   update   equivalent [37].
(A)   (B)   (C)

Thank you, and I look forward to hearing from you soon.

Sincerely,

Ken Pham

Ken Pham

---

29 (A) (B) (C) (D)   32 (A) (B) (C) (D)   35 (A) (B) (C) (D)
30 (A) (B) (C) (D)   33 (A) (B) (C) (D)   36 (A) (B) (C) (D)
31 (A) (B) (C) (D)   34 (A) (B) (C) (D)   37 (A) (B) (C) (D)

Go to the next page ▷

F LISTENING ASSESSMENT: A Job Interview

Read and listen to the questions. Then listen to the interview and answer the questions.

38. What does the interviewer think about Ken?

  (A) He thinks he has too many weaknesses.
  (B) He thinks he isn't qualified.
  (C) He thinks he needs more training.
  (D) He thinks he is a good applicant.

39. What does Ken consider his greatest strength?

  (A) He loves learning.
  (B) He's qualified.
  (C) He communicates well.
  (D) He takes good notes.

40. How many weaknesses does Ken talk about?

  (A) None.
  (B) One.
  (C) Two.
  (D) Three.

G WRITING ASSESSMENT: A Resume

Complete these sections of a resume. List your work experience and your education history.

WORK EXPERIENCE (LIST MOST RECENT FIRST)

Dates _____   Position, Place of Employment, City, State _____

Description of job duties _____

Dates _____   Position, Place of Employment, City, State _____

Description of job duties _____

Dates _____   Position, Place of Employment, City, State _____

Description of job duties _____

EDUCATION HISTORY

Dates _____   Degree or certificate _____

School, City, State _____

Dates _____   Degree or certificate _____

School, City, State _____

H SPEAKING ASSESSMENT

I can ask and answer these questions:

Ask Answer

☐ ☐ Are you working now? If so, what is your position? What are your duties?
☐ ☐ Where would you like to work? In what position? Why?
☐ ☐ What skills or training do you need to advance in your career?
☐ ☐ What do you consider your greatest strength?
☐ ☐ What is your greatest weakness?
☐ ☐ What are your long-term goals for the future?
☐ ☐ Have you ever asked someone for career advice? Explain.

---

38    **39**   **40** Ⓐ Ⓑ Ⓒ Ⓓ

A EMPLOYMENT AND BENEFITS

Example:

Employees turn in their _____ on Friday.
- ● timesheets
- Ⓑ paychecks
- Ⓒ benefits
- Ⓓ pay stubs

1. Mario takes care of his wife, his mother, and his two children. They are his _____.
   - Ⓐ independents
   - Ⓑ siblings
   - Ⓒ dependents
   - Ⓓ offspring

2. If you are *eligible* for benefits, it means you _____.
   - Ⓐ are able to receive them
   - Ⓑ aren't able to receive them
   - Ⓒ must pay the full price for them
   - Ⓓ must apply for them

3. _____ insurance provides money to an employee's family members if the employee dies.
   - Ⓐ Health
   - Ⓑ Dental
   - Ⓒ Tax
   - Ⓓ Life

4. A 401(k) is a type of _____.
   - Ⓐ retirement savings plan
   - Ⓑ vacation plan
   - Ⓒ bonus payment
   - Ⓓ state tax

5. Employees' _____ usually include paid sick leave and vacation days.
   - Ⓐ medical plans
   - Ⓑ benefits
   - Ⓒ taxes
   - Ⓓ bonuses

6. An employee who works for the same company for many years shows _____.
   - Ⓐ flexibility
   - Ⓑ promotion
   - Ⓒ dedication
   - Ⓓ respect

7. It's easy to _____ a friendly person.
   - Ⓐ get over
   - Ⓑ defer
   - Ⓒ carry over
   - Ⓓ get along with

8. Jake has good _____ qualities. He encourages his employees to work as a team and motivates them to do their best.
   - Ⓐ friendship
   - Ⓑ leading
   - Ⓒ leadership
   - Ⓓ network

9. A new employee usually needs training and _____ during the first weeks.
   - Ⓐ procedure
   - Ⓑ feedback
   - Ⓒ investment
   - Ⓓ dedication

1 Ⓐ Ⓑ Ⓒ Ⓓ   4 Ⓐ Ⓑ Ⓒ Ⓓ   7 Ⓐ Ⓑ Ⓒ Ⓓ

2 Ⓐ Ⓑ Ⓒ Ⓓ   5 Ⓐ Ⓑ Ⓒ Ⓓ   8 Ⓐ Ⓑ Ⓒ Ⓓ

3 Ⓐ Ⓑ Ⓒ Ⓓ   6 Ⓐ Ⓑ Ⓒ Ⓓ   9 Ⓐ Ⓑ Ⓒ Ⓓ

Go to the next page ▷

Example:

Could you tell me what
_____ wrong?
- Ⓐ am I doing
- Ⓑ I do
- Ⓒ do I
- ● I'm doing

11. Oh. I _____ that.
- Ⓐ didn't know
- Ⓑ don't know
- Ⓒ wouldn't know
- Ⓓ hadn't known

10. Sure. You're supposed
_____ the original face
down.
- Ⓐ put
- Ⓑ to put
- Ⓒ putting
- Ⓓ you put

12. If you put it face down, the
copier _____ correctly.
- Ⓐ would have worked
- Ⓑ worked
- Ⓒ will work
- Ⓓ has worked

13. Could you tell me
when I _____ personal
days?
- Ⓐ use
- Ⓑ will use
- Ⓒ used
- Ⓓ can use

15. If I add my wife to my
health plan, what
_____ my premium be?
- Ⓐ is
- Ⓑ will be
- Ⓒ will
- Ⓓ wouldn't

17. Life insurance is free
for all employees,
_____?
- Ⓐ it is
- Ⓑ is it
- Ⓒ it isn't
- Ⓓ isn't it

14. Yes. They _____ for
doctor appointments and
family illness.
- Ⓐ can use
- Ⓑ can be used
- Ⓒ could use
- Ⓓ could have used

16. It _____ from $160 to
$340 a month.
- Ⓐ increase
- Ⓑ will increase
- Ⓒ is increasing
- Ⓓ would have increase

18. Yes, _____. We also offer
a 401(k) plan.
- Ⓐ it is
- Ⓑ is it
- Ⓒ they are
- Ⓓ are they

....

10 Ⓐ Ⓑ Ⓒ Ⓓ	**13** Ⓐ Ⓑ Ⓒ Ⓓ	**16** Ⓐ Ⓑ Ⓒ Ⓓ
11 Ⓐ Ⓑ Ⓒ Ⓓ	**14** Ⓐ Ⓑ Ⓒ Ⓓ	**17** Ⓐ Ⓑ Ⓒ Ⓓ
12 Ⓐ Ⓑ Ⓒ Ⓓ	**15** Ⓐ Ⓑ Ⓒ Ⓓ	**18** Ⓐ Ⓑ Ⓒ Ⓓ

Side by Side Plus Book 4
Unit 9 Achievement Test (Page 2 of 6)

222

© 2009 Pearson Education, Inc.
Duplication for classroom use is permitted.

Go to the next page ⟶

Look at the description of employee benefits. Then do Numbers 19 through 24.

RIVERSIDE FLOORING COMPANY   **Employee Benefits at a Glance**

Full-time employees are eligible for the benefits listed below. The insurance costs are taken out of your paycheck every two weeks. The Health Maintenance Organization (HMO) has specific doctors that you must use. The Preferred Provider Organization (PPO) has a large network of doctors who give discounted prices. With the PPO, you may choose any doctor. Both plans pay for prescription drugs.

Type of Coverage	HMO	PPO	Dental
Employee	$63.82	$63.82	$ 4.25
Employee + spouse	$113.71	$115.09	$10.83
Employee + child	$113.71	$115.09	$11.30
Employee + family	$154.23	$157.40	$17.42

Benefits at no additional cost:
Life Insurance: Provides payment equal to your annual salary.
Employee Assistance Program: Provides short-term mental health counseling and career planning services.

Other Benefits:
401(k) Plan: Employees are eligible to enroll in the 401(k) plan immediately upon employment. Please see Human Resources for a complete description of the plan.
Vacation Days: Employees receive 10 days of vacation per year during the first 5 years of employment.
Personal Days: Employees are eligible for 3 personal days per year.
Sick Time: Employees receive 5 paid sick days per year. Sick days may be carried over to the next year.

---

19. The chart shows how much the insurance costs _____.
   Ⓐ every month
   Ⓑ every week
   Ⓒ every two weeks
   Ⓓ twice a weeks

20. If you want to have _____ when choosing your doctor, you should choose a PPO.
   Ⓐ fewer choices
   Ⓑ more choices
   Ⓒ the lowest prices
   Ⓓ the highest prices

21. If you are married with three children and you choose a PPO and dental coverage, your biweekly deduction will be _____.
   Ⓐ $154.23
   Ⓑ $157.40
   Ⓒ $164.82
   Ⓓ $174.82

22. The _____ is a good way to save money for retirement.
   Ⓐ HMO
   Ⓑ PPO
   Ⓒ 401(k) plan
   Ⓓ life insurance

23. If you don't use all of your _____, you can use them during the next year.
   Ⓐ sick time
   Ⓑ vacation days
   Ⓒ personal days
   Ⓓ holidays

24. If you have a very difficult family problem, you might use the _____ benefit.
   Ⓐ sick time
   Ⓑ dental
   Ⓒ life insurance
   Ⓓ Employee Assistance Program

---

19 Ⓐ Ⓑ Ⓒ Ⓓ   21 Ⓐ Ⓑ Ⓒ Ⓓ   23 Ⓐ Ⓑ Ⓒ Ⓓ

20 Ⓐ Ⓑ Ⓒ Ⓓ   22 Ⓐ Ⓑ Ⓒ Ⓓ   24 Ⓐ Ⓑ Ⓒ Ⓓ

Read the article. Then do Numbers 25 through 28.

RIVERSIDE HOSPITAL NEWS

Riverside Hospital Employees on the Move!

Selena Costa has recently been promoted to the position of head nurse on the surgery floor of the hospital. Ms. Costa has been an employee of Riverside Hospital since 2001, and most recently she was the head night nurse on the pediatric floor. Ms. Costa has shown strong leadership in her previous position and successfully led the pediatric department through the change to new software. Throughout the hospital, she is known as a problem-solver. She always meets challenges with a positive attitude. In addition, she is a very effective communicator and has worked with the Human Resources department to improve the communication procedures at nursing stations on all hospital floors.

Richard Nguyen will move up to the position of Vice President of Operations for the hospital at the end of this month. Mr. Nguyen joined our staff in 2007 as Operations Manager. He has held that position since that time, and his responsibilities have grown along with the growth of the hospital. As Operations Manager, he has overseen the day-to-day operations of the hospital, including equipment, repairs, training, and safety procedures. In his new position as Vice President of Operations, Mr. Nguyen will focus on improving hospital management and office procedures for the highest quality of patient care. He will be responsible for equipment budgets. Mr. Nguyen has great dedication to the hospital, and he has the respect of all the employees in his department.

---

25. We know from the article that when Selena worked on the pediatric floor, she worked _____.
- Ⓐ part time
- Ⓑ during the day
- Ⓒ at night
- Ⓓ on weekends

26. Which personal characteristic is NOT mentioned about Selena?
- Ⓐ dependability
- Ⓑ positive attitude
- Ⓒ good communicator
- Ⓓ problem-solver

27. You can infer that the hospital has _____ since 2007.
- Ⓐ become more crowded
- Ⓑ become larger
- Ⓒ lowered prices
- Ⓓ changed insurance plans

28. In his new position, Richard will NOT be responsible for _____.
- Ⓐ office procedures
- Ⓑ budgets
- Ⓒ improving management
- Ⓓ training doctors

....

25 Ⓐ Ⓑ Ⓒ Ⓓ   27 Ⓐ Ⓑ Ⓒ Ⓓ

26 Ⓐ Ⓑ Ⓒ Ⓓ   28 Ⓐ Ⓑ Ⓒ Ⓓ

224
     Go to the next page ⟩

Choose the correct answers to complete the article.

TIPS FOR CAREER   EARNINGS   ADVANCEMENT   INSURANCE
Ⓐ   ●   ©

Many career counselors agree that the best time to think about your next job is when you are comfortable in your present job. Don't wait until you are sick unhappy efficient 29 in your job.
Ⓐ   Ⓑ   ©

Plan ahead for your career advancement! Prepare for a promotion task investment 30 at
Ⓐ   Ⓑ   ©

your present place of employment. If there are no ways to match advance defer 31 where
Ⓐ   Ⓑ   ©

you work, you may need to look at other companies or organizations. Here are some tips for advancing.

1. Talk to your employer. Have a conversation with your boss about your future in the company. Explain your chain sales vision 32 for your career.
Ⓐ   Ⓑ   ©

   Your boss will have respect experience profits 33 for your confidence and planning.
Ⓐ   Ⓑ   ©

2. Show that you are interested in learning new skills. Businesses are always changing, so it is important to be punctual adaptable online 34.
Ⓐ   Ⓑ   ©

3. Improve your communication skills. Listen carefully to others. Be helpful and
   pleased famous friendly 35.
Ⓐ   Ⓑ   ©

4. Make Take Leave 36 friends with other people in your profession. Get to know people in
Ⓐ   Ⓑ   ©

   other companies—you will be more likely to hear about other jobs.

5. If you would like to be a manager, develop your marketing leadership flexibility 37 skills.
Ⓐ   Ⓑ   ©

   Learn how to supervise other employees.

29 Ⓐ Ⓑ © Ⓓ   32 Ⓐ Ⓑ © Ⓓ   35 Ⓐ Ⓑ © Ⓓ

30 Ⓐ Ⓑ © Ⓓ   33 Ⓐ Ⓑ © Ⓓ   36 Ⓐ Ⓑ © Ⓓ

31 Ⓐ Ⓑ © Ⓓ   34 Ⓐ Ⓑ © Ⓓ   37 Ⓐ Ⓑ © Ⓓ

Go to the next page ➡

Read and listen to the questions. Then listen to the conversation and answer the questions.

38. What procedure is the person showing the new employee?
- Ⓐ How to check out.
- Ⓑ How to lock the door.
- Ⓒ How to break into the building.
- Ⓓ How to turn on the security alarm.

39. How do you know that the security alarm is on?
- Ⓐ The top light is red.
- Ⓑ The top light is blue.
- Ⓒ All of the buttons are red.
- Ⓓ You are the last person to go home.

40. What is the last step?
- Ⓐ Ringing the alarm.
- Ⓑ Selecting the office areas.
- Ⓒ Pushing the red button.
- Ⓓ Pushing the on-off button.

G   WRITING ASSESSMENT: Instructions for a Procedure

Write instructions for how to do a procedure.

_____

_____

_____

_____

_____

_____

_____

_____

H   SPEAKING ASSESSMENT

I can ask and answer these questions:

Ask Answer
- ☐ ☐ Which of your personal qualities will be most helpful for career advancement? Why?
- ☐ ☐ Have you ever received a promotion? Explain the situation. Why were you promoted?
- ☐ ☐ If you are working now, what job would you like to be promoted to? If you aren't working now, what job would you like to have?
- ☐ ☐ What skills or experience do you need for this promotion or job?
- ☐ ☐ What is a complicated procedure that you often follow at work or at home?
- ☐ ☐ Do you learn procedures best by reading, by listening to an explanation, or by doing it?
- ☐ ☐ What benefits do you (or your family) currently receive at work?
- ☐ ☐ What benefit would you like to receive? Why?
- ☐ ☐ Who do you often give feedback to? Give an example of feedback you have given recently.
- ☐ ☐ Who do you receive feedback from? Is the feedback helpful? Why or why not?

38 Ⓐ Ⓑ Ⓒ Ⓓ   39 Ⓐ Ⓑ Ⓒ Ⓓ   40 Ⓐ Ⓑ Ⓒ Ⓓ

A CIVIC RESPONSIBILITIES; COMMUNITY LEGAL SERVICES

Example:

If a person is born in the United States, he or she is automatically _____.

- Ⓐ a naturalized citizen
- Ⓑ an immigrant
- ● a legal citizen
- Ⓓ a voter

1. _____ is NOT a privilege of U.S. citizenship.
   - Ⓐ The right to vote
   - Ⓑ The right to serve on a jury
   - Ⓒ Visiting any foreign country
   - Ⓓ A fair trial

2. You must _____ to become a naturalized citizen.
   - Ⓐ pass a citizenship test
   - Ⓑ be born in the U.S.
   - Ⓒ be a homeowner
   - Ⓓ serve on a jury

3. The general meaning of *citizen* is _____ who lives in a city or state.
   - Ⓐ a permanent resident
   - Ⓑ any person
   - Ⓒ a taxpayer
   - Ⓓ a registered person

4. _____ tax is based on a person's earnings.
   - Ⓐ Resident
   - Ⓑ Property
   - Ⓒ Service
   - Ⓓ Income

5. Local and state governments do NOT use tax money to pay for _____.
   - Ⓐ schools
   - Ⓑ fire and police departments
   - Ⓒ national defense
   - Ⓓ local roads

6. Citizens should read the newspaper or watch the news to stay _____ about issues.
   - Ⓐ informed
   - Ⓑ expected
   - Ⓒ required
   - Ⓓ called

7. Although hiring an attorney is expensive, most communities have free _____.
   - Ⓐ judges
   - Ⓑ legal services
   - Ⓒ counselors
   - Ⓓ trials

8. The jury observes the trial and then reaches _____.
   - Ⓐ an offense
   - Ⓑ a judge
   - Ⓒ innocence
   - Ⓓ a verdict

9. All tenants have certain _____ that are protected by the law.
   - Ⓐ conditions
   - Ⓑ buildings
   - Ⓒ landlords
   - Ⓓ rights

1 Ⓐ Ⓑ Ⓒ Ⓓ   4 Ⓐ Ⓑ Ⓒ Ⓓ   7 Ⓐ Ⓑ Ⓒ Ⓓ

2 Ⓐ Ⓑ Ⓒ Ⓓ   5 Ⓐ Ⓑ Ⓒ Ⓓ   8 Ⓐ Ⓑ Ⓒ Ⓓ

3 Ⓐ Ⓑ Ⓒ Ⓓ   6 Ⓐ Ⓑ Ⓒ Ⓓ   9 Ⓐ Ⓑ Ⓒ Ⓓ

Go to the next page ⟩

Example:

_____ trouble understanding this letter. Could you look at it?
- Ⓐ I would have
- ● I'm having
- Ⓒ I am
- Ⓓ I was having

10. This is a letter about jury duty. You _____ on a jury next month.
- Ⓐ have served
- Ⓑ would serve
- Ⓒ have to serve
- Ⓓ served

11. Can I be on a jury if I _____ a permanent resident?
- Ⓐ was
- Ⓑ will be
- Ⓒ were
- Ⓓ am

12. Yes, you can. If you are called for jury duty, you _____ to serve on a jury.
- Ⓐ are required
- Ⓑ were required
- Ⓒ are requiring
- Ⓓ require

13. _____ you _____ to vote yet?
- Ⓐ Are . . . registering
- Ⓑ Do . . . register
- Ⓒ Could . . . register
- Ⓓ Have . . . registered

14. No, I _____. I should register before next week.
- Ⓐ have
- Ⓑ hadn't
- Ⓒ haven't
- Ⓓ would have

15. Last night my landlord said she _____ me!
- Ⓐ was going to evict
- Ⓑ evicted
- Ⓒ evicting
- Ⓓ will be evicted

16. Really? But you always _____ your rent on time. How can she evict you?
- Ⓐ are paying
- Ⓑ will pay
- Ⓒ pay
- Ⓓ paying

17. I don't know. Maybe I _____ the community legal services office.
- Ⓐ must call
- Ⓑ should call
- Ⓒ might call
- Ⓓ will have called

18. Good idea. If I _____ you, I _____ right away.
- Ⓐ am . . . will call
- Ⓑ were . . . would call
- Ⓒ are . . . will call
- Ⓓ weren't . . . wouldn't call

10 Ⓐ Ⓑ Ⓒ Ⓓ   13 Ⓐ Ⓑ Ⓒ Ⓓ   15 Ⓐ Ⓑ Ⓒ Ⓓ   17 Ⓐ Ⓑ Ⓒ Ⓓ

11 Ⓐ Ⓑ Ⓒ Ⓓ   14 Ⓐ Ⓑ Ⓒ Ⓓ   16 Ⓐ Ⓑ Ⓒ Ⓓ   18 Ⓐ Ⓑ Ⓒ Ⓓ

12 Ⓐ Ⓑ Ⓒ Ⓓ

Go to the next page

C READING: Taxes

Read the civics textbook lesson. Then do Numbers 19 through 24.

A LOOK AT TAXES

Who pays taxes?

Every person who works in the United States must pay federal income tax. The amount due depends on how much income is earned in a year (for example, from salary).

Federal, state, and local taxes

Federal taxes are used for the federal government, federal programs, national defense, national parks, and money that the federal government assigns to special projects in states. Federal income tax supports programs on a national level. State and local taxes support our public schools, the public health system, local hospitals, parks, streets, highways, and so on.

Tax levels

For federal, state, and local taxes, a person is not required to pay income tax if his or her income is very low. This level is called the "threshold" level. If the income is less than the "threshold" level, no income tax is due. Each year, states set their own income levels for state income taxes.

As an example, the chart below shows 2008 tax threshold levels in California. If a single mother with one child earns less than $25,145, she owes no state income tax. If a family of four with two children has an income of less than $47,715, they owe no state income tax.

Personal Income Tax Thresholds	
	Tax Threshold
Single, no children	$14,845
Married, no children	$26,690
Head of household, one child	$25,145
Head of household, two children (or more)	$32,870
Married, one child	$39,990
Married, two children (or more)	$47,715

19. Taxpayers pay local, state, and _____ taxes.
   - Ⓐ federal
   - Ⓑ income
   - Ⓒ threshold
   - Ⓓ property

20. The term *tax threshold* refers to _____.
   - Ⓐ a person's salary
   - Ⓑ the level where no income tax is due
   - Ⓒ the amount of federal tax due
   - Ⓓ the amount of state tax due

21. People with a very _____ might not have to pay taxes.
   - Ⓐ small family
   - Ⓑ high income
   - Ⓒ low income
   - Ⓓ large salary

22. In the chart, *head of household* means _____.
   - Ⓐ a single mother
   - Ⓑ a single father
   - Ⓒ a landlord
   - Ⓓ a single parent

23. According to the chart, if a husband and wife have no children and have a combined income of _____, they do not need to pay income tax.
   - Ⓐ $26,000
   - Ⓑ $27,000
   - Ⓒ $30,000
   - Ⓓ $35,000

24. For a head of household, the difference between the threshold for one child and the threshold for two children is _____.
   - Ⓐ $1,545
   - Ⓑ $2,545
   - Ⓒ $7,725
   - Ⓓ $8,725

19 Ⓐ Ⓑ Ⓒ Ⓓ   21 Ⓐ Ⓑ Ⓒ Ⓓ   23 Ⓐ Ⓑ Ⓒ Ⓓ
20 Ⓐ Ⓑ Ⓒ Ⓓ   22 Ⓐ Ⓑ Ⓒ Ⓓ   24 Ⓐ Ⓑ Ⓒ Ⓓ

Go to the next page ⟩

Read the brochure. Then do Numbers 25 though 28.

Community Services for North County Residents

Health

Daly City Youth Health Center
Medical services for youth 6-18
623-2240

Spring Street Mental Health Association
Clinic for persons with mental illness
623-3345

Drug Abuse Recovery Services
Substance abuse prevention and treatment
623-3945

North County Health Services Agency
Medical services available to the public
623-9876

Legal Services

Legal Aid Society of North County
Legal services for tenant/landlord disputes
623-0915

North County Immigration Services
Assistance with immigration procedures
623-7654

Family Law Center
Legal counseling and referral for legal issues affecting families
623-9191

Housing

Rebuilding Together
Home repairs for low-income homeowners
623-6597

Fair Housing Program
Fair housing counseling for renters
623-6291

Human Services

Center for Domestic Violence Prevention
Services for domestic violence victims
623-0800

North County Family Counseling Agency
Mental health counseling for individuals and families
623-0555

Friends for Youth
A variety of programs for youth
623-2867

Project Read
Adult literacy tutoring
623-3871

---

25. Substance abuse refers to _____.
- Ⓐ housing problems
- Ⓑ immigration procedures
- Ⓒ addiction to drugs
- Ⓓ domestic violence

26. If your landlord doesn't make important repairs, call _____.
- Ⓐ the Family Law Center
- Ⓑ the Center for Domestic Violence Prevention
- Ⓒ Rebuilding Together
- Ⓓ the Legal Aid Society of North County

27. If your teenager needs a doctor, call _____.
- Ⓐ Abuse Recovery Services
- Ⓑ the Daly City Youth Health Center
- Ⓒ Friends for Youth
- Ⓓ Project Read

28. If a man and a woman want legal advice about getting a divorce, they should call _____.
- Ⓐ the Legal Aid Society of North County
- Ⓑ the Spring Street Mental Health Association
- Ⓒ the Family Law Center
- Ⓓ the North County Family Counseling Agency

---

25 Ⓐ Ⓑ Ⓒ Ⓓ   **26** Ⓐ Ⓑ Ⓒ Ⓓ   **27** Ⓐ Ⓑ Ⓒ Ⓓ   **28** Ⓐ Ⓑ Ⓒ Ⓓ

Side by Side Plus Book 4
Unit 10 Achievement Test (Page 4 of 6)

230

© 2009 Pearson Education, Inc.
Duplication for classroom use is permitted.

Go to the next page ▷

Choose the correct answers to complete the flyer.

Citizenship **Voter** **Legal** Registration Drive, Saturday, October 2, 10 AM–2 PM
Ⓐ ● Ⓒ

Westside Community Center

Are you **registered** **due** **signed** 29 to vote? Voting gives you a **speech** **voice** **status** 30
Ⓐ Ⓑ Ⓒ Ⓐ Ⓑ Ⓒ

in our **traffic** **jury** **government** 31. You must register to vote by October 2 so that you can
Ⓐ Ⓑ Ⓒ

reach **participate** **assemble** 32 in the **local** **small** **neighborhood** 33 and state
Ⓐ Ⓑ Ⓒ Ⓐ Ⓑ Ⓒ

verdict **election** **elected** 34 on November 4. To be eligible to vote, you must be a
Ⓐ Ⓑ Ⓒ

taxpayer **individual** **citizen** 35 of the United States and at least 18 years old.
Ⓐ Ⓑ Ⓒ

In the upcoming election, you can vote for the following positions: members of the City

Department **Council** **Committee** 36, members of the School **Jury** **Agency** **Board** 37,
Ⓐ Ⓑ Ⓒ Ⓐ Ⓑ Ⓒ

the mayor, your state senator, and your state representative.

Candidates' Night will be on October 10, 6:00–9:00 P.M. at City Hall

Read and listen to the questions. Then listen to the phone call and answer the questions.

38. What agency is the person calling?
Ⓐ City Hall.
Ⓑ Community Legal Aid.
Ⓒ Immigration.
Ⓓ Domestic Violence.

39. What number do you press for immigration?
Ⓐ 1
Ⓑ 2
Ⓒ 3
Ⓓ 4

40. Which office does the person want to reach?
Ⓐ Immigration.
Ⓑ Domestic violence.
Ⓒ Fair housing.
Ⓓ Family law.

29 Ⓐ Ⓑ Ⓒ Ⓓ   32 Ⓐ Ⓑ Ⓒ Ⓓ   35 Ⓐ Ⓑ Ⓒ Ⓓ   38 Ⓐ Ⓑ Ⓒ Ⓓ

30 Ⓐ Ⓑ Ⓒ Ⓓ   33 Ⓐ Ⓑ Ⓒ Ⓓ   36 Ⓐ Ⓑ Ⓒ Ⓓ   39 Ⓐ Ⓑ Ⓒ Ⓓ

31 Ⓐ Ⓑ Ⓒ Ⓓ   34 Ⓐ Ⓑ Ⓒ Ⓓ   37 Ⓐ Ⓑ Ⓒ Ⓓ   40 Ⓐ Ⓑ Ⓒ Ⓓ

231

Go to the next page

Fill in the voter registration application with your information.

Voter Registration Application

Are you a citizen of the United States of America?	☐ Yes ☐ No	This space for office use only.	
Will you be 18 years old on or before election day?	☐ Yes ☐ No		

If you checked "No" in response to either of these questions, you are not eligible to vote.

1 (Check one) ○ ○ ○ ○ Mr. Mrs. Miss Ms.

Last Name | **First Name** | **Middle Name(s)**

(Check one) ○ ○ ○ ○ ○ Jr. Sr. II III IV

2 Home Address | Apt or Lot# | City/Town | State | Zip Code

3 Address Where You Get Your Mail If Different From Above | City/Town | State | Zip Code

4 Date of Birth — Month Day Year

5 Telephone Number (optional)

6 ID Number (Social Security or driver's license number)

7 Choice of Party (Democrat, Republican, or other)

8 Race or Ethnic Group (Optional)

9 I have reviewed my state's instructions and I swear/affirm that:
- I am a United States citizen.
- I meet the eligibility requirements of my state and subscribe to any oath required.
- The information I have provided is true to the best of my knowledge under penalty of perjury. If I have provided false information, I may be fined, imprisoned, or (if not a U.S. citizen) deported from or refused entry to the United States.

Please sign full name (or put mark) ▲   Date: ____ / ____ / ____
                                                      Month   Day   Year

I can ask and answer these questions:

Ask Answer
- ☐ ☐ If you had legal problems with a landlord, who would you call in your community?
- ☐ ☐ If you had a legal question about a family matter, who would you call?
- ☐ ☐ If you had a legal question concerning immigration, who would you call?
- ☐ ☐ Do you vote in elections? Why or why not?
- ☐ ☐ Have you ever served on a jury? Explain.
- ☐ ☐ How do you keep informed about your town or city?
- ☐ ☐ What services and privileges do you enjoy in your community?
- ☐ ☐ Do you participate in your community? If so, how do you participate? If not, how could you participate?
- ☐ ☐ Do you pay taxes? If so, who prepares the forms for your tax returns?
- ☐ ☐ Describe something in your community that is probably paid for through *local* taxes
- ☐ ☐ Describe something in your community that is probably paid for through *state* taxes.

STOP

Side by Side Plus 4
Unit Achievement Tests Listening Script

UNIT 1 TEST

Section F

Read and listen to the questions.

38. Who is leaving a message?
39. What grade is the student in?
40. Why is the student absent?

Now listen to the parent's message and answer the questions.

School message machine: Hello. You have reached the Westmont High School automated attendance line. After the tone, please leave your name and your student's name and grade. Then give the reason for the absence and your phone number. When you are finished, press pound to hang up, or press zero to talk to the school secretary. [*beep*]

Parent: Hello. This is Helen Shaw. I'm calling about my son, Greg Shaw. He's in the ninth grade. Greg hurt his ankle yesterday during the baseball game, so he won't be in school today. I'm going to take him to the doctor. Again, my name is Helen Shaw, and my phone number is 516-5353. Thank you.

UNIT 2 TEST

Section F

Read and listen to the questions.

38. Why did the person call?
39. Which directions does the recording give?
40. Which buses stop at the mall?

Now listen to the recording and answer the questions.

Hello. Thank you for calling Big Bucks Department Store at the Valley Mall. For store hours, press 1. For the store address and directions, press 2. For customer service, press 3. For questions about your account, press 4. [*pause*]

Store address and directions. Big Bucks Department Store is in the Valley Mall. We are located at 2801 Stevens Avenue.

If you are taking public transportation, Bus numbers 19 and 21 stop In front of Big Bucks.

From the north, take Interstate 880 south to the Stevens Avenue exit. Turn right on Stevens Avenue and you will see the mall on the right. Big Bucks is in the center of the mall.

From the south, take Route 17 north to Interstate 880 north. Exit at Stevens Avenue. Turn left and you will see the mall on the right. Big Bucks is in the center of the mall.

UNIT 3 TEST

Section F

Read and listen to the questions.

38. What subject won't be on the test?
39. When did the United States enter World War I?
40. Who did the Allies fight against?

Now listen to the conversation and answer the questions.

A. As you know, we will have a test on Friday. It will cover the material we've studied in class this month, starting with World War I through the end of World War II. So, let's review some questions to prepare you for the test. Who can tell me about World War I? What countries were in this war? Ana?

B. England, France, and Russia were allies. They fought against Germany.

A. That's right. But what other country did the Allies fight against?

B. Austria-Hungary.

A. Correct. And when did the United States enter the war? Kevin?

C. In 1917. The war ended in 1918.

A. That's right. In 1917, the U.S. joined the Allies in their fight against Germany and Austria-Hungary. Think about the years after World War I. What important event happened in the U.S. In 1929? Sonya?

D. The Great Depression. It started with the stock market crash in October, 1929.

A. Very good.

UNIT 4 TEST

Section F

Read and listen to the questions.

38. Why is the customer calling the store?
39. How long has she had the refrigerator?
40. What does the salesman offer to do?

Now listen to the conversation and answer the questions.

A. Good morning. Best Appliance Company. How may I help you?
B. Hello. This is Anita Wong. I bought a new refrigerator from you about three months ago. The refrigerator light isn't working correctly.
A. Do you mean the inside light?
B. Yes, the inside light. It doesn't go on when I open the door.
A. I'm sorry to hear that. Have you checked the owner's manual?
B. Yes, I have. I tried to fix it, but it still isn't working.
A. I see. Well, your refrigerator is still under warranty. We can make an appointment for a repairperson to come to your home tomorrow to fix it. Let's see. Our repairperson can come in the afternoon between one o'clock and four. Will someone be home at that time?
B. Yes. I'll be here. Thanks very much.

UNIT 5 TEST

Section F

Read and listen to the questions.

38. Why is the person calling 9-1-1?
39. What happened to the caller's husband?
40. What does the operator tell the caller to do?

Now listen to the conversation and answer the questions.

A. Nine-one-one emergency operator. What is your emergency?
B. My husband has cut his hand very badly.
A. What is your address?
B. 127 West Adams Avenue, Apartment 3B.
A. I can help you. But first, tell me what happened.
B. He was cutting meat in the kitchen and he cut his thumb. It's a very deep cut.
A. Is he breathing?
B. Yes.
A. And is he sitting down?
B. No. He's standing by the sink.

A. Okay. Don't hang up the phone. Follow my instructions. I'll tell you the first-aid procedure. First, have him sit down right away.
B. Okay. He's sitting down.
A. Can he talk?
B. Yes. He can talk.
A. Good. Now take a clean, dry towel. I want you to press the towel against the cut.
B. All right. I can do that.
A. Next, elevate his hand.
B. Elevate his hand? What do you mean?
A. You need to hold it up. His hand needs to be higher than his heart.
B. Okay.
A. Can your husband hold the towel on his thumb and keep it on the cut?
B. Yes, he can do that.
A. Can you drive him to the hospital or clinic, or do you want me to call the ambulance?
B. Oh no, don't call an ambulance. I can drive him to the clinic right now.
A. Okay. Tell him to keep his hand up and keep the towel on the cut.
B. All right. Thank you so much.
A. You're welcome.

UNIT 6 TEST

Section F

Read and listen to the questions.

38. Why is this person calling the bank?
39. What number does the person give to get account information?
40. What account information does the person listen to?

Now listen to the phone call and answer the questions.

A. Welcome to Central Bank. For bank locations and hours, press or say 1. For checking account information, press or say 2. For savings account information, press or say 3. For current interest rates on our checking and savings accounts, press or say 4. To speak with a customer service representative, press or say 5.
B. Two.
A. For checking account information, please enter or say your account number.
B. Two–four–seven, three–nine–one, zero–five–six.

(continued)

A. For security purposes, please enter or say your personal identification number.

B. Three–one–nine–three.

A. Thank you. Please hold while I get your account information. For today's account balance, press or say 1. For information on the last three deposits, press or say 2. For information on the last three withdrawals, press or say 3.

B. Three.

A. Check number . . . one–four–two–two . . . was posted on . . . July ten . . . in the amount of . . . 36 dollars and 40 cents. An ATM withdrawal was posted on . . . July 12 . . . in the amount of . . . 200 dollars and zero cents. Check number . . . one–four–three–two . . . was posted on . . . July 13 . . . in the amount of . . . 170 dollars and zero cents.

UNIT 7 TEST

Section F

Read and listen to the questions.

38. How did the woman hurt herself?
39. What doesn't the nurse tell her to do?
40. What should the woman do if her back isn't better in a few days?

Now listen to the phone call and answer the questions.

A. Hello. This is Paul, Doctor Wilson's nurse. How may I help you?

B. I hurt my back.

A. Oh, that's not good. How did it happen?

B. Well, I work at an automobile factory, and there was a heavy box that I needed to move. I shouldn't have tried to lift it, but I was in a hurry so I did it myself.

A. Oh, so this happened at work. Do you know that all workplace injuries should be reported to your employer?

B. Yes, I do. I've reported it. I stayed home today, but my back hurts a lot.

A. What are your symptoms?

B. It's in my lower back, and every time I move my back hurts.

A. You've probably pulled a muscle. The best treatment is rest, ice, and a pain reliever medication like ibuprofen. When you are resting, lie flat on your back. Put a pillow under your head and another pillow under your knees. Once an hour, put an ice pack on your back for about ten minutes.

B. Okay.

A. That should relieve the symptoms. If you don't feel better in a few days, please call back to make an appointment with Doctor Wilson.

B. All right. I'll call back if it isn't better. Thanks.

A. You're very welcome.

UNIT 8 TEST

Section F

Read and listen to the questions.

38. What does the interviewer think about Ken?
39. What does Ken consider his greatest strength?
40. How many weaknesses does Ken talk about?

Now listen to the interview and answer the questions.

A. Well, Ken, I can see from your resume that you are very qualified for this position.

B. I'm glad to hear that.

A. I see you've also received additional training in computer programs.

B. Yes. I always enjoy learning new things.

A. I can see that is one of your strengths. What do you consider your GREATEST strength?

B. My greatest strength is communicating well with others. It's so important in healthcare services to communicate well with patients and co-workers. I think I'm a very good listener.

A. Communication is very important. Now, what about your weaknesses? What do you think some of your weaknesses are?

B. Well, in my first position, it was difficult for me to take good notes. There was so much patient information to write down. I've gotten much better, though. My notes are more complete now, and I'm working to improve them.

A. Any other weaknesses?

B. Well, I need to improve my time management. When I'm working with a patient, I sometimes forget about the time, and the appointment takes longer than it should.

A. That's a common problem here, too. Managing our time with patients is very important, and we always try to improve that.

UNIT 9 TEST

Section F

Read and listen to the questions.

38. What procedure is the person showing the new employee?
39. How do you know that the security alarm is on?
40. What is the last step?

Now listen to the conversation and answer the questions.

A. Since you are a new employee, I need to show you how to turn on the security alarm.

B. All right.

A. If you're the last person to leave the building at night, you need to turn on the security alarm before you go home. If someone tries to break into the building, the security alarm will ring and the police will come.

B. Okay.

A. So, here's the alarm on the wall next to the copy machine. The top light is blue, so that means the security alarm is off. If it's red, the security alarm is on.

B. I see. During the day the light will be blue, won't it?

A. That's right. So, right now, the light is blue and the alarm is off. Here's how to turn on the alarm. First, push the buttons for our three office areas.

B. Okay. One . . . two . . . three.

A. So now you've pushed three area buttons and they're flashing red.

B. Right.

A. Now, push the bottom buttons to enter the security code. It's four–one–one–three.

B. Four–one–one–three. Okay.

A. Good. The last step is to push the on-off button. Here it is at the top. When you do this, the on-off button will start flashing red.

B. All right.

A. Now the security alarm is on. You have thirty seconds to leave the building.

B. Okay. I understand.

UNIT 10 TEST

Section F

Read and listen to the questions.

38. What agency is the person calling?
39. What number do you press for immigration?
40. Which office does the person want to reach?

Now listen to the phone call and answer the questions.

A. Hello. Thank you for calling the Westside Community Legal Aid office. Our office hours are Monday through Friday, 9 A.M. to 12 P.M. and 1 P.M. to 5 P.M. For English, press or say 1. For Spanish, press or say 2. For Mandarin, press or say 3.

B. One.

A. Please listen carefully for our departments and services: For immigration, press or say 1. For fair housing and tenant rights, press or say 2. For family law, press or say 3. For domestic violence, press or say 4. If you wish to hear this menu again, press or say 5.

B. Five.

A. Please listen carefully for our departments and services: For immigration, press or say 1. For fair housing and tenant rights, press or say 2. For family law, press or say 3.

B. Three.

A. You have reached the Family Law office of Westside Community Legal Aid. All of our lines are busy right now. Please leave your name and phone number, and we will call you back as soon as possible.

Side by Side Plus 4
Unit Achievement Tests Answer Key

UNIT 1 TEST

A–F.

1. A	11. C	21. D	31. C
2. D	12. C	22. B	32. A
3. C	13. A	23. D	33. A
4. B	14. D	24. A	34. B
5. C	15. B	25. A	35. C
6. D	16. A	26. C	36. A
7. A	17. C	27. B	37. C
8. D	18. B	28. D	38. B
9. B	19. C	29. A	39. A
10. B	20. B	30. B	40. D

UNIT 2 TEST

A–F.

1. C	11. C	21. C	31. A
2. B	12. A	22. B	32. C
3. A	13. C	23. C	33. B
4. D	14. A	24. B	34. A
5. A	15. D	25. A	35. A
6. B	16. B	26. C	36. B
7. B	17. D	27. B	37. B
8. D	18. C	28. D	38. B
9. C	19. D	29. A	39. A
10. B	20. C	30. B	40. D

UNIT 3 TEST

A–F.

1. C	11. C	21. D	31. C
2. A	12. B	22. B	32. B
3. C	13. C	23. A	33. C
4. A	14. D	24. D	34. C
5. B	15. B	25. C	35. A
6. D	16. D	26. B	36. B
7. B	17. A	27. D	37. A
8. A	18. C	28. B	38. D
9. B	19. C	29. B	39. B
10. A	20. A	30. A	40. C

UNIT 4 TEST

A–F.

1. B	11. C	21. D	31. B
2. D	12. B	22. A	32. C
3. B	13. D	23. D	33. B
4. A	14. A	24. C	34. B
5. C	15. D	25. A	35. A
6. D	16. B	26. B	36. C
7. A	17. C	27. A	37. A
8. B	18. A	28. B	38. D
9. A	19. C	29. A	39. C
10. C	20. B	30. C	40. B

UNIT 5 TEST

A–F.

1. A	11. B	21. B	31. B
2. D	12. C	22. D	32. C
3. C	13. D	23. A	33. B
4. B	14. A	24. B	34. A
5. B	15. A	25. C	35. C
6. A	16. D	26. C	36. A
7. D	17. B	27. A	37. C
8. C	18. B	28. B	38. D
9. D	19. C	29. B	39. C
10. C	20. A	30. C	40. B

UNIT 6 TEST

A–F.

1. C	11. D	21. C	31. C
2. A	12. A	22. B	32. A
3. B	13. B	23. D	33. A
4. C	14. D	24. C	34. B
5. A	15. B	25. B	35. C
6. D	16. C	26. D	36. C
7. D	17. D	27. C	37. B
8. A	18. C	28. A	38. D
9. B	19. B	29. A	39. B
10. C	20. A	30. B	40. D

UNIT 7 TEST

A–F.

1. D	11. D	21. B	31. C
2. C	12. B	22. D	32. A
3. B	13. C	23. C	33. B
4. D	14. B	24. C	34. A
5. A	15. C	25. A	35. C
6. D	16. D	26. B	36. C
7. A	17. B	27. B	37. B
8. C	18. A	28. D	38. B
9. B	19. C	29. B	39. D
10. C	20. A	30. A	40. C

UNIT 9 TEST

A–F.

1. C	11. A	21. D	31. B
2. A	12. C	22. C	32. C
3. D	13. D	23. A	33. A
4. A	14. B	24. D	34. B
5. B	15. C	25. C	35. C
6. C	16. B	26. A	36. A
7. D	17. D	27. B	37. B
8. C	18. A	28. D	38. D
9. B	19. C	29. B	39. A
10. B	20. B	30. A	40. D

UNIT 8 TEST

A–F.

1. C	11. D	21. C	31. B
2. A	12. C	22. A	32. A
3. D	13. B	23. B	33. B
4. B	14. D	24. B	34. B
5. D	15. A	25. C	35. C
6. A	16. D	26. C	36. B
7. B	17. C	27. A	37. A
8. C	18. A	28. D	38. D
9. D	19. B	29. A	39. C
10. B	20. D	30. C	40. C

UNIT 10 TEST

A–F.

1. C	11. D	21. C	31. C
2. A	12. A	22. D	32. B
3. B	13. D	23. A	33. A
4. D	14. C	24. C	34. B
5. C	15. A	25. C	35. C
6. A	16. C	26. D	36. B
7. B	17. B	27. B	37. C
8. D	18. B	28. C	38. B
9. D	19. A	29. A	39. A
10. C	20. B	30. B	40. D

SIDE BY SIDE PLUS 4
Unit Achievement Tests Answer Sheet

Student's Name _____ I.D. Number _____

Course _____ Teacher _____ Date _____

1 Ⓐ Ⓑ Ⓒ Ⓓ
2 Ⓐ Ⓑ Ⓒ Ⓓ
3 Ⓐ Ⓑ Ⓒ Ⓓ
4 Ⓐ Ⓑ Ⓒ Ⓓ
5 Ⓐ Ⓑ Ⓒ Ⓓ
6 Ⓐ Ⓑ Ⓒ Ⓓ
7 Ⓐ Ⓑ Ⓒ Ⓓ
8 Ⓐ Ⓑ Ⓒ Ⓓ
9 Ⓐ Ⓑ Ⓒ Ⓓ
10 Ⓐ Ⓑ Ⓒ Ⓓ
11 Ⓐ Ⓑ Ⓒ Ⓓ
12 Ⓐ Ⓑ Ⓒ Ⓓ
13 Ⓐ Ⓑ Ⓒ Ⓓ
14 Ⓐ Ⓑ Ⓒ Ⓓ
15 Ⓐ Ⓑ Ⓒ Ⓓ
16 Ⓐ Ⓑ Ⓒ Ⓓ
17 Ⓐ Ⓑ Ⓒ Ⓓ
18 Ⓐ Ⓑ Ⓒ Ⓓ
19 Ⓐ Ⓑ Ⓒ Ⓓ
20 Ⓐ Ⓑ Ⓒ Ⓓ

21 Ⓐ Ⓑ Ⓒ Ⓓ
22 Ⓐ Ⓑ Ⓒ Ⓓ
23 Ⓐ Ⓑ Ⓒ Ⓓ
24 Ⓐ Ⓑ Ⓒ Ⓓ
25 Ⓐ Ⓑ Ⓒ Ⓓ
26 Ⓐ Ⓑ Ⓒ Ⓓ
27 Ⓐ Ⓑ Ⓒ Ⓓ
28 Ⓐ Ⓑ Ⓒ Ⓓ
29 Ⓐ Ⓑ Ⓒ Ⓓ
30 Ⓐ Ⓑ Ⓒ Ⓓ
31 Ⓐ Ⓑ Ⓒ Ⓓ
32 Ⓐ Ⓑ Ⓒ Ⓓ
33 Ⓐ Ⓑ Ⓒ Ⓓ
34 Ⓐ Ⓑ Ⓒ Ⓓ
35 Ⓐ Ⓑ Ⓒ Ⓓ
36 Ⓐ Ⓑ Ⓒ Ⓓ
37 Ⓐ Ⓑ Ⓒ Ⓓ
38 Ⓐ Ⓑ Ⓒ Ⓓ
39 Ⓐ Ⓑ Ⓒ Ⓓ
40 Ⓐ Ⓑ Ⓒ Ⓓ

Student's Name _____ I.D. Number _____

Course _____ Teacher _____ Date _____

Test Sections & Scoring Guidelines/Rubrics: Score:

A–F. MULTIPLE-CHOICE QUESTIONS

Parent/School Communication
Helping Children Succeed in School
Grammar in Context: School Communication
Reading: A School Announcement
Reading: Notes to School
Cloze Reading: A Letter from the Principal
Listening Assessment: Reporting an Absence

_____ correct x **2** points   _____ (80)

G. WRITING ASSESSMENT: A Note to School

For each of the following criteria, score **2** (Good), **1** (Fair), or **0** (Unsatisfactory):

Appropriateness of Content: _____

Spelling, Punctuation, Capitalization: _____

Correct Note/Letter Form: _____

Grammar: _____

Completeness of Sentences: _____   _____ (10)

H. SPEAKING ASSESSMENT

Score <u>separately</u> the student's ability to ask and answer the questions based on appropriateness, grammatical correctness, and comprehensibility:

Score **5** (Excellent), **4** (Good), **3** (Fair), **2** (Poor), or **1** (Unsatisfactory):

Asking the Questions: _____

Answering the Questions: _____   _____ (10)

TOTAL SCORE: _____ (100)

SIDE BY SIDE PLUS
Learner Assessment Record

Test Sections & Scoring Guidelines/Rubrics: **Score:**

A–F. MULTIPLE-CHOICE QUESTIONS

Driving Rules; Directions
Grammar in Context: Driving Rules; Directions; Schedules
Reading: Bus and Train Schedules
Reading: Neighborhood Watch
Cloze Reading: Directions
Listening Assessment: Recorded Directions to a Place

_____ correct x **2** points   _____ (80)

G. WRITING ASSESSMENT: A Personal Letter with Directions

For each of the following criteria, score **2** (Good), **1** (Fair), or **0** (Unsatisfactory):

Appropriateness of Content: _____

Spelling, Punctuation, Capitalization: _____

Correct Letter Form: _____

Grammar: _____

Completeness of Sentences: _____   (10)

H. SPEAKING ASSESSMENT

Score <u>separately</u> the student's ability to ask and answer the questions based on appropriateness, grammatical correctness, and comprehensibility:

Score **5** (Excellent), **4** (Good), **3** (Fair), **2** (Poor), or **1** (Unsatisfactory)

Asking the Questions: _____

Answering the Questions: _____   _____ (10)

TOTAL SCORE: _____ (100)

SIDE BY SIDE PLUS
Learner Assessment Record

Student's Name _____ I.D. Number _____

Course _____ Teacher _____ Date _____

Test Sections & Scoring Guidelines/Rubrics: **Score:**

A–F. MULTIPLE-CHOICE QUESTIONS

United States History
Grammar in Context: Talking about U.S. History
Reading: U.S. Presidents
Reading: Dr. Martin Luther King, Jr.
Cloze Reading: A History Textbook Lesson
Listening Assessment: Classroom Discussion

_____ correct x **2** points   _____ (80)

G. WRITING ASSESSMENT: A Personal Timeline

Score <u>globally</u> the student's ability to complete the timeline with appropriate detail and correct form:

Score **10** (Excellent), **8** (Good), **6** (Fair), **4** (Poor), or **2** (Unsatisfactory)

_____ (10)

H. SPEAKING ASSESSMENT

Score <u>separately</u> the student's ability to ask and answer the questions based on appropriateness, grammatical correctness, and comprehensibility:

Score **5** (Excellent), **4** (Good), **3** (Fair), **2** (Poor), or **1** (Unsatisfactory)

Asking the Questions: _____

Answering the Questions: _____   _____ (10)

TOTAL SCORE: _____ (100)

| Student's Name _____ | I.D. Number _____ |
| Course _____ Teacher _____ | Date _____ |

Test Sections & Scoring Guidelines/Rubrics: **Score:**

A–F. MULTIPLE-CHOICE QUESTIONS

Consumer Complaints and Warranties
Grammar in Context: Returning and Exchanging Defective Products
Grammar in Context: A Web Page with Consumer Protection Information
Reading: A Consumer Action Newspaper Advice Column
Cloze Reading: A Product Complaint Letter
Listening Assessment: Calling a Store about a Problem

_____ correct x **2** points   _____ (80)

G. WRITING ASSESSMENT: A Warranty Registration Form

For each of the following lines on the form:
    Score **1** if completed correctly.
    Score **0** if incorrect or missing.

Date: _____

Name: _____

Address: _____

City / State: _____

Zip: _____

Phone Number / Email Address: _____

Name of Store: _____

Date of Purchase: _____

Model Number / Serial Number: _____

Signature: _____   _____ (10)

H. SPEAKING ASSESSMENT

Score <u>separately</u> the student's ability to ask and answer the questions based on appropriateness, grammatical correctness, and comprehensibility:

Score **5** (Excellent), **4** (Good), **3** (Fair), **2** (Poor), or **1** (Unsatisfactory)

Asking the Questions: _____

Answering the Questions: _____   _____ (10)

TOTAL SCORE: _____ (100)

Student's Name _____ I.D. Number _____

Course _____ Teacher _____ Date _____

Test Sections & Scoring Guidelines/Rubrics: Score:

A–F. MULTIPLE-CHOICE QUESTIONS

Home Fire Safety and Emergency Procedures
Grammar in Context: Home Safety; Reporting an Emergency
Reading: A News Article
Reading: A Fire Safety Notice
Cloze Reading: A Workplace Fire Safety Memo
Listening Assessment: Reporting an Emergency

_____ correct x **2** points   _____ (80)

G. WRITING ASSESSMENT: A Fire Escape Plan

Score <u>separately</u> the student's ability to draw an escape plan and write instructions:

Score **5** (Excellent), **4** (Good), **3** (Fair), **2** (Poor), or **1** (Unsatisfactory)

Drawing the Escape Plan: _____

Writing the Instructions: _____   _____ (10)

H. SPEAKING ASSESSMENT

Score <u>separately</u> the student's ability to ask and answer the questions based on appropriateness, grammatical correctness, and comprehensibility:

Score **5** (Excellent), **4** (Good), **3** (Fair), **2** (Poor), or **1** (Unsatisfactory)

Asking the Questions: _____

Answering the Questions: _____   _____ (10)

TOTAL SCORE: _____ (100)

Student's Name _____ **I.D. Number** _____

Course _____ **Teacher** _____ **Date** _____

Test Sections & Scoring Guidelines/Rubrics: **Score:**

A–F. MULTIPLE-CHOICE QUESTIONS

Bank Services; Budget Planning
Grammar in Context: Requesting Bank Services; Budget Planning
Reading: Comparing Checking Accounts
Reading: A Bank Statement
Cloze Reading: A News Article
Listening Assessment: Recorded Bank Account Information

_____ correct x **2** points _____ (80)

G. WRITING ASSESSMENT: A Bank Account Application

Score <u>globally</u> the student's ability to complete the sections of the form:

Score **10** (Excellent), **8** (Good), **6** (Fair), **4** (Poor), or **2** (Unsatisfactory)

_____ (10)

H. SPEAKING ASSESSMENT

Score <u>separately</u> the student's ability to ask and answer the questions based on appropriateness, grammatical correctness, and comprehensibility:

Score **5** (Excellent), **4** (Good), **3** (Fair), **2** (Poor), or **1** (Unsatisfactory)

Asking the Questions: _____

Answering the Questions: _____

_____ (10)

TOTAL SCORE: _____ (100)

SIDE BY SIDE PLUS
Learner Assessment Record

Student's Name _____ I.D. Number _____

Course _____ Teacher _____ Date _____

Test Sections & Scoring Guidelines/Rubrics: **Score:**

A–F. MULTIPLE-CHOICE QUESTIONS

Health Care; Nutrition; Safety
Grammar in Context: Describing Symptoms; Following Medical Advice
Reading: Nutrition Facts on Food Labels
Reading: Medicine Labels
Cloze Reading: A Workplace Safety Notice
Listening Assessment: Calling for Medical Advice

_____ correct x **2** points   _____ (80)

G. WRITING ASSESSMENT: A Medical History Form

Score <u>globally</u> the student's ability to fill out the sections of the form:

Score **10** (Excellent), **8** (Good), **6** (Fair), **4** (Poor), or **2** (Unsatisfactory)

_____ (10)

H. SPEAKING ASSESSMENT

Score <u>separately</u> the student's ability to ask and answer the questions based on appropriateness, grammatical correctness, and comprehensibility:

Score **5** (Excellent), **4** (Good), **3** (Fair), **2** (Poor), or **1** (Unsatisfactory)

Asking the Questions: _____

Answering the Questions: _____   _____ (10)

TOTAL SCORE: _____ (100)

246

Student's Name _____   I.D. Number _____

Course _____   Teacher _____   Date _____

Test Sections & Scoring Guidelines/Rubrics: **Score:**

A–F. MULTIPLE-CHOICE QUESTIONS

Job Interviews; Career Advancement
Grammar in Context: Talking about Job Interviews
Reading: Help Wanted Ads
Reading: A Resume
Cloze Reading: A Cover Letter
Listening Assessment: A Job Interview

_____ correct x **2 points**   _____ (80)

G. WRITING ASSESSMENT: A Resume

Score <u>globally</u> the student's ability to complete the work experience and education history sections of the resume:

Score **10** (Excellent), **8** (Good), **6** (Fair), **4** (Poor), or **2** (Unsatisfactory)

_____ (10)

H. SPEAKING ASSESSMENT

Score <u>separately</u> the student's ability to ask and answer the questions based on appropriateness, grammatical correctness, and comprehensibility:

Score **5** (Excellent), **4** (Good), **3** (Fair), **2** (Poor), or **1** (Unsatisfactory)

Asking the Questions: _____

Answering the Questions: _____   _____ (10)

TOTAL SCORE: _____ (100)

Student's Name		I.D. Number
Course	Teacher	Date

Test Sections & Scoring Guidelines/Rubrics: Score:

A–F. MULTIPLE-CHOICE QUESTIONS

Employment and Benefits
Grammar in Context: Feedback about Following Procedures; Benefits
Reading: An Employee Benefits Manual
Reading: An Employee Newsletter
Cloze Reading: A Magazine Article
Listening Assessment: Following a Procedure

_____ correct x **2** points   _____ (80)

G. WRITING ASSESSMENT: Instructions for a Procedure

For each of the following criteria, score **2** (Good), **1** (Fair), or **0** (Unsatisfactory):

Appropriateness of Content: _____

Spelling: _____

Punctuation & Capitalization: _____

Grammar: _____

Completeness of Sentences: _____   _____ (10)

H. SPEAKING ASSESSMENT

Score <u>separately</u> the student's ability to ask and answer the questions based on appropriateness, grammatical correctness, and comprehensibility:

Score **5** (Excellent), **4** (Good), **3** (Fair), **2** (Poor), or **1** (Unsatisfactory)

Asking the Questions: _____

Answering the Questions: _____   _____ (10)

TOTAL SCORE: _____ (100)

SIDE BY SIDE PLUS
Learner Assessment Record

Student's Name _____ I.D. Number _____

Course _____ Teacher _____ Date _____

Test Sections & Scoring Guidelines/Rubrics: Score:

A–F. MULTIPLE-CHOICE QUESTIONS

Civic Responsibilities; Community Legal Services
Grammar in Context: Jury Duty; Voting; Tenant Rights
Reading: Taxes
Reading: A Community Services Brochure
Cloze Reading: A Voter Registration Information Flyer
Listening Assessment: Recorded Community Services Information

_____ correct x **2** points   _____ (80)

G. WRITING ASSESSMENT: A Voter Registration Formn

Score <u>globally</u> the student's ability to complete the sections of the form:

Score **10** (Excellent), **8** (Good), **6** (Fair), **4** (Poor), or **2** (Unsatisfactory)

_____ (10)

H. SPEAKING ASSESSMENT

Score <u>separately</u> the student's ability to ask and answer the questions based on appropriateness, grammatical correctness, and comprehensibility:

Score **5** (Excellent), **4** (Good), **3** (Fair), **2** (Poor), or **1** (Unsatisfactory)

Asking the Questions: _____

Answering the Questions: _____   _____ (10)

TOTAL SCORE: _____ (100)

SIDE BY SIDE PLUS
Learner Progress Chart

BOOK 4

Student's Name _____ I.D. Number _____

Course _____ Teacher _____ Term _____

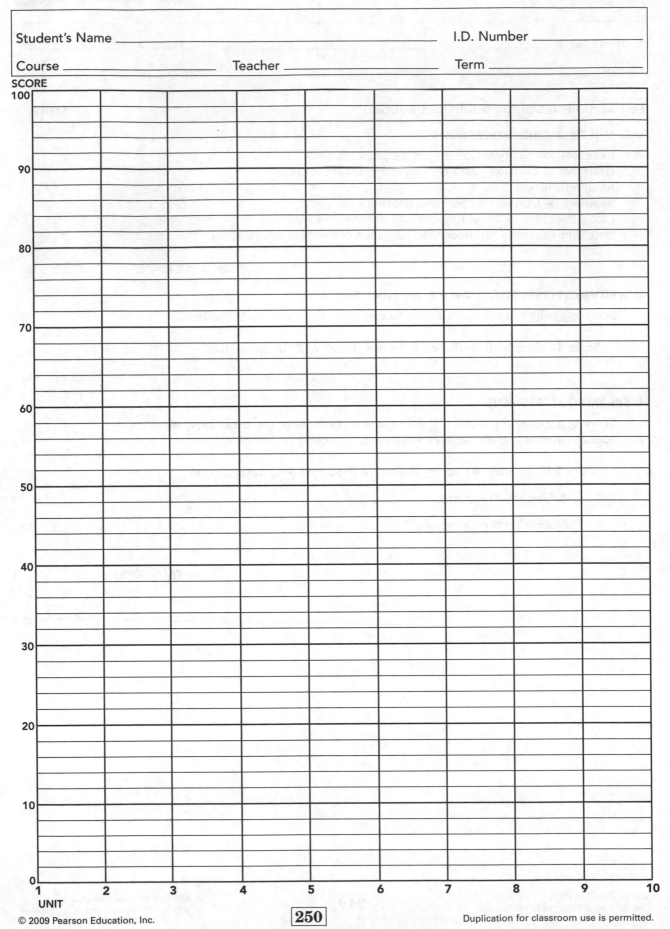